Black

Self-Genocide

What Black Lives
Matter Won't Say

Black

Self-Genocide

What Black Lives Matter Won't Say

WELLINGTON
BOONE

APPTE Publishing
Duluth, Georgia

Black Self-Genocide

What Black Lives Matter Won't Say

© 2016 Wellington Boone

www.WellingtonBoone.com

APPTE Publishing

703 Beaufort Circle, Duluth, GA 30096

The following abbreviations are used to identify versions of the Bible used in this book:

KJV *King James Version,* also known as the *Authorized Version.*

NASB Scripture quotations taken from the New American Standard Bible®,
Copyright © 1960, 1962, 1963, 1968, 1971, 1972, 1973,
1975, 1977, 1995 by The Lockman Foundation
Used by permission. (www.Lockman.org)

NLT Scripture quotations are taken from the Holy Bible, New Living Translation, copyright ©1996,
2004, 2007, 2013, 2015 by Tyndale House Foundation. Used by permission of Tyndale House
Publishes, Inc., Carol Stream, Illinois. 60188. All rights reserved.

NKJV Scripture taken from the New King James Version®. Copyright © 1982
by Thomas Nelson. Used by permission. All rights reserved.

The Message Scripture quotations from THE MESSAGE. Copyright © by
Eugene H. Peterson 1993, 1994, 1995, 1996, 2000, 2001, 2002. Used by
permission of NavPress. All rights reserved. Represented by Tyndale House
Publishers, Inc.

Nouns and pronouns referring to Deity are capitalized throughout the text of this
book unless they are included within a direct quotation, in which case the
original capitalization is retained.

Includes Footnotes, References, Historical Charts, Index
Print Edition. ISBN-13: 978-0977689255
Print Edition. ISBN-10: 0977689255
Library of Congress Control Number: 2016957952
© 2016 Wellington Boone

Printed in the United States of America
November 2016

CONTENTS

INTRODUCTION

REVERSING BLACK SELF-GENOCIDE

S omewhere in Black America is a deep sorrow that was born in the belly of slave ships. It should have ended with emancipation, but continued because of segregation and discrimination. Now it manifests itself in the end result—the deathstyle that characterizes too many Black Americans today.

No one has to kill Black Americans any more by racial genocide. It is now Black self-genocide and cultural self-hatred.

Doll Test in *Brown v. Board of Education*

In the landmark 1954 *Brown v. Board of Education* case brought before the United States Supreme Court by the NAACP to integrate public schools, Dr. Kenneth Clark used a "doll test" to prove that Black children suffered from cultural self-hatred as a result of segregation. Here's a description from the Library of Congress archives:

"In the 'doll test,' psychologists Kenneth and Mamie Clark used four plastic, diaper-clad dolls, identical except for color. They showed the dolls to black children between the ages of three and seven and asked them questions to determine racial perception and preference. Almost all of the children readily identified the race of the dolls.

"However, when asked which they preferred, the majority selected the white doll and attributed positive characteristics to it. The Clarks also gave the children outline drawings of a boy and girl and asked them to color the figures the same color as themselves. Many of the children with dark complexions colored the figures with a white or yellow crayon. The Clarks concluded that 'prejudice, discrimination, and segregation' caused black children to develop a sense of inferiority and self-hatred."[1]

---

[1] Library of Congress exhibit on the 50th anniversary of *Brown v. Board of Education*. Online at http://www.loc.gov/exhibits/brown/brown-brown.html.

1

Thurgood Marshall, chief counsel for the NAACP Legal Defense Fund who argued the case and later became the first Black American to serve as a justice of the Supreme Court, issued a challenge. He said that the Court should rule against the admission of Black children to public schools only if Blacks were actually inferior to others. We know that Blacks are not inferior, because God created all races the same, but as the doll test showed, Black children *feel* inferior because of the way their race has been treated from the slavery era to the present.

VISION FOR BLACK AMERICA:

AMERICANS WILL REPENT BECAUSE RACISM IS WRONG AND HAS CAUSED CULTURAL SELF-HATRED.

". . . to separate them from others of similar age and qualifications solely because of their race generates a feeling of inferiority as to their status in the community that may affect their hearts and minds in a way unlikely ever to be undone."

Brown v. Board of Education[2]

New doll test—startling signs of lingering cultural self-hatred

In 2005, a high school student from New York named Kiri Davis recreated the doll test for a Reel Works Teen Filmmaking project. She tested Black children ages four and five and filmed her results in a documentary she produced called "A Girl Like Me."

To her surprise, the reaction of Black children to the dolls demonstrated that cultural self-hatred still existed in young children 50 years after *Brown v. Board of Education*. She found that 15 of 21 Black children still favored the White dolls. When a girl on film was asked to choose which doll was "bad," she chose the Black one.[3]

Reversing the curse on Black Americans by saying "I'm sorry"

For centuries, people have spoken a curse over Black Americans. It is time to reverse this curse—to speak life so consistently and so often that Blacks everywhere are being spoken about as examples of Christ-likeness.

---

[2] *Brown v. Board of Education,* 347 U.S. 483 (1954). 347 U.S. 483. Online at https://www.ourdocuments.gov/doc.php?flash=true&doc=87&page=transcript.
[3] Kiri Davis, "A Girl Like Me." Online at https://www.youtube.com/watch?v=z0BxFRu_SOw. Accessed October 2016.

But I didn't do it! Jesus said in Matthew 23, Yes, you did! And *"you testify against yourselves that you are indeed the descendants of those who murdered the prophets. . . . I tell you the truth, this judgment will fall on this very generation."* [4] White Americans who take responsibility for the mistreatment of Blacks by past generations and repent on their behalf have the right spirit. They demonstrate godliness and a desire to understand and correct the past. They can reverse the curse on this generation.

When Uganda began independent self-rule, it is said that the British left behind a curse that Ugandans would never make it without them. Whites who think inner-city Black Americans can't make it without them call them the "permanent underclass."

Not us! We say, "God bless Black America!"

Restoring Hope and Self-Worth to a People Group

You can do something about Black self-genocide. You are called to influence people. Your life is a seed into somebody else's destiny. Your words and deeds can restore self-worth to the people group of Black Americans and reverse their downward trends.

Jesus told His disciples to go into the world and preach the Gospel because they carried His name and He wanted the integrity of His name to bring hope to their generation.

This generation of Black Americans needs your hope and your faith in Christ. Their hope depends on your obedience. They will receive you if you go to them in His name.

Civil government must protect inalienable rights of Blacks

America was forced to grant *civil rights* to Black Americans, but another kind of rights that they deserve have not been acknowledged—Black Americans' *inalienable rights* as people created in the image of God. Civil rights are granted by man, but the inalienable rights affirmed in the founding document of America—the Declaration of Independence—are granted by God to Blacks as well as White Americans. Those are the rights Blacks should seek and that should have been faithfully protected for Blacks by our civil government, but were not.

---

[4] Matthew 23:31, 36 NLT.

3

"We hold these truths to be self-evident, that all men are created equal, that they are endowed by their Creator with certain unalienable Rights, that among these are Life, Liberty and the pursuit of Happiness.—That to secure these rights, Governments are instituted among Men."[5]

Power to Bless the Nations of the Earth

God told Abram in Genesis 12 that He would make Abram a great nation and all the families of the earth would be blessed through him. Abraham's significance and the future significance of Israel and other nations would be determined by his obedience to the destiny of God.

We give men credit and applause as being important because of their bank statements or because they are CEOs over major corporations or because of their natural athletic or singing ability, but God determines their level of importance by *what they do for others in His name.*

God is looking for genuine Christians willing to restore Black people in despair and release them from the past oppression and devaluation that has been aimed at them in this country for centuries. When that happens, it will be an irrefutable declaration of the power of God the Father, Jesus Christ, the Son and our Savior, and Holy Ghost our Friend.

Likewise, Black Americans will be released to become an example of the miracle-working power of God by the way they obey God and bless others in His name—what Jesus called a city on a hill for all to see.

"You are the light of the world, like a city on a hilltop that cannot be hidden."[6]

"If you obey the commands of the LORD your God and walk in his ways, the LORD will establish you as his holy people as he solemnly promised to do.

"Then all the nations of the world will see that you are a people claimed by the LORD, and they will stand in awe of you."[7]

---

[5] "Declaration of Independence: A Transcription." Online at https://www.archives.gov/founding-docs/declaration-transcript.
[6] Matthew 5:14 NLT.
[7] Deuteronomy 28:9-10 NLT.

CHAPTER 1

BLACK AMERICAN AMBASSADORS

From American Tragedy to Global Triumph

*"And all things are of God, who hath reconciled us to himself by Jesus Christ, and hath given to us the **ministry of reconciliation**; . . . that God was in Christ, reconciling the world unto himself, not imputing their trespasses unto them; and hath committed unto us the **word of reconciliation**."*[8]

INTRODUCTION TO CHAPTER 1

John Winthrop (1588-1649) was a Puritan lay leader in England being persecuted for his faith when he made the journey to the New World on the ship *Arbella* in the spring of 1630. He became the first colonial governor of the Massachusetts Bay Colony, which had been given a unique opportunity to establish self-government and a Bible-based Christian community in America. On board ship with Winthrop were others seeking religious freedom. Before they landed, Winthrop shared his biblical vision for the New World. He said God has a destiny for us to become a Christ-like example to others—as individuals and as a people group.

> *"We shall find that the God of Israel is among us, when ten of us shall be able to resist a thousand of our enemies; when he shall make us a praise and glory that men shall say of succeeding plantations, 'the Lord make it like that of New England.' For we must consider that we shall be as a city upon a hill.[9] The eyes of all people are upon us."*[10]

---

[8] 2 Corinthians 5:18-19 KJV.
[9] See Matthew 5:14.
[10] John Winthrop, "A Modell of Christian Charity" (1630). Hanover Historical Texts Project. Corrected to match modern usage. Original online at http://history.hanover.edu/texts/winthmod.html.

In this chapter you will learn more about Winthrop and also a chain of events 233 years later involving another godly Christian from Massachusetts, William Carney (1840-1908). Carney fought in the Civil War and became the first Black soldier to earn the Congressional Medal of Honor for courage on the field of battle.

Unfortunately, too many Black Americans today lack the assertiveness of a Carney, who was determined to fulfill God's plan regardless of obstacles, and lack the assurance of a John Winthrop, that God absolutely has a plan for their lives and their people. They don't yet understand that God in His sovereign will has determined their race, their gender, their parents, and the place they were born, and that regardless of their trials God has chosen them for such a time as this.

Black Americans once understood that regardless of mistreatment in their historical experience, that didn't change God's creative purpose. He allowed it to happen, He sustained them with hope while they were going through it, and in the end, *"God causes everything to work together for the good of those who love God and are called according to his purpose for them."*[11] It's not what you're going through that counts but how you're going through it. That's what prepares you for greatness.

The American Civil War began in April 1861, one month after Abraham Lincoln was installed as President of the United States. Lincoln had been elected president in November 1860 as the candidate of the new Republican Party that had been created on a platform of ending the extension of slavery. As soon as the election results were confirmed, first South Carolina and soon these additional Southern states seceded from the Union: Mississippi, Florida, Alabama, Georgia, Louisiana, Texas, Virginia, Arkansas, North Carolina, and Tennessee.

The South wanted slavery to continue as it was.

---

[11] Romans 8:28 NLT.

Fight to Keep Slavery as It Was, Even at Price of Civil War

On July 4, 1776, the founders of the Southern states had signed a Declaration of Independence with the founders of the Northern states and made this pledge to one another before God:

"And for the support of this Declaration, with a firm reliance on the protection of divine Providence, we mutually pledge to each other our Lives, our Fortunes and our sacred Honor."[12]

However, on December 20, 1860, South Carolina became the first state to break that pledge when it seceded from the Union, the United States of America. Although historians for more than 150 years have misrepresented what happened next, the truth is readily available and it must be admitted. It was a fight to keep slavery that was never resolved.

DID YOU KNOW? Secession by Slave States and Civil War

December 20, 1860	South Carolina secedes.
January 9-26, 1861	Mississippi, Florida, Alabama, Georgia, Louisiana secede.
February 1, 1861	Texas secedes. Seven states form the Confederate States of America (also called "the South" and "the Confederacy"). Montgomery, Alabama, is selected as the temporary capital.
February 9, 1861	Jefferson Davis is selected provisional president of the Confederacy. Davis remains in office until the end of the Civil War.
March 4, 1861	Abraham Lincoln inaugurated U.S. President (also called "the North" and "the Union"). Lincoln remains in office until the end of the Civil War. He is assassinated and dies April 15, 1865, six days after the Confederacy surrenders.
March 11, 1861	Seven states that have seceded to date sign the Constitution of the Confederate States of America

[12] Declaration of Independence. The full text is online at http://www.archives.gov/exhibits/charters/declaration_transcript.html. Accessed October 2016.

April 12, 1861	Confederate forces fire on Union installation at Fort Sumter, South Carolina, launching the Civil War.
April, May, June 1861	Virginia, Arkansas, North Carolina, and Tennessee secede.
April 9, 1865	Confederate General Robert E. Lee surrenders to Union General Ulysses S. Grant at Appomattox Court House, Virginia, to end the Civil War four years after it began.

Loss of life in Civil War greater than any other American war

The Civil War lasted four long years with 750,000 to 850,000 deaths. Of that number, 40,000[13] who died were Blacks or "Colored Troops" who fought bravely to the end for the Union Army. Some historians of the day calculated smaller numbers but since then more accurate work has been done to determine the correct count.[14] The number who died by any computation was far greater than any other war in our history, before or since. Brother fought brother. Families were torn apart.

Civil War Could Have Been Averted by 1857 Revival

It is important to look back and review what else was happening during that time in history to see if our ancestors were following the leading of God. Indeed, the great spiritual awakening of the 1857 Revival could have been the impetus for peace instead of war. It was God's way of saying, "I want all my creation set free."

A New York businessman named Jeremiah Lanphier on a mission for a local church saw the desperate need of our troubled nation and he knew prayer would be the answer. He handed out a prayer bill to local businessmen calling for a weekly hour of prayer. Beginning with that first businessmen's prayer meeting in New York City, the awakening quickly spread through the city, the state, and on to other states. For two years, people across the country were praying and giving their lives to the Lord

---

[13] "Teaching With Documents: The Fight for Equal Rights: Black Soldiers in the Civil War." Online at https://www.archives.gov/education/lessons/blacks-civil-war/. Accessed October 2016.

[14] J. David Hacker, "Disunion. Miscounting the Dead." New York Times, September 20, 2011. Online at http://opinionator.blogs.nytimes.com/2011/09/20/recounting-the-dead/#more-105317. Accessed October 2016. This source also includes a bibliography.

*How Often
Shall I Pray?*

*Handbill
distributed by
Jeremiah
Lanphier before
revival hit New
York City, 1857[15]*

"As often as the language of prayer is in my heart; as often as I see my need of help; as often as I feel the power of temptation; as often as I am made sensible of any spiritual declension or feel the aggression of a worldly spirit.

"In prayer we leave the business of time for that of eternity, and intercourse with men for intercourse with God.

"A day Prayer Meeting is held every Wednesday, from 12 to 1 o'clock, in the Consistory building in the rear of the North Dutch Church, corner of Fulton and William Streets (entrance from Fulton and Ann Streets).

"This meeting is intended to give merchants, mechanics, clerks, strangers, and business men generally an opportunity to stop and call upon God amid the perplexities incident for those who may find it inconvenient to remain more than five or ten minutes, as well as for those who can spare the whole hour."

America at that time was a nation of devout, church-going people, yet they would not deal with the number one national sin of slavery. As a country they still would not yield. If the people had prevailed in prayer, freedom for the slaves would have been based on the price that Jesus paid on the cross for all men to be free because Jesus not only set people free from the bondage of sin but also from the bondage of sinners like the slave owners who kept other human beings unjustly in chains.

However, Americans refused to resolve their differences by revelation, so what they wouldn't do by revelation they had to do by tribulation. What they refused to do by Christ's blood shed they did by their own blood shed.

National Strife Continued After the South Lost the War

It is vital to understand both biblical principles and practical explanations of what happens in history so that we can keep a biblical

---

[15]J. Edwin Orr, *The Light of the Nations Evangelical Renewal and Advance in the Nineteenth Century* (Grand Rapids, MI: Eerdmans, 1963).

perspective. Interpreting events by the Bible keeps us from being limited to the historical realm. It gives us revelation understanding and practical principles that we can put to use today to resolve the current crisis.

After the Civil War, there was a period of Reconstruction when the losing South had to endure occupation by the Northern troops. The U.S. Congress, which was dominated by "Radical Republicans" who supported rights of the freedmen (the liberated slaves), stationed Union troops in the South, which was dominated by Democrats, to protect the Blacks' rights.

Even though Lincoln was a Republican, in those days there was not a one-party ticket in a Presidential election. Lincoln's Vice President, Andrew Johnson, was a Democrat. He took office as President after Lincoln was assassinated. Even though Johnson had not joined the Southern Democrats when they seceded from the Union, the Southern governors definitely had his sympathies. This set up so much antagonism between the President and Congress that Johnson was almost impeached.

Newly freed Black Americans became Republicans and ran for office

Since the Civil War was truly about slavery, when the Southern states lost the war, all of their slaves were finally free. The states had to write and ratify new state constitutions specifying that the slaves were free. In Congress, three amendments were eventually added to the United States Constitution that also spelled out the terms of Black Americans' freedom.

For the next 12 years, the former Black slaves, who were now free citizens, joined the Republican Party, the party of Lincoln, and could vote, run for office, and serve at the local, state, and national level. Their former masters were predominantly Democrats.

Contrary to prejudice and depictions of the freedmen that would come later, these former slaves were dignified, intelligent people. They were predominantly Christian, partly because of their exposure to the Gospel through attending church with their masters but mainly because God had made Himself known to them in the midst of their trials. Even though the Southern states had laws against Black literacy, many slaves and free Blacks secretly learned to read so they could read the Bible. They were also managing plantations for their masters and had the skills necessary to run businesses and handle their masters' affairs. Behind the scenes, Northern groups like the American Missionary Association were also sending teachers for years to educate them.

Contested Presidential election of 1876 ends Reconstruction

In the Presidential election of 1876, there was no clear winner of a majority of Electoral College votes. National conditions were still chaotic because of the ongoing antagonism between the South and the North during Reconstruction. In the end, pride had its day and the Blacks lost.

DID YOU KNOW? 1877 Compromise Disenfranchises Blacks Again

Presidential election of 1876 ends with no clear winner	Republican candidate Rutherford B. Hayes 20 votes short of electoral college win
	Democratic Candidate Samuel J. Tilden Won popular vote, 1 vote short in electoral college
Three Southern states withhold 20 Electoral votes	Florida, Louisiana, South Carolina still have Republican electoral boards in charge of vote certification who accuse Democrats of violence against Black voters.
March 1877	Just before date set for Inauguration of next President, in a secret compromise the three states allow Hayes to win if he is willing to meet their terms
South offers secret deal that becomes known as the 1877 Compromise	• Withdraw federal troops from the South and restore "home rule" (control by Whites) • Enact federal legislation that would spur industrialization in the South • Appoint Democrats to patronage positions in the South • Appoint a Democrat to the president's cabinet. .
Hayes agrees, is pronounced winner	Final Electoral College votes: Hayes, 185; Tilden 184

America Needs to Understand and Apologize for Its Racial History

White Southern officeholders were taken out of office by Blacks but inside their hearts aren't changed. It was only a matter of time before they threw out the Blacks and took over again.

When the Northern Republicans caved in and removed the troops from the South to win an election with help from the Democrats, Blacks were not only thrown out of office but also thrown into the era of Jim Crow laws and segregation for the next 100 years. Ku Klux Klan and other terrorism flourished that prevented Blacks from even voting, especially if they tried to vote as a Republican, let alone allowing them to run for office.

Blacks in the North were unjustly treated, too. Lynchings, mostly of Blacks, took place in every state except four New England states: Massachusetts, Rhode Island, New Hampshire and Vermont.

Until I started going through this racial history of America, I didn't understand it the way I am able to talk about it now. If I didn't understand it, and I have been preaching racial reconciliation for 40 years, I know that scores of people of all races still don't get it.

Character of Christ-likeness has been missing, North and South

When I looked at the history of the 1857 Revival that preceded the Civil War and then the number of people who died fighting, I realized that God had tried to avert this national destruction but people would not listen. As a result, a tithe—ten percent—of their men of military age died.[16]

The South started the Civil War to keep slavery as it was and lost. The North fought to free the slaves and won, but did not have the substance of the character of Christ-likeness to support the freedmen in their quest for true freedom.

As a result, today there is an antagonistic racial climate in this nation. Black Americans are not free in terms of their civil liberties and resentment and White Americans are not free in terms of repentance from their racist past.

Both sides need to repent.

Black Americans have a unique identity, value, and God-given destiny that this nation needs. America's racial problems can be solved both biblically and practically, but we must all look honestly at historical attacks against Black Americans and reawaken their spiritual strengths so they can once again rise above them. Then the world will see why they are alive today for such a time as this.

---

[16] The Civil War death statistics estimated a century ago were too low because of many difficult conditions in those days for recording facts. The Confederacy was in disarray. There were no systematic ways to count the dead or even bury them all. Many died after the war was over from wounds suffered and disease.

Let's Look Back Together so that Everyone Can Win

If all of us look back at history together and honestly try to understand what happened, all of us can win and we will internally be at peace as a nation. Then we will have the substance to bring peace to people of other countries.

How the South Laid a Foundation to Start a War Over Slavery

After the Southern states seceded, they wrote words into their Constitution of the Confederate States of America that still explain today better than any historian the reasons why the South started the Civil War.

Their Constitution was filled with no less than ten guarantees that the South could continue slavery.[17]

When the South seceded and formed a new nation, the lives of generations of Black Americans were affected by the South's broken pledge to the Union, their Constitution, the war dead, and more than a century of persecution, terror, and disenfranchisement of the Black community that followed.

Southern slaves understood the reason for the war and escaped

Within months after seceding and forming a new government with its national capital in Montgomery, Alabama, the South initiated hostilities against the North. The Civil War began in April 1861 when the South fired on Fort Sumter, a Union installation in Charleston, South Carolina.

The South's slaves had no confusion about the reasons for the war, contrary to the historians who would later write about the war. They knew it was a war over slavery. As soon as Northern Union troops began entering Southern territory, droves of slaves who had escaped from their masters ran to them to join the Union Army.

Some Union generals were confused about whether they should return the slaves to their Southern masters, but Brigadier General Benjamin Butler was not confused. He labeled the slaves who escaped to him as

---

[17] The Confederate Constitution is available online at the University of Georgia http://www.libs.uga.edu/hargrett/selections/confed/const.html. Accessed October 2016.

"contraband" of war and kept them with him as free men. This earned him the wrath of Confederate President Jefferson Davis, who issued a war order that Butler should be immediately hanged if captured.[18]

Southern slaves "forever free" after Emancipation Proclamation

On January 1, 1863, President Abraham Lincoln officially resolved the issue of what to do with slaves escaping to the Union Army. He honored them by declaring that all slaves in the Confederacy were "thenceforward, and forever free." It was a stunning blow to the South, which needed their slave labor to win, and an ingenuous legal maneuver.

Lincoln had been a beacon of light against slavery for years. However, because of the separation of powers in the U.S. Constitution, as President he did not have constitutional authority to interfere with state sovereignty and free the slaves in the Union states. He used the solution of an Emancipation Proclamation against the South because it was a time of war. He could issue a proclamation freeing the slaves of an enemy combatant—the rebellious South.

". . . all persons held as slaves within any State or designated part of a State, the people whereof shall then be in rebellion against the United States, shall be then, thenceforward, and forever free." [19]

President Lincoln's Emancipation Proclamation, effective January 1, 1863

Slaves in Union "border states" became free later

At the same time, Lincoln could not legally intervene and free the slaves in any sovereign Northern slave state because they were not at war against the Union. Maryland, Delaware, Kentucky, and Missouri were border slave states that remained in the Union. West Virginia seceded from Virginia in 1861 and in 1863 was admitted to the Union as a free state. Because of the Emancipation Proclamation, slavery technically ended in all

---

[18] Jefferson Davis, President of the Confederate States of America, "General Orders, No. 111" (Richmond, Virginia, December 24, 1862). Source: The Freedmen and Southern Society Project. Online at http://www.history.umd.edu/Freedmen/pow.htm.
[19] "Emancipation Proclamation." National Archives. Online at http://www.ourdocuments.gov/doc.php?doc=34. Accessed October 2016.

the Confederate states as soon as they lost the Civil War. Then, in December 1865, after 27 of the 36 states voted to ratify the Thirteenth Amendment, slavery officially ended in all states.

Blacks encouraged to enlist in Union Army

Early in the war years, most soldiers on both sides of the Civil War were White. However, in the same document where Lincoln freed the Confederate slaves in the Emancipation Proclamation he also invited Blacks to join the Union Army.

> *"And I further declare and make known, that such persons of suitable condition, will be received into the armed service of the United States to garrison forts, positions, stations, and other places, and to man vessels of all sorts in said service."*

Lincoln's Emancipation Proclamation, effective January 1, 1863

Gaining Insight from the Movie *Glory*

You may recall that a movie released in 1989 called *Glory* was based on the true Civil War story of the Massachusetts 54th Infantry, a group of 600 "colored" soldiers who became some of the first Black heroes of the Civil War. Denzel Washington won an Oscar for Best Supporting Actor for his portrayal of one of the Black soldiers, Private Silas Trip.

The Black soldiers of the 54th were commanded by Colonel Robert Gould Shaw (played by Matthew Broderick), who was a young White man and the son of wealthy Boston abolitionists. Shaw was persuaded by Black statesman Frederick Douglass and Governor John Andrew of Massachusetts to take this commission.

Confederate death edict did not stop Blacks from seeking liberty

The Black men who fought for the Union in the Civil War were fighting for the same liberties that slave owners 80 years earlier had proclaimed as they signed the Declaration of Independence. Those White men took up arms in the American Revolution to fight for liberty against

England. However, most of those founding patriots never granted liberty to their slaves.

By the time of the Civil War, many of the Northern states had freed their slaves, but the South was willing to fight *another* war to keep liberty away from their slaves.

To this day the South makes the ridiculous claim at their annual Confederate History celebrations that people of other races wanted to help the South win the Civil War. Although some Black slaves were kind enough to stay to help the families that had enslaved them, many slaves ran away at the first opportunity to be free. They knew that captured runaway slaves faced torture and death at the hands of their owners, but liberty called them, and, as one of America's Founders, Patrick Henry, had said:

> *"Is life so dear or peace so sweet as to be purchased at the price of chains and slavery? Forbid it, Almighty God! I know not what course others may take, but as for me, give me liberty, or give me death!"*

Patrick Henry
St. John's Church, Richmond, Virginia (March 23, 1775)[20]

Confederate President Jefferson Davis warned of harsh treatment

As the movie *Glory* explains, Blacks who became Union soldiers faced even greater dangers than the White Union soldiers if captured by the Confederacy. In response to the pending release of the Emancipation Proclamation by Lincoln, Jefferson Davis, president of the Confederacy, had issued his own harsh proclamation in December 1862. It stated that whenever Black Union soldiers were captured they would be turned over to the Southern states, which meant they would be treated with the brutality inflicted on escaped slaves and returned to slavery or killed. They would never become prisoners of war.

---

[20] The text of Patrick Henry's speech is online at https://www.history.org/almanack/life/politics/giveme.cfm. Accessed October 2016.

Likewise, White officers who commanded colored troops, like General Butler mentioned earlier, would be treated like common criminals who had incited a slave revolt and would be executed.[21]

Courageous Black assault on Fort Wagner

Under the command of Colonel Shaw, the Black soldiers of the Massachusetts 54th who had risked everything to fight for their country were ordered to make a direct frontal attack on Fort Wagner in Charleston Harbor. This required that they advance across open sand and scramble up sand dunes straight into the line of fire.

On the day of battle, with little sleep but filled with faith after a celebration of Jesus Christ the night before, in the movie *Glory* the men of the 54th marched past White soldiers who would be responsible for the next wave of assault. The Whites had previously mocked the Black soldiers, but this time they broke out in cheers. In the movie they shout and wave their hats in the air as a rare show of honor toward this under-appreciated race.

This was the first time that Black soldiers saw major action in a battle of the Civil War, but it would not be the last time that White soldiers cheered them for their courage. These "colored troops," despised and rejected and acquainted with grief,[22] like their Savior, Jesus, would become an indomitable force with a fierce resolve as great as any White man as they faced danger with relentless courage. In every war, the courage and accomplishments of Blacks in the military have been exemplary.

Carrying the Flag, Singing the National Anthem

Every time soldiers go into battle, one man is chosen to carry the flag. He is called the color bearer or standard bearer. The flag embodies the cause that the soldiers are fighting for. It is a visible rallying point that gives courage and purpose to the troops. In our national anthem the words of the describe the thrill on the triumphant morning after a battle in the War of 1812 when "our flag was still there."

---

[21] "General Orders, No. 111" (Richmond, Virginia, December 24, 1862). Source: The Freedmen and Southern Society Project. Online at http://www.history.umd.edu/Freedmen/pow.htm.
[22] See Isaiah 53:3.

"And the rocket's red glare, the bombs bursting in air,
Gave proof through the night that our flag was still there."[23]

Blacks who sit down to dispute and dishonor their country

Currently Black Americans are protesting injustices in America by some signal such as sitting or kneeling when America's national anthem is played at sporting events. During the Civil Rights Movement, some raised a black fist when the national anthem was played at the Olympics after they had won a medal.

An important issue needs to be addressed here.

As we shall see, the problems in Black America are not entirely the fault of White Americans, even though we do need to address injustice.

I am a Black American man. If I walk down the streets of any inner-city in America, I am in far more danger from people of my own race than from any White police. This is not a new phenomenon.

I am a senior citizen now, but even when I was a child 60 years ago it was not safe for me to walk to school in Newark, New Jersey, and then in Baltimore, Maryland. Gangs of older Black boys would stand on the corner and wait for me every day, then take my lunch money unless I could outrun them. I was Black and living among other Blacks but I lived in fear. The same conditions exist in the inner cities today.

The Black community needs more policemen, not less. Sure, the police and Black Americans need to guard against injustices and prejudice and work out their differences, but the streets of the inner cities are unsafe for Blacks primarily because of other Blacks. That's why they need a spiritual solution that changes their hearts and brings them to Christ.

Blacks should sit down for the "Black National Anthem" instead

Black sports figures and others who protest injustice by sitting down during the *Star Spangled Banner* ought to sit down instead for the Black National Anthem, *Lift Every Voice and Sing.* +

---

[23] The full text of our national anthem is at the Smithsonian, online at http://amhistory.si.edu/starspangledbanner/the-lyrics.aspx. Accessed October 2016.

James Weldon Johnson (1871-1938) wrote the words to *Lift Every Voice and Sing* in 1900 as a poem to celebrate Abraham Lincoln's birthday. His brother, John Rosamond Johnson (1873–1954), set the words to music. Through the support of the NAACP,[24] where Johnson was active for many years, *Lift Every Voice and Sing* became an alternative anthem for Blacks that is still used today at Black college sporting events and other public occasions.

Lift Every Voice concludes with a warning in the form of a prayer:

"Keep us forever in the path, we pray.
Lest our feet stray from the places, our God, where we met Thee."[25]

Many Black Americans have strayed from the path of the Christian faith, as Johnson feared. Blacks have made the inner cities of America unsafe by their own sins. Let them take a stand and sit down.

Black Americans Can Raise a New Flag of Freedom

In 2 Corinthians 5:17, the Apostle Paul said that the Gospel is so powerful that even the worst sinners can begin a new life if they come to Christ. In fact, they can not only live according to God's standards for themselves but also they can become ambassadors who rally the troops to follow them as they follow Christ.

God is offering Black Americans a new flag—God's standard—for them to carry once again, if they will turn to Jesus and be saved. That's the vision.

Black Americans, who currently lead in some of the worst social indicators of sin, such as crime, murder, imprisonment, abortion, disease, and premature death, could instead lead in social indicators of health such as wholeness, health, marriage and family, education, and most important of all—spiritual prosperity.

---

[24] National Association for the Advancement of Colored People.
[25] James Weldon Johnson, "Lift Every Voice and Sing." Online at http://www.pbs.org/black-culture/explore/black-authors-spoken-word-poetry/lift-every-voice-and-sing/. Accessed August 2016.

From leaders in sin to raising a flag of righteousness

This is an achievable vision—Black Americans becoming bold ambassadors of Christ to the nations. Someday soon all nations will cheer them as they raise the flag of hope and truth.

"Smooth out the road; pull out the boulders; raise a flag for all the nations to see."[26]

Sin in the Black community as it exists now may be an embarrassment to God, but someday God will celebrate their restoration.

". . . you yourselves became an example to all the Christians . . . And now the word of the Lord is ringing out from you to people everywhere . . . for wherever we go we find people telling us about your faith in God."[27]

The Psalmist uses the analogy of a banner as a rallying point for God's people after they have come out of sin. They have failed Him, but when they return and honor Him, He raises a banner to encourage them to win in the face of an attack.

"You have been very hard on us, making us drink wine that sent us reeling. But you have raised a banner for those who fear you—a rallying point in the face of attack."[28]

Courageously Carrying the American Flag—Carney

William Carney was born a slave in Norfolk, Virginia, and secretly educated by a minister. He loved the Lord and considered entering the ministry himself. However, after being freed upon the death of his master, he moved north to Massachusetts where he later joined the Union Army. He said, "I felt I could best serve my God by serving my Country and my oppressed brothers."[29]

Carney was a soldier in the 1863 military battle for Fort Wagner mentioned earlier. Although his role was not mentioned in the movie

---

[26] Isaiah 62:11 NLT.
[27] 1 Thessalonians 1:7-8 NLT.
[28] Psalm 60:1-4 NLT.
[29] William H. Carney's personal account is available on the website of the elementary school in New Bedford, Massachusetts, that is named after him. Online at http://www.newbedford.k12.ma.us/elementary/whc.htm.

Glory, his deeds were later honored and celebrated for years. This former slave not only won the Congressional Medal of Honor but also continued to stand proudly for his country wherever he was asked to speak at patriotic celebrations.

Here are some details of his heroism and that of his fellow "colored troops" of the Massachusetts 54th Infantry.

> *"On July 18, 1863, these brave black soldiers led the charge and attack on Fort Wagner. During the heat of the battle the color guard, John Wall, was struck by a fatal bullet. He staggered and was about to drop the flag. Carney saw him. He threw down his gun, seized the flag, and held it high throughout that fierce and bloody battle."*[30]

In the movie *Glory*, the American flag lies ignominiously in the dirt beside the troops waiting to resume the battle, but it was actually a point of honor for soldiers to keep the flag of their country off the ground.

When Carney survived the battle and returned behind the Union lines with the flag, the men broke out in cheers. This is how he described it.

> *"An officer came, and taking my name and regiment, put us in charge of the hospital corps, telling them to find my regiment. When we finally reached the latter the men cheered me and the flag. My reply was, 'Boys, the old flag never touched the ground.'"*[31]

The flag now safe, his mission complete, Carney collapsed from his multiple wounds and was carried away.

Congressional Medal of Honor to Black American hero

Until the battle of Fort Wagner, too many Whites did not believe that Black men could fight and lead. They thought that Black men lacked intelligence, had bad character, and were ill prepared to handle such

---

[30] Jane Waters, "William H. Carney." New Bedford Black Heritage Trail. Online at http://nbhistoricalsociety.org/Important-Figures/sergeant-william-h-carney/. Accessed September 2016.
[31] Carney, *op. cit.*

extreme danger, but Carney was promoted to sergeant on the basis of his actions and became a hero and a popular speaker at patriotic events.

Although the movie states that the fort was never taken, in reality Union troops occupied Fort Wagner only two months later when it was abandoned by the Confederates. One of the Confederacy's military leaders who had observed the charge that day later admitted that the Black soldiers showed unusual courage and commitment.

William Carney was the first Black soldier to be awarded the Congressional Medal of Honor in the Civil War. It was awarded 40 years later, a delay that was not uncommon in those days.

The flag that he carried is kept in Boston's Memorial Hall and his face is immortalized in a sculpture honoring the men of the 54th with Colonel Robert Gould Shaw. The memorial resides in Boston Common across from the Massachusetts State House on the Black Heritage Trail.

Why Africans Don't See Black Americans as African Americans

Black Americans often achieve recognition in situations led by Whites, such as the memorial in Boston, but unique world recognition of Blacks as a people group is often missing. I sum this up in three statements:

1. Black Americans are not recognized as a people group by a world body, even though their historical experience is unique.
2. There is a disconnect that causes Black Africans not to acknowledge the African roots of Black Americans.
3. Africans wonder why Blacks have not come to help them *en masse*, because they see all Americans as resource-based, not need-based.

The last time I was in East Africa, I met privately with Black Anglican Archbishops who oversee the spiritual life of their nations. They challenged the term "African American" with these three questions:

1. "What tribe are you from?
2. "What original language do you speak?
3. "What geographical area did you live in? "

Black Americans would have to answer to all three questions, "I don't know."

Then the Africans summarized:

1. "You have no tribe.
2. "You have no original language,
3. "You have no geographical land base.

"Therefore, you are not African-American. You are Black American."

Then they draw this conclusion, "You can help us."

Blacks already have an identity as Americans

Black Americans are going to Africa to seek their identity while the Africans think they already have one. They are Americans who happen to be Black.

While Blacks are looking for their identity within the designation of "African Americans," they should be thinking of themselves as American-based resource people to the nations of the world, and especially to Africa.

Those Africans understood that if Black Americans continue to link their identity to Africa and allow others to identify them that way, they will miss the staggering implications of being born in America.

Blacks should be missionaries but they are still a mission field

I have come to this conclusion. While Blacks should be missionaries they are still a mission field. Most studies on world missions related to the Black community count less than 500 full time Black missionaries outside the United States.

Africans ask Blacks, *"Why have you not come to help us?"*

The Africans add this, "You are not African-Americans. You are Black Americans. You can help us. *Why have you not come to help us?"*

They gave me their own answer to that question:

"Here is why you have not come to help us.

1. "You haven't forgiven us for selling you into slavery.
2. "You think you are better than we are because you were born in America.
3. "You don't think we are worth it because we are not rich. You think we are like monkeys still hanging on the trees."

Blacks still plead for recognition from the government

Those Africans don't realize that Blacks Americans do not see themselves as a resource people group. Blacks are still pleading, trying to get the government to recognize them and help them. Blacks also put a low value to their lives among themselves, as indicated by the abortion rate of Black babies that is more than triple the abortion rate of White babies; also the Black-on-Black murder rate.

God brought every Black American to life

Blacks won't realize the call of God on their lives as a people group until they look to God as the explanation for their coming into existence. The Bible says in John 1 that God brought all life into existence.

> *"In the beginning was the Word, and the Word was with God, and the Word was God. The same was in the beginning with God. All things were made by him; and without him was not any thing made that was made. In him was life; and the life was the light of men. And the light shineth in darkness; and the darkness comprehended it not."[32]*

Blacks have to find their God-given destiny as a people, regardless of how they came into the world or what they have experienced since.

I say about my own ghetto and gutter background—
I came the wrong way, but I am the right result.

---

[32] John 1:1-5 KJV.

IDENTITY, VALUE, AND RECOGNITION

Three medals of liberation we need to award to Black America

When you always focus on the problem, you can't see the solution. With all of the injustices Blacks have suffered in this nation, none of them outweighs the advantages of being born and raised in America, the greatest nation on earth.

Sure, Black Americans have suffered and their accomplishments have often not been recognized, but even if everyone in America acknowledged how much Blacks had been mistreated and praised them for the many things they have accomplished, all of that would still be empty unless they firmly established their identity, value, and recognition on the foundation of God. Then they can walk in their assignment as ambassadors for Christ in the world.

IDENTITY. Black Americans are not recognized as a valid people group by any world body, even though their experience is unique.

VALUE. Blacks helped build state capitals and the national capital in Washington. They fought bravely in American wars despite prejudice in the ranks, including, for example, the Revolutionary War and the Civil War. Blacks have proven their value.

RECOGNITION. Blacks developed many inventions and discoveries where they never received credit. For every William Carney who won the Congressional Medal of Honor there are many others who did not receive recognition because they were Black.

IDENTITY

Black America is suffering from an identity crisis. When you don't know who you are and what you have to contribute to this life, you will lack a sense of purpose and personal identity.

You don't need to have White people give you identity if you are Black. When White people say things to deny who you are, unless your identity comes from God, you will strike back and try to force them to speak better of you. You won't guard your identity as a righteous person and keep yourself morally and intellectually strong. You will fulfill their unrighteous expectations instead of proving them wrong.

25

God created you for a purpose. You have a call on your life as an American created in the image of God. In order to thrive as a human being, you need to drop everything else you are doing until you discover what that purpose is and how God wants you to fulfill it. When you have the right vision for your life, that vision has power to transform everything. The world looks different to everyone who knows in his heart that God created him for a purpose.

Everyone else but God identifies you by outward signs. The most obvious outward way that people identify Black Americans is by pigmentation. The next is by their way of life.

- Black families—49% fatherless and led by unwed mothers. Percentage is much higher in the projects.
- Schools—illiteracy and high drop-out rates
- Productivity—high unemployment, selling drugs
- How you treat people—crime and murder rates
- Communities where you live—poor, living in the ghetto, trashing the environment

Even if White Americans failed you, God still holds *you* responsible

In every one of those categories I can show you how Blacks' treatment by White America has contributed to the problem, but that is not an excuse that God will give you. When you stand before God at Judgment Day you will not be able to say, "White people made me do it."

God created you as an individual with a will and an ability to change your environment. You are not helpless. You can clean up your life, your family, your community, and yourself. Blacks historically built and maintained systems and structures, from plantation homes to the White House. That is a fact of Black history.

The conditions in your inner cities should identify you as people of God who are safe and thriving, like Goshen in the Bible. When God was judging the Egyptians with plagues for their rebellion against Him and their mistreatment of His people Israel, he set aside Goshen as a place where there were no plagues and all the people could live in safety.

"But this time I will spare the region of Goshen, where my people live. No flies will be found there. Then you will know that I am the LORD and that I am present even in the heart of your land."[33]

---

[33] Exodus 8:22 NLT.

White people have historically doubted if you could become civilized without them. Prove them wrong. During the Blacks' first centuries in America, many in the White majority refused to identity Blacks even as human beings, let alone as free citizens. Jefferson Davis, in the proclamation mentioned earlier, called out slaves who escaped to join the Union Army as "savages" who committed "the most merciless atrocities."[34] Show them your exemplary character and first class behavior.

Your identity should come from your father's name but he is missing. Currently the Black community is largely fatherless and lacking true family identity. I didn't grow up with my natural father in the home. I don't carry his name. I carry my granddaddy's name. However, I didn't allow that to define me. I made my own way by learning how to be a father from the Scriptures and from my relationship with my heavenly Father.

Some of the best fathers in American history have been Black. Black fathers in slavery valued their children so much that they were willing to risk their lives to protect them.[35] Some fathers escaped through the Underground Railroad with their families so that they and their families would be free. After the Civil War, fathers who had been slaves were known to walk hundreds of miles searching for lost wives and children who had been sold to other slave owners.[36]

You can recapture your identity if you go back to God and allow Him to define you.

> *"Once you had no identity as a people; now you are God's people. Once you received no mercy; now you have received God's mercy."*[37]

VALUE

For centuries Black Americans have been a nation within a nation, devalued by every other people group. Even when the great Black American hero Booker T. Washington was a brilliant student and tutor of

---

[34] Jefferson Davis, President of the Confederate States of America, "General Orders, No. 111" (Richmond, Virginia, December 24, 1862). Source: The Freedmen and Southern Society Project. Online at http://www.history.umd.edu/Freedmen/pow.htm. Accessed August 2016.
[35] Thomas Sowell, *Ethnic America: A History* (New York, Basic Books, 1981), p. 186-190.
[36] Ibid.
[37] 1 Peter 2:10 NLT.

Native Americans at Hampton Institute, as it was called then, the Native Americans looked down on him. Blacks were the lowest of the low.

White people have historically degraded Blacks.

- The U.S. Constitution listed Blacks as "other persons" who were counted in the census for purposes of election strength only, and then merely as "three fifths" of White citizens.[38]
- The U.S. Supreme Court decision in *Dred Scott* labeled Blacks as subhuman, a "subordinate and inferior class of beings, who had been subjugated by the dominant race."[39]
- Margaret Sanger, notorious founder of Planned Parenthood, famously set out to decrease the number of births in the *"inferior classes, . . . the feeble minded, the mentally defective, the poverty-stricken."[40] (See also Chapter 6 and Chapter 7.)*

Black men and women degrade themselves. Many Black men no longer see themselves with the kind of God-centered, generational vision that fathers need in order to believe that their lives have value—their lives or their children's lives. They allow their own media to depict them as sex-driven and submitted to women while the women allow the media to depict them as half-naked, lust-filled whores. Wake up!

Black American men need to recapture the vision that they are made in God's image and that their wives and children are people of value with potential for greatness. Nothing is too much for a father to do to give his child a sense of value, of being cherished, of being important to his dad. Each generation needs fathers like that or the race will die out, as you see now in Black America.

God is the Father who never fails us. He showed us how much He valued us when He gave us His only Son so that we could have eternal life.

"For God so loved the world, that he gave his only begotten Son, that whosoever believeth in him should not perish, but have everlasting life."[41]

---

[38] All quotations from the United States Constitution online at http://www.ourdocuments.gov/doc.php?flash=true&doc=9&page=transcript. Accessed October 2016.

[39] *Dred Scott vs. John F. A. Sandford* (1857). Online at http://www.ourdocuments.gov/print_friendly.php?page=transcript&doc=29&title=Transcript+of+Dred+Scott+v.+Sanford+percent281857percent29. Accessed October 2016.

[40] Ibid.

[41] John 3:16 KJV.

RECOGNITION

William Carney did not receive the Congressional Medal of Honor to make him feel better as a Black American or to manipulate him to sacrifice more for his country. He was recognized because he deserved recognition. He exhibited outstanding bravery in the field of battle when he honored his country by preserving the flag.

Black Americans should be receiving awards all the time for honoring their native land, leading godly, high-achieving families, and developing inventions and other legitimate accomplishments greater than anyone else on earth.

Blacks in history should be recognized, even posthumously, for their contributions to science, medicine, the arts, government—almost every field. This recognition was often stolen from them by White people in power who took it for themselves but God saw it and will reward them.

DID YOU KNOW? Black Accomplishments and Inventions

Ambassador to foreign nations	Frederick Douglass (1817-1895) served as a foreign ambassador from the United States to Haiti and the Dominican Republic. One of the most famous Black Americans of the 19th century. Author, access to U.S. Presidents, promoter of Black soldiers in Civil War.
Automatic gear shift, car directional signals, brakes	Richard Spikes (1878-1965). Modifications of the automatic gear shift, automatic safety brake used for school buses
Beauty products, first Black millionaire	Madame C.J. Walker (1867-1919) Invented beauty products for Blacks, became first Black millionaire, wealthy donor to Black charities. Sales staff promoted her philosophy of "cleanliness and loveliness"[42] to advance status of Blacks.

---

[42] "Madame C. J. Walker." Online at http://www.biography.com/people/madam-cj-walker-9522174#success-and-philanthropy. Accessed October 2016.

Blood plasma research and first blood bank	Dr. Charles Richard Drew (1904-1950) Advanced degrees in medicine and surgery from McGill University in Montreal, Quebec, in 1933 and from Columbia University in 1940. Research in separating plasma in blood and setting up the first blood bank.
Dry cleaning process	Thomas L. Jennings (1791-1859). First Black to hold a U.S. patent (1821, dry-cleaning process). He was a free Black but had to fight against patent laws denying patents to slaves. Abolitionist who successfully challenged segregation in transportation.
Electric lamp and carbon filament, telephone	Lewis Howard Latimer (c.1848-1928) Invented an electric lamp and a carbon filament for light bulbs (patented 1881, 1882). Only Black in Thomas Edison's engineering laboratory and also worked on telephone with Alexander Graham Bell.
Evaporator for refining sugar, soap	Norbert Rillieux (1806-1894). Invented a safe and efficient evaporator for refining sugar (patented 1846) still used today in sugar and soap industries.
First woman to charter a bank	Maggie Walker (1864-1934), first woman to charter and lead a bank in the United States—St. Luke Penny Savings Bank, Richmond, Virginia. She was also a publisher and department store developer. During segregation, Richmond built the Maggie L. Walker High School for Blacks.
Gas mask, three-part traffic signal	Garrett Augustus Morgan (1877-1963) Invented gas mask (1914) that protected soldiers from chlorine fumes in World War I; patent (1923) for a traffic signal that featured automated STOP and GO signs (later replaced by traffic lights); hair products
Hospital founder, heart surgeon, pioneer in using sterile technique	Dr. Daniel Hale Williams. (1856-1931). Founder of integrated training hospital, Provident Hospital in Chicago. Introduced Louis Pasteur's sterilization procedures. Performed one of first open-heart surgeries (1893) on a man with a stab wound and it was successful.

HVAC inventor, heating system Radio City Music Hall	David Crosthwait, Jr. (1898-1976) Designed heating system for Radio City Music Hall in New York, 40 HVAC patents
Layout for Washington, DC, almanac, astronomy	Benjamin Banneker (1731-1806) from a free Black family taught himself advanced mathematics and astronomy. Published a yearly almanac. Was chosen by Thomas Jefferson to assist with the layout of Washington, DC.
Open heart surgery pioneer, trainer of famous heart surgeons	Vivien Thomas (1910-1985) Helped pioneer open-heart surgery for "blue babies" (four heart defects called Tetralogy of Fallot) while assistant to Dr. Alfred Blalock at Johns Hopkins (see HBO film *Something the Lord Made*). Trained heart surgeons
Psychologist, research on insects, educator	Charles Henry Turner (1867-1923) Ph.D. (1907) University of Chicago. First Black psychologist. Authority on insects, first to prove insects can hear. Chose to become an educator of young Black Americans in a St. Louis high school in addition to his research.
Second female medical school grad, protector of unborn children	Rebecca Cole (1846-1922). Second black female graduate of a medical school (1867, Women's Medical College of Pennsylvania, founded by Quakers). She co-founded the Women's Directory Center for the poor and worked to prevent feticide (killing a fetus) and infanticide.
Steam engine	Benjamin Bradley (1830?-?) Slave who as a teenager built a steam engine out of junk metal. He developed the first steam engine for a warship. Although as a slave he could not obtain a patent, his slave master allowed him to sell it to purchase his freedom.
Steam engine lubricator	Elijah McCoy (1844-1929). He and his family escaped from slavery. He patented a lubricator for steam engines (1872) and 56 other patents including lawn mower and lawn sprinkler.

Synthetic cortisone, physostigmine	Percy Julian (1899-1975) first to synthesize cortisone, greatly reducing the cost. He also helped synthesize physostigmine for the treatment of glaucoma. 115 patents, 20 honorary doctorates. DePauw University renamed its science building in his honor
Telegraph between moving trains, safety cut-off switch,	Granville T. Woods (1856-1910). Known as the "Black Edison," he also successfully defended himself in a lawsuit by Thomas Edison. He invented telegraph communication between moving trains, automatic cut-off switch, He held about 60 patents for his many inventions.
Truck refrigeration	Frederick McKinley Jones (1893-1961). Self-educated. Invented automatic refrigeration system for long-haul trucks used for food and blood during World War II. Held more than 60 patents in refrigeration, cars, and sound. First Black to receive National Medal of Technology awarded posthumously in 1991 by President George H.W. Bush.
Uses of peanut, best practices in agriculture	George Washington Carver (1865?-1943) Born a slave, brilliant researcher who openly honored God, became director of agricultural research at the Tuskegee Institute in 1896. Developed hundreds of applications of peanut, sweet potato, soybean, and pecan. Taught farmers best agricultural methods. A national monument was dedicated in his honor in 1943 by President Franklin Roosevelt.
Yale Physics Doctorate	Edward Alexander Bouchet (1852-1918). One of first Blacks to earn doctorate from Yale (1876, Physics). Member of Phi Beta Kappa. Educator. Edward A. Bouchet Graduate Honor Society was created in 2005 by Yale along with Howard University.

They had a destiny. Have you identified yours?

You might look at those examples and say you can understand why God brought those people into the world, but you also need to ask God why He brought *you* into existence. Should you be recognized for something you have accomplished that proves why He created you? Are you seeking God for His purpose for your life? Is there something on Earth that needs to be done and only you can accomplish it?

Black Ambassadors for Christ and America

When you know your calling and you honor God and country, you can become an honored ambassador to other nations.

A person who understands his high calling in God is a great asset to his country. He is not influenced by the temptation to sin and betray His King, Jesus, and he is not a candidate to betray or embarrass his country.

When you are an ambassador to the world, you don't let the world influence you to go against your nation or against what Jesus expects of you and what you know is right.

You are reconciled to God and He has given you the ministry of reconciliation and the word of reconciliation. *"[43]*

Ambassadors responding to the Great Commission

All Christians are called to be ambassadors for Christ to nations. Jesus gave the Great Commission to all of His apostles. This is not a secular calling, either. He told them to make Christian disciples of nations. Is that calling always manifested in overt ways? Not necessarily, but every Black American should consider how to become an ambassador who is inwardly motivated by the call of Jesus to be an example of Christ-likeness before world powers.

---

[43] 2 Corinthians 5:18-19 KJV.

*"Jesus came and told his disciples, 'I have been given all
authority in heaven and on earth. Therefore, go and make
disciples of all the nations, baptizing them in the name of
the Father and the Son and the Holy Spirit. Teach these
new disciples to obey all the commands I have given you.
And be sure of this: I am with you always,
even to the end of the age."*[44]

Ambassadors empowered by the Holy Spirit can bring restoration

Your righteousness is obvious to the world according to the level of an ambassador's call on your life and also according to the work of the Holy Spirit in your life.

God measures the heavens by the span of His hand.[45] There is nothing on Earth that God doesn't understand. When you talk to God in prayer, you can turn everything on your mind not just into a prayer but also into a discussion you would have with your Best Friend.

Holy Ghost wants to use somebody who is willing to show that God is alive. He can show up mystically. He can show up in the atmosphere and the atmosphere is charged.

However, Jesus gets the most credit on earth when Holy Ghost shows up inside a Christian. You must be the person He shows up in. You can bring restoration by your consecration and your Friendship with Holy Ghost. God's abundant life through Jesus Christ can be yours, and abundant life can be restored to earth—through you.

*"If God be for us, who can be against us? He that spared not
his own Son, but delivered him up for us all, how shall he not
with him also freely give us all things? Who shall lay any
thing to the charge of God's elect? It is God that justifieth.
Who is he that condemneth? It is Christ that died, yea rather,
that is risen again, who is even at the right hand of God, who
also maketh intercession for us. Who shall separate us from*

---

[44] Matthew 28:18-20 NLT.
[45] See Isaiah 40:12

> *the love of Christ? shall tribulation, or distress, or*
> *persecution, or famine, or nakedness, or peril, or sword?*
> *"As it is written, For thy sake we are killed all the day long;*
> *we are accounted as sheep for the slaughter.*
> *"Nay, in all these things we are more than conquerors*
> *through him that loved us."[46]*

An ambassador is a giver instead of a taker—he loves to give

An ambassador isn't sent to a nation to become righteous. He is sent to a nation because he *is* righteous. Christians find people in the world who need what they have and give it away. They can't keep being takers when they have something that somebody else needs. Christians are not takers. They are givers. ***They love to give.***

Your spirit man already knows that you are an ambassador, but your insecure mind keeps rejecting it. When you hear the word that you are an ambassador, your spirit bears witness with that. You can identify with that statement because it is already real inside of you. You haven't just accepted it mentally. You have the witness of the Bible confirming in your mind what is true in your spirit. With your mind you have self-consciousness. With your spirit you have God-consciousness.

Creating inner-city environments like heaven as heaven's ambassador

A foreign ambassador establishes the environment of the embassy. It can be totally different from the country where he lives. Within that compound, he has diplomatic immunity. He can set rules. He can carry on the affairs of state entrusted to him.

Black Americans should be able to create inner-city environments that are like heaven. As ambassadors foreign to the lusts of the world, they should create embassies on earth like heaven.

When you walk by faith, Jesus can call you to walk on water or to represent the greatest nation on earth and you will do it. The Bible says that the Kingdom of God is within you, so you carry it with you. You are able

---

[46] Romans 8:31-37 KJV.

to change the environment everywhere you go. Because of you, earth's atmosphere is changed.

You don't develop confidence from thinking about *going to heaven*. You believe that you *come from heaven* and you are bringing heaven to the earth.

Take authority—you have the right credentials

> *"The earth is the LORD's, and everything in it. The world and all its people belong to him. For he laid the earth's foundation on the seas and built it on the ocean depths."[47]*

When you are sent somewhere on earth as an ambassador, you take dominion every place you go—not just in one section of the earth. The whole earth is yours, and you run it like God's government in heaven.

Christianity is not a liability for an American ambassador

You are not illegal. Don't let anybody doubt your credentials. You bring everything in line. Jesus' adversaries are the ones who are illegal. These are a Christian's adversaries, too, as described in John 1:

> Jesus *"was in the world, and the world was made through Him, and the world did not know Him. He came to His own, and His own did not receive Him."[48]*

If Jesus comes to someone who does not acknowledge or receive Him, they are not in line with the Creator of the earth. If you approach someone and you represent Jesus, they are out of line if they don't receive you. God will have to deal with them but you need to keep your place.

Black Americans Out of Darkness, God's Light to the World

The Bible says that Christians are a holy nation, God's chosen people. They are not supposed to stumble in sin like other people. They demonstrate God's goodness as they walk in His favor.

---

[47] Psalm 24:1-2 NLT.
[48] John 1:10-11 NKJV.

". . . you are a chosen people. You are a kingdom of priests, God's holy nation, his very own possession. This is so you can show others the goodness of God, for he called you out of the darkness into his wonderful light."[49]

Black American Christians served in the U.S. Congress briefly after the Civil War, but then they were thrown out and blocked from becoming a new guard of national leaders because of prejudice and oppression. There are still not many in national leadership in spite of the Civil Rights movement. Something is still missing.

God is still calling Christians, especially pastors and laymen who live by the Bible, to take the lead and solve national and international challenges of the day, both in principles and practice.

Blacks have lost some of the world's favor by their sins

Twice in history, the eyes of the world have been on Black America with favor. Now Blacks are sometimes in disfavor. However, soon they will be delivered from their own sins.

Slavery and the Civil War. As people read *Uncle Tom's Cabin* in nations around the world and listened to international speakers like the former slave Frederick Douglass, they realized that American slavery was evil, and wept and prayed for Black Americans until they were free.

Civil Rights Movement. Because of the advances of television news during the Civil Rights era, the world saw Black Americans beaten and attacked by dogs, and they won others over to the cause of their freedom.

Now—deliverance from their own evil through Jesus Christ. With few exceptions, most Black Americans don't have the international spotlight today, and the thousands being murdered each year by other Blacks in the inner cities don't even make the local news. Blacks need to be delivered from evil, then lead in righteousness.

"And lead us not into temptation, but deliver us from evil."[50]

A few Black candidates, athletes, and movie stars work hard and know how to get media attention, but there is no current groundswell of admiration and support towards Black Americans as a race. There are too

---

[49] 1 Peter 2:9 NLT.
[50] Matthew 6:13 KJV.

many failures. They need to look to God for their success so that He can raise them up.

A day is coming when Blacks will be delivered from evil. God will exalt them, and the eyes of the world will be on them once again with favor. If they can get clean this time, they can lead a spiritual revolution that everyone will want to follow. I am not just talking about following spiritual leaders while in church, but in all of society—the highest positions of political and economic leadership in this country and the world led by strong Christian leaders.

Blacks seeing themselves as standard bearers

Black Americans, you need to regain a vision of yourselves as standard bearers and Jesus' faithful foot soldiers in the fight against evil. Not only White Americans and your fellow Blacks will cheer you on but also the witnesses in heaven who are even now watching to see how nobly you will fight in the battle of the ages.

> *"Since we have such a huge crowd of men of faith watching us from the grandstands, let us strip off anything that slows us down or holds us back, and especially those sins that wrap themselves so tightly around our feet and trip us up; and let us run with patience the particular race that God has set before us."[51]*

The world will say, Lord, make us like Black America

Someday soon people will say about Black Americans, to paraphrase the words of John Winthrop's message at the beginning of this chapter, "The Lord make us like Black America, for we must consider that we shall be as a city upon a hill. The eyes of all people are upon us."

That day is coming, but first Black Americans must become like Jesus. That was Winthrop's message to the colonists, and it is the message you need to heed today.

---

[51] Hebrews 12: 1 TLB.

Blacks Couldn't Set American Agenda in Past, But That Can Change

Jesus never let anyone else set the agenda when people came around Him. Sinners were drawn to Him, but they found that when they got close to Him they couldn't bring up all their issues and dominate Him. No one could usurp His authority. It was impossible. He was always in charge. He never let anyone else set the conditions for His relationships.

Black Americans are hardly ever in charge, outside of their own race. Blacks held state and federal elected offices during Reconstruction, but those opportunities were quickly taken away 12 years after the Civil War by the 1877 Compromise and kept out of reach for the next century. That can only change if they become like Jesus.

DID YOU KNOW? Black Setbacks from 1877 Compromise

Before 1877 Compromise

1865   April 26, surrender of Confederate General Robert E. Lee to Union General Ulysses S. Grant. Slaves in Confederate states were freed by the Emancipation Proclamation previously issued by Lincoln. Texas slaves were last to hear the news on June 19, 1865, which is still celebrated as "Juneteenth." Lincoln assassinated. Union Army begins to govern the defeated South.

1865   Congress establishes the U.S. Bureau of Refugees, Freedmen, and Abandoned Lands ("Freedmen's Bureau") to aid four million Black Americans moving from slavery to freedom.

1865   Thirteenth Amendment abolishing slavery is ratified by 27 of 36 states in December 1865.

1866   Massachusetts is first state to elect Blacks to its legislature. Many other Northern states do not allow blacks to vote for many years.

1866   The states of the former Confederacy pass "black code" laws to replace the social controls removed by Emancipation Proclamation and Thirteenth Amendment to the U.S. Constitution

1866   Ku Klux Klan formed in Pulaski, Tennessee, led by Lieutenant General Nathan Bedford Forrest (1821-1877), notorious for Confederate massacre of Black Union soldiers at Fort Pillow in the Civil War. KKK is characterized by violence, whippings, murder, including lynchings.

1867   One of first Reconstruction Acts provided for free elections in every former Confederate state to determine if it should rewrite its constitution and be readmitted to the Union. This was the first election where Blacks could vote in the South. Thousands registered, sometimes outnumbering White voters. Almost all Blacks were Republicans, "the party of Lincoln."

1867   New legislatures voted for free public schools for all, a new concept in the aristocratic South where even Whites were often uneducated. Much debate about mixing races.

1867   Mississippi delegates: 18 Blacks, 80 Whites. Louisiana delegates: half of delegates were Blacks. South Carolina Blacks included speaker of house and president of White-controlled senate. Blacks were criticized, but proved intelligent and effective. Passed laws to aid the poor and sick. Spoke against fraud. Never took vengeance for the years they had been enslaved.

1868   The Fourteenth Amendment to the Constitution is ratified, guaranteeing equal protection under the law.

1868   Fourth Reconstruction Act provided that instead of two-thirds, a simple majority of voters could ratify state constitutions. New state constitutions were then passed in Alabama, Georgia, Louisiana, North Carolina, South Carolina; and Mississippi.

1868   South Carolina General Assembly convenes with 85 Black and 70 White representatives, first state legislature with a Black majority.

1870   Congress passes Enforcement Act and Ku Klux Klan Act in 1870 and 1871

1870   Hiram R. Revels of Mississippi becomes first Black U.S. Senator.

1870   Last state holdouts are readmitted to Union: Mississippi, Florida, and Texas.

1870   Joseph Rainey of South Carolina is the first Black American elected to the U.S. House of Representatives.

1870   The Fifteenth Amendment of the U.S. Constitution is ratified, guaranteeing the right to vote regardless of "race, color, or previous condition of servitude."

1870   Blacks hold public office as sheriff, mayor, prosecuting attorney, justice of peace, superintendent of education.

1871   Mississippi House: 38 Blacks and 77 Whites. Total of 7 blacks
        became state senators.

1872   John R. Lynch, former slave, studied at night: speaker of the
        Mississippi House of Representatives, elected to the U.S.
        Congress. Commended by all for leadership.

1873   P. B. S. Pinchback elected U.S. senator from Louisiana but never
        allowed to take his seat. As Lieutenant Governor, governed state
        for 35 days when governor removed from office.

1874   Blanche K. Bruce sent to U. S. Senate from Mississippi, the last
        Black U.S. senator until Edward Brooke of Massachusetts in 1966.

1875   Civil Rights Act promoted for years by Senator Charles Sumner of
        Massachusetts (R) passed after his death. Guaranteed rights in inns,
        public conveyances, theaters, and place of amusement. This was
        last major act to protect blacks' rights for nearly 100 years.

After 1877 Compromise

1877   Resurgence in Black lynchings: 100 or more each year until 1900.

1879   More loss of support for Black leaders. Southern states rewrote
        constitutions and added poll taxes to be paid before people could
        vote. The "grandfather clause" allowed only those who had voted
        prior to 1861 and their descendants to vote.

1881   Tennessee becomes the first state to enact Jim Crow legislation,
        which requires Blacks and Whites to ride in separate railroad cars.

1884   Connecticut, Iowa, New Jersey, and Ohio pass laws permitting
        discrimination in public accommodations.

1885   Colorado, Illinois, Indiana, Michigan, Minnesota, Nebraska, Rhode
        Island pass similar laws.

1887   Pennsylvania passes similar laws.

1890   Washington state passes similar laws. *Plessy v. Ferguson* (case for
        separate but equal railroad accommodations in Louisiana) affirmed
        by U.S. Supreme Court.

1890   Mississippi: Black voters outnumber Whites by 200,000. Whites
        rewrite constitution to disenfranchise Blacks.

Long Time Coming, But Makeover for Blacks Not Impossible

Black Americans can lead an agenda that benefits the entire homeland if they launch an aggressive makeover program to become more like Jesus. If they become like Him, God will back them. They will be qualified to become elders in the gates—not only on the basis of man's qualifications but on the basis of the higher laws of God. Nothing is impossible with God.

> *"Jesus looked at them intently and said, 'Humanly speaking, it is impossible. But not with God. Everything is possible with God.'"*[52]

It doesn't have to take a long time. God said that a nation can be born in a day.[53] The Greek word for nation in the Bible is *ethnos*, thus our word "ethnic." It also means a people group, race, or tribe. According to the Bible a new ethnic group can be born in a single day whom others will look upon and be glad.

> *"Has a nation ever been born in a single day? Has a country ever come forth in a mere moment? . . . When you see these things, your heart will rejoice. Vigorous health will be yours! Everyone will see the good hand of the Lord on his people."*[54]

When a spiritual awakening sweeps through the inner cities of Black America and multitudes are born again, God can entrust American leadership roles to Blacks in a fiat. Blacks would have to lead from a position of humility and righteousness, based on the Bible and their relationship with Jesus Christ. Then they would have real power.

God Could Make Blacks into Leaders by Fiat

"Fiat" comes from the Latin root that means "Let it be done." God creates by divine fiat things that never existed before. No effort by man can stop what God chooses to do, as God reminded Job in this passage:

---

[52] Mark 10:27 NLT
[53] See Isaiah 66:8.
[54] Isaiah 66:8, 14 NLT.

"Where were you when I laid the foundations of the earth? Tell me, if you know so much. Do you know how its dimensions were determined and who did the surveying? What supports its foundations, and who laid its cornerstone as the morning stars sang together and all the angels shouted for joy? Who defined the boundaries of the sea as it burst from the womb, and as I clothed it with clouds and thick darkness? For I locked it behind barred gates, limiting its shores. I said, 'Thus far and no farther will you come. Here your proud waves must stop!'"[55]

For those who obey Him, Jesus opens doors that no man can shut.[56] America needs leaders with that kind of power today. They need to get in the face of God, become transformed into His likeness, and then change the world according to His plan. It's radical, but it's reality. America's founders did it, and that's why we are all here today, because God has been with us as a nation.

Can Black Americans Come Together in Love?

John Winthrop's shipboard message at the beginning of this chapter where he quoted Jesus' words about becoming a city on a hill was called "A Modell of Christian Charity."

"Charity" is the old King James word for "love" in 1 Corinthians 13. Sometimes you have to go back to an old definition to learn what something means without its modern corruption. Black America today still reveres the language of the King James Bible, with good reason.

Today's loose definitions of love include a guy who says "I love you" to trick a girl to have sex with him without giving her the covenant of marriage.

In 1 Corinthians 13, true love is described as "charity"—selfless love toward others for *their* benefit. In other words, when you love, you are like God. That chapter would make a good platform for political parties in the next election.

John Winthrop said people characterized by the kind of love described in 1 Corinthians 13 could become a unified and powerful nation

---

[55] Job 38:4-11 NLT.
[56] Revelation 3:8-9 NLT.

that was an example for the world to see. He must have been talking about Black America.

Martin Luther King's message of loving others

The Rev. Dr. Martin Luther King, Jr., wrote a book called *Strength to Love*. Under his leadership, the Black citizens of Montgomery, Alabama, the first capital of the Confederacy, decided to stop riding segregated buses and became unified by love. They were not unified by hatred of White people or even hatred of the Jim Crow laws that segregated public transportation in Alabama, forcing them to ride in the back of the bus.

King taught Blacks to love White people instead of hating them. They learned to love one another in order to share their cars and walk all those miles for months until the system of segregation began to crumble. They needed love to go to those church services where they would sing and pray and listen to brave men tell them to be strong because God was with them, never knowing when they would be beaten, hit by spit or rocks, jailed, or blown up by bombs.

The Puritans' message of love and unity

Winthrop and the Puritans who came to Massachusetts had endured persecution, too. That was one reason their New England descendants eventually had so much compassion for slaves. Depending on which king or queen was in power in England, Puritans could be thrown in jail for their faith or given a royal position. It was that extreme.

The Puritans came to New England to establish a new nation—not only so they could practice freedom of religion for themselves personally but also to build a unified Christian society based on God and His love. Their successes and failures helped them lay a unified foundation for what America became in later years.

"Behold, how good and how pleasant it is for brethren to dwell together in unity!"[57]

---

[57] Psalm 133:1 NKJV.

Can Black Communities Become a New "City Upon a Hill"?

If Black Americans can recapture the faith of their fathers and build a better nation based on the Bible and Jesus Christ, Black America can become the world's new city upon a hill that the entire world is watching. God will delight in them and so will others who come to see their transformation and what a wonder they have become. Their change will cause even skeptics to begin praising God.

Winthrop gave the New England settlers a vision for such a great community that God would command a blessing on it. He said:

> *"So shall we keep the unity of the spirit in the bond of peace. The Lord will be our God, and delight to dwell among us, as his one people, and will command a blessing upon us in all our way."*[58]

Fixing Yourselves So You Can Fix the Government

Blacks have the potential to restore love to the body of Christ and Christ-like love to the public forum.

First they should fix themselves. Second, they should fix America. And finally, they can start fixing the world. God is great enough for that accomplishment to come to pass. He could use the least likely people group to start a worldwide spiritual revolution that restores a biblical worldview to government.

When unlikely people bring the next awakening, God will get the glory.

Some Blacks have lost their credibility as Christians because of the stuff that they have done, but when they pull this off everybody will know it must have been God who did it. He came upon them and what could they do but lift Him up? Everything changed because they were willing to change and do things God's way.

Black America has a great testimony coming. It's going to give them such great leverage that when they want to talk about Jesus, people will listen. If they die to themselves by being born again, they won't care about public benefits or public opinion. They will only care about God's benefits and His opinion.

---

[58] John Winthrop, op. cit. Original online at http://history.hanover.edu/texts/winthmod.html.

Blacks Unifying to Conquer the World with Love

In 1996, Coach Bill McCartney, co-founder of Promise Keepers, asked me to speak at a Pastors' Conference that he was hosting in Atlanta, Georgia. While I was speaking to the several thousand men, I was suddenly distracted. I looked over at another one of the speakers that day, a Black pastor named Dr. Tony Evans of Oak Cliff Fellowship in Dallas, Texas.

The impression was so strong that I interrupted my message. I began confessing to the crowd of pastors—most of whom were White—that there is jealousy and division in Black America, including division among Black churches. I even said that some of that jealousy had been unjustly targeted at Tony. I turned to him and said, "If I had some water, I would wash your feet."

I tried to return to my message, but it was too late. Something I said had caught the hearts of the men. They started running up to the platform and throwing bottles of water and towels up on the stage. Men in the stands were shouting and clapping.

Randy Phillips of Promise Keepers, who is White, and Bishop Phillip Porter, who is Black, brought Tony over to me on the stage and sat him down in a chair. Tony couldn't believe this was happening! I took off his shoes and socks and washed his feet. The crowd went wild. Tony was totally embarrassed, but he managed to say, "No greater honor has ever been given to me, especially from someone of my own race."

Black Americans need to restore their love for one another

Why should it be so amazing that one Black man would humble himself to show his love for another Black man? Because many Blacks have lost the ability to love one another unconditionally.

Blacks didn't get that divisive spirit from being close to Jesus. Jesus told us to follow His example when He washed the disciples' feet at the Last Supper. That's why I washed Tony's feet. I was following the example of Jesus. He did it to a bunch of guys who were into disunity, too, and it broke something in them. He told them to follow His example.

"If I then, your Lord and Master, have washed your feet;
ye also ought to wash one another's feet. For I have given
you an example, that ye should do as I have done to
you."[59]

---

[59] John 13:14-15 KJV.

Devil divides, God unites

The devil has been dividing Blacks ever since there were house slaves and field slaves, so instead of washing one another's feet they stay awake nights thinking of new ways to put down their brothers.

Disunity keeps Black Americans weak. Unity will make them strong enough to rule nations. As a unified group within a nation they honor, Black Americans will take their place among the nations of the world when they move from competing to completing, when they wash one another's feet and honor one another instead of competing with one another and with White America. As one nation under God they will fulfill the divine destiny of their people to become true world leaders.

Faith to Rule Nations

America's Founders were influenced by people in their history who had said England had a destiny to rule the nations as representatives of Christ. One of those men was Samuel Purchas, a pastor, author, and compiler of information on world-wide exploration. His book *Purchas his Pilgrimage* (1613) was a survey of world travel and pagan religions, which he compared to the superior standards of Christianity.

This book was so popular that he published another version incorporating the records of Richard Hakluyt. Hakluyt was another Englishman with a passion for world exploration who had helped develop the settlement of Virginia. It was called *Hakluytus Posthumus, or Purchas His Pilgrims* and was published in 1625.

These books contained hundreds of stories from people who had traveled the world, which was no small feat in their day. They had witnessed pagan rituals in foreign lands and contrasted that with their own civilized society as Christians. They concluded, by faith, that they had an extraordinary advantage and something redemptive to offer the heathen. Those who read it were not just reading history and geography but getting a vision for Englishmen changing the world because they were Christians.

Christian world vision of godly dominion

Black American Christians need to recapture that vision of godly dominion that believes that they can conquer the world for good. As long as they keep a ghetto mentality they will keep shooting each other dead and trading insults with people with whom they disagree. They will lose sight of the potential in a world they are called to conquer. They won't see the forest for the trees.

Christians don't have to become colonialists who kill the people in the nations they conquer, break treaties, and institute slavery, as some of the explorers and settlers did in North America. They can focus on fulfilling Jesus' prayer that earth will become like heaven. They can fulfill the Bible-based conqueror's mentality because what they have to offer the world is something better than what it has now.

The Lord Will Make You the Head, Not the Tail

Moses taught Israel that obedience to God brought blessings in all areas of life. He also said that when you obey God you get the upper hand. You become the head and not the tail.

> *"The Lord will give you an abundance of good things in the land he swore to give your ancestors—many children, numerous livestock, and abundant crops. The Lord will send rain at the proper time from his rich treasury in the heavens to bless all the work you do. You will lend to many nations, but you will never need to borrow from them. If you listen to these commands of the Lord your God and carefully obey them, the Lord will make you the head and not the tail, and you will always have the upper hand. You must not turn away from any of the commands I am giving you today to follow after other gods and worship them."[60]*

Getting rid of ingratitude, becoming brothers

Sometimes Blacks become bitter and ungrateful because of legitimate wrongs that White people have done to them, but if they readjust their lenses they will see that not everyone has tried to hurt them. The founders of America and their descendants weren't perfect in their treatment of Blacks. Some even owned slaves and sold slaves, but others did a lot of good for Blacks, especially in the early years of their freedom.

White Americans were on the front lines fighting to end slavery and some even gave their lives to free them and educate them. Many Blacks of the past and many Blacks today owe a lot to their White brothers,

---

[60] Deuteronomy 28:11-14 NLT.

just as Whites owe a lot to Blacks for helping to build America from the ground up. We need each other. We are one nation under God together.

Every time ungrateful Black leaders rail against the government or blame White people for their problems and demand more respect or more money, if they are proud, unrepentant for their own sins and the sins of Blacks, they are pounding another nail in the coffin of the bad image of Black America. The more the government gives them, the weaker they seem to get. They need to focus humbly on restoration and their role in it.

Mobilizing a team effort to beat the devil

The devil is fighting a war for the souls of Black people. This is no time to be a pacifist in spiritual warfare. Everyone needs to fight this war.

We need to initiate action against the devil and fight him together. We can't fight one another and the devil at the same time. The enemies of God are becoming more aggressive every day. They are on the move. They will overtake us and the rest of the nation unless we rise up and become soldiers for Jesus Christ and His righteousness.

> *"Put on all of God's armor so that you will be able to stand firm against all strategies and tricks of the Devil. For we are not fighting against people made of flesh and blood, but against the evil rulers and authorities of the unseen world, against those mighty powers of darkness who rule this world, and against wicked spirits in the heavenly realms."*[61]

Throughout American history, whenever there was a war, Blacks were right there ready to fight for their country. That was amazing, because there was always another war they had to win first against the prejudice of their fellow White soldiers and commanders. In spite of that handicap, as said earlier, it has been historically documented that Black soldiers always proved to be men of outstanding courage and discipline.

How many soldiers are fighting the devil the way they know how to fight? A few brave souls are doing the work that every Christian ought to be doing. It's our time now. People will look around and suddenly, instead of a small company of believers, they will see a mighty army.

---

[61] Ephesians 6:11-12 NLT.

According to the 2010 U.S. census, the population of Black Americans is about 42 million people.[62] Where are they headed? To the battlefield! To arms against the enemies of God! They are about to cut off the heads of the Goliaths of false teaching that are killing them. They will not kill people any more. They will kill the devil's schemes and anti-Christ mentalities. Watch out for them. They are awakened.

Prayer for God to Help Black America

Father, in Jesus' name, I ask You by the anointing of the Holy Spirit to take Black Americans to this new level that You are seeing as ambassadors for Christ. May every intention of heaven be fulfilled. May every spoken word be backed by the Holy Spirit, every heart be good ground for Your Word. I am asking You, Lord, out of an intensity of spirit that You have given us, come upon us. Don't let us just talk about the revivals of old and what you have done in the past, for this is the day that You have made. Let this moment be a time where the Holy Spirit shows up and Your name is glorified in us. Don't let us be an embarrassment to You. Don't let us compare ourselves with other Christians we know. Let us see Your face and get Your approval, Your rebuke, and Your intentions so that You can bring the transformation necessary. Break the yoke of racial distinctions. Help us to know that we are culturally conscious but not culturally controlled. Move on these who have been sick and dying. Raise them up and cause the spirit of revelation and wisdom to come upon them. Give them a desire for Your Word. And Lord, in Your wrath remember mercy. Deal with them according to Your mercy.

In Jesus' name I pray. Amen.

---

[62] "The Black Population:2010. 2010 Census Briefs." Online at https://www.census.gov/prod/cen2010/briefs/c2010br-06.pdf. Accessed October 2016.

CHAPTER 2

COLLEGE STUDENTS:

THE NEW EMERGING LEADERSHIP

"Blessed are those who are persecuted for righteousness' sake,
For theirs is the kingdom of heaven.
Blessed are you when they revile and persecute you, and say all
kinds of evil against you falsely for My sake.
Rejoice and be exceedingly glad, for great is your reward in
heaven, for so they persecuted the prophets
who were before you." [63]

INTRODUCTION TO CHAPTER 2

Any change that happens in Black America will be affected by the zeal of young Black men and women, especially those in college.

This chapter issues a call to the Church to reach Black students on the college campuses, and also calls the students to reach out to their peers and those in need with a message of hope.

Many college champions of the past paid a price so that people of all races could enjoy equal justice. Their sacrifices—sometimes even their deaths as martyrs—made this country better.

Jesus called all of us to die—not always a physical death as a martyr but always to die to self. Those who make a difference cannot be self-centered and focused on their sex lives and other lusts. They have to be dedicated to winning the battle for people's souls.

The quality of life in the inner city and the statistics on abortion, poverty, disease, and death in Black America show that this people group still lacks total deliverance. They are almost there. They need to rekindle the passion that students had in the Civil Rights Movement and a century earlier in the abolition of slavery, and apply it to generational deliverance for the inner cities in our lifetime into their inalienable rights.

---

[63] Matthew 5:10-13 NKJV.

The Civil War and the Constitutional Amendments ended slavery, but without advocates fighting for them against genocidal forces, Blacks quickly lost their rights to live as free Americans. The Civil Rights Movement and Civil Rights Bills ended segregation and Jim Crow laws, but the work was again unfinished. The inner cities and statistics regarding the deathstyle in Black America cry out for one more all-out battle, and young people need to be there in the war.

One of the places where motivated young Black students can be reached is the Historically Black Colleges and Universities. Forty percent of Black students in higher education attend those schools, even though the schools represent only four percent of all higher-education institutions.

College can be a life-changing step toward success for young people who have known only poverty, fear, and a life devoid of vision, especially if Christians are there to ensure that they receive the Gospel and grow in the grace of the Lord.

College students need to see that they can know God as their Father, Jesus as their Lord, and the Holy Spirit as their constant Companion.

They need a picture of marriage as the relationship between Christ and the Church.

They need a vision for social action and what they can accomplish in the world as Christians, and the Church needs their willing hearts and energetic minds to accomplish the Lord's work.

The year began with tragedy in Boston's inner-city neighborhoods with the murders of three young men. They were senseless murders by people without hope or vision. The streets had become a combat zone. Children as young as 11 years old were protecting themselves with guns. Where did this mess come from? Where will it end?

The inner cities are in trouble. Blacks need a generation of new emerging Christian leaders, Black and White, like the students who dedicated their lives to the Civil Rights Movement and the abolition of slavery. A spiritual revolution among college students can change the inner cities and restore the Black community. I've seen it before.

On the campuses of the 100-plus Historically Black Colleges and Universities (HBCUs) in this nation are many of the students who go on to higher education. Most of the schools need a greater Christian presence and a more activist challenge to do good works.

Some of the greatest transformations that I have seen have come through college students who heard the Word and became changed people. I am dedicating this chapter to the college students of the past and present who have proven themselves champions against the enemies of Black America. Black America needs you, students, in the coming great awakening that will bring this nation and the inner cities back in shape.

> *"Listen as wisdom calls out! Hear as understanding raises her voice! She stands on the hilltop and at the crossroads. At the entrance to the city, at the city gates, she cries aloud, 'I call to you, to all of you!*
>
> *"'I am raising my voice to all people. How naive you are! Let me give you common sense. O foolish ones, let me give you understanding. Listen to me!'"*[64]

Student population leaves nearby community needs unmet

For example, Boston, the city with those nearby inner-city murders, has one of the largest populations of college students per capita of any major city in America. That's one reason this intellectual capital is nicknamed "The Hub."

> *"There are 114 higher education institutions in Massachusetts, according to the Carnegie Classification of Institutions of Higher Education. More than 50 of those are in the greater Boston metropolitan area, which is home to more than 250,000 students."*[65]

In another generation, Martin Luther King, Jr., met his future wife Coretta Scott when he was a doctoral student at Boston University and she was studying voice and violin at the New England Conservatory. They later gave their lives to the cause of bettering Black America.

Boston students attend area schools such as Harvard, MIT, Tufts, Boston University, Northeastern University, Bentley, Brandeis, Simmons, Gordon-Conwell, and Boston College—household words in the fields of

---

[64] Proverbs 8:1-6 NLT.
[65] Allison Pohle, "Massachusetts is the 8th most popular destination for college students." Online at http://www.boston.com/news/education/2015/09/01/massachusetts-is-the-8th-most-popular-destination-for-college-students. Accessed September 2016.

technology, law, medicine, business, and even sports. How many of these students are aware of the desperate need for intervention just a few miles away? A few pilot projects and internships are no doubt underway, but how many college students have a concern for today's inner cities?

New Englanders Who Made a Difference Against Racism

Before the Emancipation Proclamation and the Civil War ended slavery, some of the key people whose lives gave evidence of the intelligence and creativity of Blacks, fought for abolition, and promoted the education of the Black freedmen came from Boston and New England. Black and White residents of the New England states were key people in the

VISION FOR BLACK AMERICA:

THEY WILL INSPIRE A NEW WAVE OF STUDENTS TO WORK WITH THEM FOR LASTING CHANGE.

"You did not choose Me, but I chose you and appointed you that you should go and bear fruit, and that your fruit should remain."

John 15:16 NKJV

rise of Black America, and they can be key leaders again. Below are a few examples of people from New England who made a difference in the era of slavery and abolition.

Early Black heroes from New England

Phillis Wheatley (1753-1784) born in Africa, slave, poet, educated by her Boston masters, who freed her after her worldwide literary success

> *"Twas mercy brought me from my Pagan land,*
> *Taught my benighted soul to understand*
> *That there's a God, that there's a Saviour too:*
> *Once I redemption neither sought nor knew.*
> *Some view our sable race with scornful eye,*
> *'Their colour is a diabolic die.'*

"Remember, Christians, Negros, black as Cain,
May be refin'd and join th'angelic train."

Phillis Wheatley, "On Being Brought from Africa to America"[66]

54th Massachusetts Infantry (see also Chapter 1; it was commemorated in the movie *Glory* with their first commander, *Robert Gould Shaw*), first unit of colored troops in the Civil War, recognized for extraordinary bravery; the free Blacks and former slaves knew that if captured they would be enslaved or killed by the Confederacy.

"Let the slaves and free colored people be called into
service, and formed into a liberating army, to march into
the South and raise the banner of emancipation among the
slaves. . . . Men of Color, To Arms!" [67]

Frederick Douglass, encouraged by President Abraham Lincoln, calling
Blacks to fight in the Civil War

Lewis Douglass, son of *Frederick Douglass,* sergeant major of the 54th Massachusetts Infantry, wounded in the Union assault on Fort Wagner, writing to his wife:

"Should I fall in the next fight killed or wounded I hope to
fall with my face to the foe. . . . My Dear girl I hope again
to see you. I must bid you farewell should I be killed.
Remember if I die I die in a good cause.
I wish we had a hundred thousand colored troops we
would put an end to this war." [68]

Sergeant Major Lewis Douglass, son of Frederick Douglass, after 54th
Infantry fought bravely at Fort Wagner in Charleston Harbor

John Russwurm, editor of first Black newspaper, *Freedom's Journal*, graduate of Bowdoin College in Maine, teacher at Boston's African Meeting House school for Black children

---

[66] Phillis Wheatley, *Memoir and Poems of Phillis Wheatley, a Native African and a Slave. Dedicated to the Friends of the Africans* (Boston: Geo. W. Light, 1834). Online at http://www.vcu.edu/engweb/webtexts/Wheatley/brought.html. Accessed October 2016.
[67] William W. Layton, "The Spring of 1863—A Call to Arms" (*The Smithsonian Associates Civil War E-Mail Newsletter*, Volume 2, Number 3). Online at http://civilwarstudies.org/articles/Vol_2/layton.htm. Accessed September 2016.
[68] Carter Woodson, *The Mind of the Negro* (Washington, D.C., 1926), 544. Quoted in History Matters, the U.S. History Course on the Web. Online at http://historymatters.gmu.edu/d/6215/. Accessed September 2016.

William Wells Brown, escaped slave who became an abolitionist and brilliant author of the first novel and first play by a Black American, in addition to other accomplishments

A Few White Abolition Heroes from New England

John Quincy Adams, sixth U.S. President and U.S. Congressman, who kept the cause of slavery before a reluctant House of Representatives and presented the winning argument for the *Amistad* slaves before the U.S. Supreme Court in 1841. His father, *John Adams,* was the second President of the United States, and never owned slaves.

Senator Charles Sumner, the "radical Republican" who was beaten senseless with a cane on the floor of the Senate for his advocacy of Black Americans, but returned three years later to lead the charge for Black rights during Reconstruction

William Lloyd Garrison, who founded the fiery anti-slavery publication *The Liberator* and pioneered the rise of former slave **Frederick Douglass**, a resident of New Bedford, Massachusetts

Arthur and Lewis Tappan, some of the largest financial donors of the abolitionist movement, including financing the *Amistad* slaves' defense and funding Oberlin College (Ohio, now Oberlin University), the first school that admitted Blacks and women and became a station in the Underground Railroad

Lyman Beecher and his children *Harriet Beecher Stowe,* who wrote *Uncle Tom's Cabin* in Brunswick, Maine, while her husband was a professor at Bowdoin College, and *Henry Ward Beecher*, who fought slavery in "Bleeding Kansas" and led in the 1857 Revival that began in New York City with Jeremiah Lanphier

The American Missionary Association, which founded several of the Historically Black Colleges and Universities, including Fisk and Atlanta University, and provided teachers and primary education for slaves as soon as they were freed, earning the gratitude of people like W.E.B. DuBois, who was born in Massachusetts and was the first Black Harvard graduate to earn a PhD.

Black Americans after the Civil War raised money for their schools mainly through the Black Church, often supplemented by Northern benevolent organizations. They also served on boards like the predominantly White American Missionary Association that funded schools and welcomed Black leadership participation.

"[T]he AMA founded more than five hundred schools and colleges for the freedmen of the South during and after the Civil War, spending more money for that purpose than the Freedmen's Bureau of the federal government."[69] These schools included the following:

- Atlanta University
- Avery Institute
- Berea College
- Fisk University
- Hampton Institute
- Howard University
- LeMoyne (now LeMoyne-Owen) College
- Straight (now Dillard) University
- Talladega College
- Tillotson (now Huston-Tillotson) College
- Tougaloo College

Multicultural Leaders Empowering Black Students

Who will answer the call to reach
Black college students in this generation?

Most Christian campus ministries today are led by predominantly White leadership and some have hundreds of full-time staff members. CRU (Campus Crusade for Christ), founded by the late Bill Bright and Vonette Bright, has recruited tens of thousands of college graduates, retired professionals, and others who have a heart to reach students. They first spend approximately one year raising support; otherwise they are volunteers. In that way their evangelism is not interrupted by economic irresponsibility. Not enough campus ministries are led by Blacks, reach out to the HBCUs, and give students Jesus Christ as the option to fraternities and godly leadership as a way of life, instead of racial posturing.

---

[69] Clara Merritt DeBoer, "Blacks and the American Missionary Association" Online at http://www.ucc.org/about-us_hidden-histories_blacks-and-the-american. Accessed October 2016.

In 1975 God gave Bill Bright and Loren Cunningham, founder of Youth With A Mission (YWAM), a revelation of Seven Mountains of influence—Family; Marketplace; Education; Arts, Entertainment and Sports; Religion; Government; and Media. From the Reformation are five sovereign spheres of individual, family, church, civil government, and free associations. We need to win Black college students to Christ, train them in the biblical worldview, including humility and a multiracial mindset, and send them out as spiritual revolutionaries into the marketplace.

Through a Bible-based campus ministry, Black students not only gain support for their area of study but also learn Christ-likeness. They learn to be like Christ and do what Jesus would do in the culture.

A Bible-based campus ministry for Black students that also embraces White students as equals offers support and accountability from other students for whom righteousness is a foundation. They learn that maintaining standards of godliness includes embracing other races, growing academically, and developing a biblical strategy to better their world. Their strategic thinking is based on both the call of God on their lives and the education that they are receiving in school.

In the early years of my ministry, New Generation Campus Ministries (NGM) made an impact on many of the Historically Black Colleges and Universities as well as other schools that were predominantly White. This was followed by an organization called Global Outreach.

White students freely joined us because our ministry didn't have a racist spirit. Since Black students are mostly an unreached people group, we decided to focus on the Black students and bring those of other races along instead of becoming a "Black arm" of a White ministry.

Blacks need leadership experience in a predominantly Black outreach

There is a difference in perception when meeting the particular needs of Black students if they are an appendage to a White organization rather than the main focus of an organization with Black leadership. Regardless of the best intentions, Black students need some experiences in leadership that are not always subservient to something led by Whites.

Historically, until the era of Black racism toward Whites, Black America's true nature has been the ability to lead while also embracing other cultures and becoming leaders after God's own heart. They need to become leaders on their own merits so that they will lead in their homes, churches, and businesses.

"We are his house, built on the foundation of the apostles and the prophets. And the cornerstone is Christ Jesus himself. We who believe are carefully joined together, becoming a holy temple for the Lord."[70]

Students who went through our campus programs, including the select groups who attended the Leadership Training Schools that we held every summer for about 20 years, are now successful adults working in society. They have great marriages and are active in their churches and communities without racist attitudes.

Christian organizations for Black students with full-time staff

God has a heart for the emerging new Black leaders on the college campuses. There must be more generational transfer of Christian values for Black students like that which is already being enjoyed by Whites.

All of America will benefit when there are Bible-based, evangelistic ministries on all Historically Black campuses as legal entities according to campus policies. Campus ministries are a great way to reach inner-city kids who had the motivation to go to college.

In order to continue the forward momentum, these young men and women need Jesus and the accountability of Christian peers to bring them up to their potential. They don't need fraternities and sororities dominated by campus drinking and sex. They need a vision for greatness in God.

I came from the ghetto and God delivered me and placed me in positions of leadership in my own predominantly Black organization that was not racist. From there, He gave me credibility with organizations led by Whites.

Other than God's favor, there is no way in my mind that I should be on the boards where I serve. I should not be talking to the people I talk to, advising the people whom I advise. I should be into racism and complaining about disenfranchisement, really getting mad with God. I should be saying, "Woe is me. He shouldn't have let all this bad stuff happen to me." Instead, everything that has happened has motivated me to find God like nobody else. I know there are young people out there with that potential and more.

---

[70] Ephesians 2:20-21 NLT.

College Crusaders vs. State-Sponsored Spy Network

During the Civil Rights Movement, both Black and White college students started organizations and volunteered to risk their lives to draw attention to the desperate state of Black America under segregation. Students were beaten and some were tortured and died, but their deaths were not in vain. They succeeded in turning around some of the greatest injustices this nation has ever seen. Slavery, Jim Crow, and segregated schools and cities were changed—but not without a fight.

Murderers of civil rights workers and their accomplices in high places escaped conviction for years because of local authorities who refused to prosecute and juries who refused to convict, even with overwhelming evidence and confessions.

It turns out that some state governments were aiding and protecting the killers, sometimes with the support of racist leaders as high the federal government. It was state-sponsored genocide of Blacks.

"Black Monday" for segregationists

In 1956 the United States Supreme Court handed down its landmark *Brown v. Board of Education* decision requiring an end to racially separate public schools. States practicing segregation then went to war to protect the "Southern way of life." That was a veiled way of saying they wanted to continue the oppression of Blacks that began in slavery and continued under segregation.

Some White Southerners called the day the *Brown* verdict was released "Black Monday." Southern states then began to use state legislation, state commissions, White citizen's councils, and even the Ku Klux Klan in their fight to keep segregated schools.

Mississippi's State Sovereignty Commission

In Mississippi, the governor and other elected officials quickly passed legislation to establish a state agency that they called the "State Sovereignty Commission." It was named after the principle of "state sovereignty"—the perceived right of each state to do basically whatever it pleases without interference from the federal government, according to their interpretation of the Tenth Amendment, which says this:

> *"The powers not delegated to the United States by the*
> *Constitution, nor prohibited by it to the States, are*
> *reserved to the States respectively, or to the people."*

Tenth Amendment, U.S. Constitution

Mississippi's covert State Sovereignty Commission enabled segregationists to take the law into their own hands and prevent the access of Blacks to integrated public education from kindergarten through college. This Commission was an incredible, state-sponsored network of spies and informants that worked to maintain segregation, regardless of the cost in human life. It continued to function for nearly two decades with the active support of some of Mississippi's governors and other elected officials.

DID YOU KNOW? Mississippi State Sovereignty Commission

1956   Mississippi Governor J.P. Coleman requests legislation to protect racial segregation after *Brown*. Legislature creates the Mississippi State Sovereignty Commission and begins to pay investigators and informants, including Blacks.

1977   Funding ends and the Commission is officially closed.

1989   Judge orders Commission files opened for public examination After lawsuits forced the state of Mississippi to unseal files from the Commission, they were made available online .[71] The following quotes from the website of the Mississippi Department of Archives and History describe how the agency started (subtitles added).

Created to maintain racial separation after Brown. "The Mississippi State Sovereignty Commission (Commission) was created by an act of the Mississippi legislature on March 29, 1956. The agency was established in the wake of the May 1954 *Brown v. Board of Education* ruling. Like other states below the Mason-Dixon Line, Mississippi responded to *Brown* with legislation to shore up the walls of racial separation."[72]

---

[71] Home page online http://www.mdah.ms.gov/arrec/digital_archives/sovcom/.
[72] MDAH "Sovereignty Commission Online: Agency History." Online at
http://www.mdah.ms.gov/arrec/digital_archives/sovcom/scagencycasehistory.php Accessed

Broad investigative powers. "The act creating the Commission provided the agency with broad powers. The Commission's objective was to 'do and perform any and all acts deemed necessary and proper to protect the sovereignty of the state of Mississippi, and her sister states . . . 'from perceived 'encroachment thereon by the Federal Government or any branch, department or agency thereof.' To exercise this loosely defined objective, the Commission was granted extensive investigative powers." [73]

Involvement of governor, president of senate, speaker, attorney general. "The governor was appointed ex-officio chairman of the Commission. Other ex-officio members were the president of the Senate, who was vice-chairman of the Commission; the attorney general; and the speaker of the House of Representatives. In addition, the Commission comprised the following members: two members from the Senate, appointed by the president of the Senate; and three members from the House of Representatives, appointed by the speaker. The governor, attorney general and legislators served on the Commission during their tenures in office. The three members appointed by the governor served for the duration of his term.[74] The agency itself was small, consisting of a director, public relations director, clerical staff and a handful of investigators."[75]

Paid Informants, Black and White

The official online files document how the Mississippi State Sovereignty Commission used paid informants, both Black and White, including NAACP workers. It exchanged information with the Ku Klux Klan, some of whose members committed murders of civil rights workers like the three men whose stories were told in the film *Mississippi Burning*.

Many killers of that era—now more than half a century ago—were never brought to justice because of secrecy, fear, jury tampering, and the state's refusal to prosecute accused murderers of civil rights sympathizers, even when provided with overwhelming evidence by the FBI

October 2016. Other information on the Mississippi State Sovereignty Commission is available from a Google search.

[73] Ibid.

[74] A footnote here refers to General Laws of the State of Mississippi, 1956, Chapter 365, 520-524. Online at http://www.mdah.ms.gov/arrec/digital_archives/sovcom/notes.php.

[75] MDAH "Sovereignty Commission Online Agency History" op. cit.

Some escaped trial because the FBI closed cases on the orders of late FBI Director J. Edgar Hoover.

The first convictions that broke the power of White supremacy against Black victims came when federal prosecutors led by John Michael Doar were able to resort to a Reconstruction[76] era federal law that prohibited "conspiring to violate the civil rights" of citizens "under color of state law."[77]

Doar joined the civil rights division of the Justice Department in 1962 and led it from 1964 to 1967. He successfully prosecuted the killers of civil rights workers James Chaney, Andrew Goodman and Michael Schwerner in Mississippi.[78] In 1967 a jury brought seven guilty verdicts and acquitted eight others. That was the beginning of a turn toward justice. In 2005, Edgar Ray "Preacher" Killen, a former Ku Klux Klan organizer who escaped conviction in the 1967 trial, was found guilty in state court of three counts of manslaughter and sentenced to 60 years in prison.

Murders in Mississippi

"For we are not fighting against people made of flesh and blood, but against the evil rulers and authorities of the unseen world, against those mighty powers of darkness who rule this world, and against wicked spirits in the heavenly realms." [79]

The Sovereignty Commission was a substantial network of high level crime in the guise of a state agency. People don't think that God will judge the blood that cries from the ground.[80] Could that be the cause of some of Mississippi's other problems such as crime, illiteracy, and a low graduation rate from high school?

---

[76] Reconstruction was the period of time after the North won the Civil War and the U. S. Congress mandated and enforced conditions of liberty for the freed slaves in the South.
[77] Douglas O. Linder, "Bending Toward Justice: John Doar and the Mississippi Burning Trial." This is an excellent resource for understanding the struggle. Online at http://law2.umkc.edu/faculty/projects/ftrials/doaressay.html. Accessed September 2016.
[78] Matt Schudel, "John M. Doar, top federal prosecutor during civil rights era, dies at 92." *Washington Post*, November 11, 2014. Online at https://www.washingtonpost.com/national/john-m-doar-top-federal-prosecutor-during-civil-rights-era-dies-at-92/2014/11/11/31399db0-69c5-11e4-a31c-77759fc1eacc_story.html. Accessed September 2014.
[79] Ephesians 6:12 NLT.
[80] See Genesis 4:10.

Assassination of Medgar Evers follows JFK civil rights speech

In 1963, Medgar Evers, the NAACP's first field officer in Mississippi, was assassinated outside his home within hours after President John F. Kennedy's speech on national television in support of civil rights:

> *"One hundred years of delay have passed since President Lincoln freed the slaves, yet their heirs, their grandsons, are not fully free. They are not yet freed from the bonds of injustice. They are not yet freed from social and economic oppression. And this Nation, for all its hopes and all its boasts, will not be fully free until all its citizens are free."*[81]

John F. Kennedy, Address to the Nation, June 11, 1963

Kennedy himself was assassinated the following November.

Background of "Mississippi Burning"

Few people outside of Mississippi knew about the secret activities of the Sovereignty Commission. A few months after the assassination of Medgar Evers, when the state was still fighting against school integration and refusing to allow Blacks to vote, college students and other young people began organizing to get involved. James Chaney, a native of Meridian, Mississippi, was Black. Michael "Mickey" Schwerner and Andy Goodman, a college student, were White. They saw Mississippi as the most dangerous state in the nation for civil rights workers.

In January 1964 the Council of Federated Organizations (COFO), a collaboration of civil rights groups, announced the Mississippi Summer Project to register Blacks to vote. In response, the next month White Knights of the Ku Klux Klan of Mississippi followed up with their first meeting to organize a plan of terrorism against COFO and other Black students and civil rights workers to keep them from enfranchising the Black citizens. Members of this racist group committed brutal beatings and murders. By the end of April, they had burned crosses at 61 separate locations across Mississippi.

From the time of slavery through segregation and the Civil Rights Movement, the Black Church has stood strong in the face of intimidation.

---

[81] John F. Kennedy, "Civil Rights Address" delivered 11 June 1963. Online at American Rhetoric http://www.americanrhetoric.com/speeches/jfkcivilrights.htm.

On Memorial Day 1964, Schwerner and Chaney spoke at the Mt. Zion Methodist Church in Neshoba County, Mississippi, urging the members of the all-Black congregation to register to vote. Then they left for training at a college in Ohio. The training was sponsored by the Congress of Racial Equality, or CORE, co-founded in 1942 by James Farmer, Jr.[82]

On June 16, armed KKK members went looking for Chaney and Schwerner at the Mt. Zion Methodist Church. When they found they were not there, they beat Blacks attending a church meeting and set fire to the building. During the summer months a total of 20 Black churches were burned, and the FBI gave their resulting investigation the code name "MIBURN" for "Mississippi Burning."

Klan members were kept informed about the activities of the civil rights workers through the Sovereignty Commission. When the files were opened, surveillance details were found such as the color and make of the CORE vehicle that Schwerner was driving.

Arrested, ambushed, and killed

On June 20, Schwerner and Chaney with their new recruit, student Andy Goodman, drove from their training sessions in Ohio to Meridian, Mississippi, where Schwerner was a field worker for CORE. He had been in Mississippi for six months, and some of the local Whites hated him for organizing a Black boycott and encouraging Blacks to register to vote. They called him "Jew boy." The next day the young men drove to see the burned-out church where they had hoped to register voters and conduct

VISION FOR BLACK AMERICA:

THEY WILL SEE KILLERS CONVICTED AND PRAY FOR THEIR SALVATION BEFORE IT IS TOO LATE.

"I tried to understand why the wicked prosper. . . .

I thought about the destiny of the wicked.

Truly, you put them on a slippery path and send them sliding over the cliff to destruction. In an instant they are destroyed."

Psalm 73:16-19 NLT

training. Deputy Sheriff Cecil Price, a member of the Ku Klux Klan, recognized their car and arrested them, taking them to the county jail in

---

[82] Farmer as a teenager was portrayed in the film *The Great Debaters* starring Denzel Washington.

Philadelphia, Mississippi. According to investigations, Price, in collusion with others, including Klan recruiter Edgar Ray Killen, released the men from jail, then he and others chased them down. They were beaten and shot, then buried in an earthen dam where their remains were found a few months later through the assistance of an informant.

Reign of terror in Philadelphia, Mississippi

In the process of searching for their bodies, officials found the remains of other missing young people. It was obvious that a reign of terror was underway in Mississippi that had been hidden from the eyes of the nation by people who seemed to hate the outside world. Eventually people changed and justice came, but it took dedicated perseverance and great sacrifice, something that is greatly needed in this day to change our nation.

Civil Rights Act passed, then death in Mississippi

On July 2, 1964, President Lyndon Johnson signed the Civil Rights Act of 1964. It had been a hard-fought battle by determined Congressmen—both Republicans and Democrats—against segregationists and states' rights advocates. A month later, on August 4, the bodies of Chaney, Goodman, and Schwerner men were uncovered. In spite of confessions and other evidence, there was so much local resistance to justice—and protection of criminals espousing segregation and states' rights—that it took four decades for some of the murderers from that era to be convicted. Some are still at large, and some day their time may come. May God have mercy on them and on those public officials who for so many years obstructed justice that was due to all people, regardless of race.

Intimidating Dr. King in Philadelphia, Mississippi

Two years after the murders, Dr. Martin Luther King, Jr., went to Philadelphia, Mississippi. When he and about 300 marchers stopped to pray at the jail where Chaney, Goodman, and Schwerner had been held the night they died, they were surrounded by a White mob that turned a hose on them and beat them with broomsticks and ax handles.

Then King was confronted by a White man in a uniform.

> *"It was Deputy Cecil Price. Price said, 'You can't come up these steps.' 'Oh, yes,' King replied. 'You're the one who had Schwerner and the other fellows in jail.'*

*'Yes, sir,' Price answered. King tried to address the crowd
above the loud jeers of white onlookers. 'In this county,
Andrew Goodman, James Chaney, and Michael Schwerner
were brutally murdered. I believe the murderers are
somewhere around me at this moment.'*

*" 'You're damn right—they're right behind you,' muttered
the Deputy. King bravely continued, 'I want them to know
that we are not afraid. If they kill three of us they will have
to kill us all.' "*

*"King described that afternoon in Philadelphia as one of
the most frightening in his life.*

*" 'This is a terrible town, the worst I've seen. There is a
complete reign of terror here.' "*[83]

The environment in Philadelphia, Mississippi, was an example of
Black genocide—killing Blacks if necessary, keeping them ignorant and
helpless as a minimum, so that Whites could reign supreme. What
character qualities did these particular White people exhibit that would
make them a model for anyone to follow as a superior race? They were
going to church every Sunday, yet in what way were they like Christ?

*"I lift my eyes to you,
O God, enthroned in heaven.
We look to the LORD our God for his mercy."* [84]

Justice in Civil Rights "Cold Cases"

In 1989, 25 years after the Mississippi murders of Chaney,
Goodman, and Schwerner, White journalist Jerry Mitchell of Jackson,
Mississippi, first became interested in reopening the story after his editor
sent him to cover the movie premiere of *Mississippi Burning*. He said the
film changed his life. Before that, he had little knowledge of the Civil
Rights era. It was a wake-up call.

Eight months later on Sunday, September 10, 1989, the *Clarion-
Ledger* carried his lead story on those murders and the potential
involvement of the Mississippi State Sovereignty Commission. Mitchell

---

[83] Douglas O. Linder, "Bending Toward Justice: John Doar and the Mississippi Burning
Trial." Originally published in *Mississippi Law Journal* (Volume 72, No. 2, Winter 2002).
Online at http://www.law.umkc.edu/faculty/projects/ftrials/trialheroes/doaressay.html.
[84] Psalm 123:1-2 NLT.

found that someone from the Commission had infiltrated the Civil Rights office of COFO and provided identifying information on volunteers and details of Civil Rights activities to state authorities. The Commission then provided local police and sheriff's departments with a description of the blue CORE vehicle and license plate number.

At the time, the Commission's records had not been made public, but Mitchell obtained access to some of them when they were mistakenly attached to another lawsuit. The files had been sealed since 1977.

High school students join crusade for reopening murder cases

On June 21, 2005, Edgar Ray "Preacher" Killen of the Ku Klux Klan (and also a Baptist minister) was found guilty of three counts of manslaughter in the Mississippi Burning case. It was the 41st anniversary of the crime. He appealed the verdict and was even released briefly after pretending to be partially paralyzed, but his punishment of 20 years in prison for each of the victims was upheld on January 12, 2007, by the Mississippi Supreme Court.

Mitchell had a role in this case and was assisted by an Illinois high school teacher named Barry Bradford and three of his female students. The girls were able to get an interview with Killen in prison where he talked about the crime and his segregationist views. Bradford and his students— Allison Nichols, Sarah Siegel, and Brittany Saltiel—produced a documentary for a National History Day contest with new evidence in the case. Their interview with Killen helped convince the state of Mississippi to reopen the investigation.

19th Century Ohio Precedent for Student Activism

Students of today who fight for civil rights or uncover evidence of wrongdoing are following a bold tradition from the past. Blacks need a lot more of them to solve today's social problems in the inner cities. They have the zeal to get things done. In the 19th Century, Oberlin College in Oberlin, Ohio, became the first American school to admit both women and Blacks. It was founded in 1833 as Oberlin Collegiate Institute and became Oberlin College in 1850.

The goal of the school's primary donors, Christian businessmen Arthur and Lewis Tappan, was an evangelical college with an anti-slavery perspective. Oberlin became a center of the abolitionist movement and a station on the Underground Railroad, providing a place of refuge for fugitive slaves. One incident was the so-called "Oberlin-Wellington rescue" of 1858 related to the Fugitive Slave Law.

Lane students call for immediate end of slavery, and pay a price

Another school, Lane (Presbyterian) Seminary in Cincinnati, Ohio, was an evangelical school also opened with funds from the Tappan brothers. Lyman Beecher was installed as president in 1832 and served until 1850. One of the Lane students in the first theological class was Theodore Weld. He had been converted to Christ under the Rev. Charles Finney while a student at Hamilton College in upstate New York. In 1834 he held an 18-day series of anti-slavery discussions at the school. Most students attended. Weld had developed a strong anti-slavery position through the influence of Finney and Charles Stuart, a retired British army officer. The series included prayer meetings, anti-slavery messages, and debates.

VISION FOR BLACK AMERICA:

THEY WILL BECOME BENEFACTORS LIKE ARTHUR AND LEWIS TAPPAN TO FINANCE NEXT MOVEMENT OF COLLEGE STUDENTS.

"Give, and it shall be given unto you; good measure, pressed down, and shaken together, and running over."

Luke 6:38 KJV

As a result of the meetings, many at Lane Seminary, including many Southerners, came to view slavery as sin and became abolitionists. They organized an antislavery group on campus and called for immediate abolition, which was contrary to the trustees' more moderate position and considered too extreme in circles that favored a gradual process.

However, Weld convinced the Lane students that slavery was desperately wrong and rallied them to the call of God to end slavery immediately to avert God's judgment.

The students also started community projects to educate local free Blacks and help them find employment services. They even offered to help them purchase the freedom of enslaved relatives. Students in other colleges and universities across the country heard about the Lane students and also became roused to action.

President Beecher met with abolitionists and Arthur Tappan but no solution was found that would change the mind of the trustees. Here is an excerpt from the report of the Lane trustees' meeting:

> *"The meeting was closed by a most appropriate and fervent prayer, offered by the colored brother, Mr. Cornish, suggested, as was felt, by the Holy Spirit. He alluded with deep pathos, to the wrongs inflicted upon his people, to the wicked prejudice and sufferings under which they groaned, to the gratitude they felt his hope of deliverance through friends raised up to plead and defend their cause, to the injurious influence of other schemes in creating hostility to the country and to Christianity, and he implored the benediction of the Almighty upon the advocates of his people, then present, and all of similar heart and mind throughout the land.*
>
> *Mr. Tappan and the other brethren felt greatly strengthened and refreshed by such an utterance. It seemed as if the whole body of the people of color was pleading at the Throne of Grace. "[85]*

Expulsion from Lane, challenge to Christians to stand up

The Lane Seminary Board voted to expel Weld and William Allen, president of the student antislavery society, to end all projects, and to stop all discussion about slavery. The students left the seminary, although some stayed on in Cincinnati to teach free Blacks, supported by funding from Arthur Tappan. A group of the students including Weld wrote "Statement of the reasons which have induced the Students of Lane Seminary, to dissolve their connection with the Institution." It was published in *The Liberator*, abolitionist William Lloyd Garrison's publication, and closed with these words:

> *". . . that men, destined for the service of the world, need, above all things, in such an age as this, the pure and impartial, the disinterested and magnanimous, the uncompromising and fearless,—in combination with the gentle and tender spirit and example of Christ; not parleying it with wrong, but calling it to repentance; not flattering the proud, but pleading the cause of the poor.*

---

[85] Lewis Tappan, *The Life of Arthur Tappan, pp. 230-231.* Hurd and Houghton, 1870. Available online from Google books.

*And we record the hope that the glorious stand taken upon
the subject of discussion, and up to the close of the last
session, maintained by the Institution, may be early
resumed, that so the triumph of expediency over right may
soon terminate, and Lane Seminary be again restored to
the glory of its beginning.* "[86]

Student "Lane Rebels" move to Oberlin College in 1835

The Lane students against slavery became known as the "Lane
Rebels." John J. Shipherd, the founder of Oberlin, reached out to students
and professors at Lane Seminary who opposed its weak position on slavery
and invited them to come to Oberlin. However, the anti-slavery students
insisted on certain standards at Oberlin that the board of trustees was
reluctant to meet. Wealthy businessmen backed them and saved the day.

Shipherd stood behind the students and wrote a persuasive letter to
the board of trustees stating that as soon as the trustees passed the
resolution the school would receive $80,000 from Arthur and Lewis
Tappan and other anti-slavery businessmen. Also, popular evangelist
Charles Finney would be appointed professor of theology.

The Oberlin Board of Trustees voted again, resulting in a tie that
was broken by the president, John Keep, in favor of the resolution for
admitting students of all races.

Students and prayer provoke leaders to renounce racism

Lewis Tappan, in his biography of his brother, Arthur, rote a
compassionate explanation of how they made the courageous decision:

*"Though they were Christians considerably in advance of
the prevailing sentiment of the churches, they had not
wholly renounced the hateful prejudice against the people
of color that so generally prevailed in the country and in
the churches. The Lane Seminary students were fully
aware of this, and determined not to go to Oberlin until*

---

[86] "Statement of the reasons which have induced the Students of Lane Seminary, to dissolve
their connection with the Institution. Cincinnati: 1834." *The Liberator*, vol. 5, no. 2, Jan. 10,
1835, pp. [5]-6. Online at
http://oberlin.edu/external/EOG/LaneDebates/RebelsDefence.htm. Accessed October 2016.

both free discussion and the right treatment of colored
students were fully secured.

"The subject so enlisted the feelings of the pious
inhabitants of Oberlin, that earnest and persevering
prayer was offered, especially by a band of godly women.
The result was an acquiescence if not entire harmony of
views in the board of trustees, and the adoption of a
resolution that students should be received and treated
irrespective of color. It was also decided that in the
boarding-houses and elsewhere, no observances should be
allowed that infringed upon this rule. CASTE has found no
asylum or toleration at Oberlin since that day." [87]

Community violence against Oberlin's righteous stand

Oberlin paid a price for its anti-slavery position. Some citizens of Ohio threatened to tear down the buildings. Finances had to be raised overseas by anti-slavery people to save the institution.

Finney became head of the Department of Theology in 1835 and president in 1850, but much of the promised aid from the Tappans to Oberlin College did not materialize at first because of the New York fire of 1835 and the financial panic of 1837.

Lane students' influence on history

One of those who attended the Lane anti-slavery debates was **Harriet Beecher**, daughter of Lane President Lyman Beecher. She later married Calvin Stowe and wrote *Uncle Tom's Cabin*.

Salmon P. Chase, a Cincinnati lawyer, went on to defend the rights of fugitive slaves in court. Chase became Secretary of the Treasury under **Abraham Lincoln** and Chief Justice of the U.S. Supreme Court. He opposed the conspiracy of the slave states to control the federal government, and gave the Free Soil Party its slogan, "Free Soil, Free Labor, Free Men."

---

[87] Lewis Tappan, *The Life of Arthur Tappan*, op. cit, p. 241.

Theodore Weld wrote the detailed expose of the evils of slavery mentioned earlier called *American Slavery As It Is* in 1839. Harriet Beecher Stowe used it as a resource for materials in *Uncle Tom's Cabin*.

Weld also assisted **John Quincy Adams** in his relentless efforts to bring the issue of slavery before the House of Representatives. Weld edited *The Emancipator*, a New York Anti-Slavery publication financed by **Arthur Tappan**.

Where are the students today who will fight genocide in the inner cities as passionately as these young people fought against slavery?

Students Could Change the Inner Cities Today

God wants to raise up a generation of righteous people, and that generation is you, today. Your season has come. God tells us in Acts 3:19 that it is time for the restoration of all things.

I don't care what you've been through. God can restore you and you can help somebody else. Whatever you are going through, God has handpicked you to be used. People in sin need a righteous person like you who can show them a righteous God Who can get them out of it.

Students, you are the chosen people of God. Get into the Word. Live by the power of the Holy Spirit. If somebody curses you, bless them. If somebody treats you bad, treat them nice. If the whole generation is against you, forgive them. That will please your Father in heaven.

God is calling out a people now. God's glory is here for your good. If God wasn't trying to do you good, He could have killed you long before this time. None of us is perfect. It's the human condition. The Bible says plainly, *"For all have sinned, and come short of the glory of God."*[88] God is a good God. He knows what you have done wrong. In spite of everything, you are the right person. Rise up!

You say, "God, I need power." He says, "I will send you the Holy Spirit." The Holy Spirit comes and gives you power and you start arising and you start getting a pep in your step and a glide in your stride, and a groove in your move. Why? Because God is with you.

---

[88] Romans 3:23.

WHAT STUDENTS COULD DO FOR THE INNER CITY

- *Friendships.* Make lasting friendships with people of all ages and races. Show that you see them as important and valuable.

- *Getting on the streets.* See also Chapter 4, "Street Revs." Start Bible clubs for children in neighborhoods.

- *Churches.* Assist the churches to be resource places for salvation, health, Bible study, family training, and prayer.

- *Education.* Tutor and teach reading and math. Help kids stay in school. Assist good teachers. Develop multimedia ways of presenting information. Be advocates for parents with the school system. Be aware of genocidal attitudes in schools. Break the mold of dropping out.

- *Technology.* Help people to get computers and use them to develop their abilities in science and technology, research, graphic design, writing. Start tech centers for after school.

- *Marriage and family.* Parenting skills. Teach young men how to be holy, responsible fathers and help them to understand fathering after marriage. Teach young women how to be Kingmakers to husbands and children.

- *Health.* Be an advocate for health. Provide info on diet and diseases, including sexually transmitted diseases. Set up clinics in churches. Teach preventive health. Volunteer in city health clinics.

- *Teen years.* Teach abstinence until marriage, how to relate in godly ways to the opposite sex. Stand against music, TV, media that flood kids with sex.

- *Finances.* Help them start business enterprises instead of dealing drugs, find creative ways to earn money, how to get and keep a job.

- *Conflict resolution.* Help them relate to people without fighting and guns.

- *Crime.* Work with parents, police, local activists, and teachers. Keep the worst offenders busy with productive activities and sports. Teach character.

- *Environment.* Clean up streets. Fix up buildings. Teach skills and habits.

- *After school.* Start or assist with programs for children after school that teach character, life skills, work skills, and how to further their education.

- *College and other education.* Give them a vision for a better future. They may get a sports or other scholarship or work their way through.

- *Safety.* Ride in patrols with police or other volunteers. Help make the streets safe for children and everyone else just by being there.

- *Women's groups.* Start discussions on how to relate to men, keep their virtue, be Kingmaker wives and mothers, succeed in a career.

- *Men's groups.* Talk about sports, how to relate to women, how to raise children, generational transfer, how to earn money, save money, own a house, go into business, understand politics.

- *Start new schools*, charter schools, Christian schools, schools funded by outside money so local people can afford them.

Student Prayer Meeting That Changed the American Church

In the early 1800s, American church denominations had little interest in foreign missions until God moved on a group of college students at Williams College in Massachusetts at an 1806 prayer meeting.

Williams had been chartered in 1793 in northwestern Massachusetts. Like many colleges of the era, it reflected the declining interest in the Gospel with a resulting increase in sin.

A small group of Christian students had begun meeting secretly in a grove of trees to pray and seek God. On this particular day, a thunderstorm drove them to find shelter in a haystack where God moved on them in a powerful way. Their zeal for Jesus Christ as a result of that "Haystack Prayer Meeting" launched the American foreign missions' movement.

The students agreed to adopt the motto "We can do this if we will," committing their lives to serve God wherever He needed them. They made a commitment to reach Asia and the Muslim nations with the Gospel. After some of the students transferred to other schools, they spread their missionary zeal far and wide.

Because of their inspiration, the Congregational churches of Massachusetts and Connecticut organized the American Board of Commissioners of Foreign Missions, which also included Presbyterian and Dutch Reformed churches. In 1812, the society sent its first group overseas, including Adoniram Judson and his wife Anne, who became missionaries to Burma, now called Myanmar.

Onboard ship Judson decided he should be baptized by immersion, transferred into the Baptist denomination, where he influenced the formation of another world missions thrust, the Baptist Missionary Union. The students' influence continued to reach far and wide.

Reaching Black college students who can become missionaries

I believe that unsaved Black students on the college campuses can be reached for Christ and turned around to become a new wave of missionaries from this nation to the world. I have seen their sensitivity to Jesus. They need to find God in a real way.

Declare the blessings of God over their lives. God isn't trying to bless their mess. When He blesses them they will feel so thankful that they will get rid of all their mess and walk in holiness.

Studies confirm the dramatic effect of higher education on lowering death rates for young Blacks, especially Black men. This is credited to a healthier lifestyle resulting in fewer deaths from AIDS, cancer, heart disease, and stroke.

If you are a college student, Black or White, expect God to do something awesome with your life on behalf of others. Begin to pray and seek God as never before, and see what He will do as you fully abandon yourself to His will.

PRAYER

Lord Jesus, may the kingdom of God become manifest this day in the lives of college students—in signs, in wonders, in diverse gifts of the Holy Spirit, in lifestyles given over to You. May there be a divine sense of the weight of glory that will not let them go until they accept a new consciousness of the kingdom. Come upon them, my Father, and birth them into a new life, the life of God. Bring forth the fruit of a new level of communion with You, and let them not desire anything more than to be like You in every way. Give them the sense that they represent a new destiny as they are pressing forth in prayer. Let the manifestation come of people being born again, people being healed, and cities being shaken. In Jesus' name, I pray. Amen.

CHAPTER 3

REVIVAL IN THE INNER CITY

". . . there are lurkers in the hedges, tramps on the highways, street-walkers and lane-haunters, whom we shall never reach unless we pursue them into their own domains. Sportsmen must not stop at home and wait for the birds to come and be shot at, neither must fishermen throw their nets inside their boats and hope to take many fish."[89]

INTRODUCTION TO CHAPTER 3

A great army is coming to life in the inner city through the great revival that is on its way. This army will arise when men searching for God hear the voice of the Lord through some minister on the streets of the inner cities and give their hearts to Jesus.

A great revival mentioned earlier began in New York City in 1857 when a businessman who believed in prayer sent out an advertisement inviting people to pray. Jeremiah Lanphier had been converted to Christ in Broadway Tabernacle (the church pastored by Charles Finney before he moved to Oberlin College). Lanphier had been given the assignment of "city missionary" for the Dutch Reformed Church in Manhattan, which, like many other churches in America in that day, was losing members. He wrote an invitation to a noonday prayer meeting and distributed it in leaflets.

"In response to his advertisement, only six people out of a population of a million showed up. But the following week there were fourteen, and then twenty-three when it was decided to meet everyday for prayer. By late winter they were filling the Dutch Reformed Church, then the Methodist Church on John Street, then Trinity Episcopal Church on Broadway at Wall Street. In February and March of 1858, every church and public hall in down town New York was filled. . . .

---

[89] Charles H. Spurgeon, "Open-Air Preaching: A Sketch of Its History and Remarks Thereon." Online at http://www.biblebelievers.com/StreetPreaching2.html. Accessed October 2016.

"Trinity Episcopal Church in Chicago had a hundred and twenty-one members in 1857; fourteen hundred in 1860. . . . Then that same revival jumped the Atlantic, appeared in Ulster, Scotland and Wales, then England, parts of Europe, South Africa and South India, anywhere there was an evangelical cause. It sent mission pioneers to many countries. Effects were felt for forty years. Having begun in a movement of prayer, it was sustained by a movement of prayer."[90]

Who is qualified to reach the unsaved? Anyone who knows Jesus Christ and is trying to live his life for Him.

If God could multiply just the seed of God in you, lives would be changed. The cities would be changed.

It doesn't take much light to brighten the darkness. God has not ordained that this generation should die out when so many Christians living nearby could save them. It's time for us to answer His call.

"Let your light so shine before men,
that they may see your good works and
glorify your Father in heaven."[91]

O ne of the Negro spirituals that became famous years ago comes from Ezekiel 37, the story of the dry bones.

"Dem bones, dem bones, dem dry bones.
Now hear the word of the Lord."

In the inner cities, I see Ezekiel's field of dry bones waiting for someone to prophesy over them, and then call for the wind of the Holy Spirit to breathe new life into the people so that they can live again.

"Then he said to me, 'Speak to these bones and say, "Dry
bones, listen to the word of the LORD! This is what the
Sovereign LORD says: Look! I am going to breathe into you
and make you live again! I will put flesh and muscles on you
and cover you with skin. I will put breath into you, and you
will come to life. Then you will know that I am the LORD." '"[92]

---

[90] J. Edwin Orr, *The Light of the Nations* (Grand Rapids, MI: Eerdmans, 1963).
[91] Matthew 5:16 NKJV.
[92] Ezekiel 37:4-6 NLT.

The world will know that God is the Lord when they see the inner cities transformed, when the blind see, the lame walk, the sick are cured, the deaf hear, and the dead come to life again. That is what the power of Jesus Christ can accomplish.

> *"Jesus told them, 'Go back to John and tell him about what you have heard and seen—the blind see, the lame walk, the lepers are cured, the deaf hear, the dead are raised to life, and the Good News is being preached to the poor.'"[93]*

God asked Ezekiel rhetorically, "Son of man, can these bones live?"[94] If you asked most people today, they would probably say no. They don't believe that the inner cities can live again, but God does. He says, "Speak to these bones!"

> *"So I spoke these words, just as he told me. Suddenly as I spoke, there was a rattling noise all across the valley. The bones of each body came together and attached themselves as they had been before. Then as I watched, muscles and flesh formed over the bones. Then skin formed to cover their bodies, but they still had no breath in them.*
>
> *"Then he said to me, 'Speak to the winds and say: "This is what the Sovereign LORD says: Come, O breath, from the four winds! Breathe into these dead bodies so that they may live again."'*
>
> *"So I spoke as he commanded me, and the wind entered the bodies, and they began to breathe. They all came to life and stood up on their feet—a great army of them."[95]*

A great army coming to life

The Bible says, *"They all came to life and stood up on their feet—a great army of them."* A great army will arise when men searching for God hear the voice of the Lord through a minister on the streets of the inner cities, or on a college campus, in a business office or sports arena, or anywhere else, and give their hearts to Jesus.

---

[93] Matthew 11:4-5 NLT.
[94] Ezekiel 37:3 KJV.
[95] Ezekiel 37:7-10 NLT.

Most pastors want to minister to those already saved, but in the next move of God they will go out and find those who are lost in sin, just as Jesus did.

Who is qualified to reach the unsaved? Even those who have been saved for a short time are still more saved than all the sinners in the world. The problem with Christians is that they don't do enough with what they have. The multiplication of even that little bit would be life-changing to someone who doesn't have anything.

It doesn't take much light to brighten the darkness, but if you don't think much of your little light the darkness will scare you off. If you ignore the darkness and look at your light, you will discover the portion of God in you that somebody else must have.

If you look at the faces of the men in the inner city, they may frighten you, but not if you look beyond them into the face of God. He has not ordained that this generation should die out when so many Christians living in the same city could save them.

Time to Take Authority Over the Streets

In the ghetto they have a saying, "It's your time. It's your world." I am saying it's our time now. It's time for Christians to take dominion authority over the streets.

"To every thing there is a season, and a time to every purpose under the heaven . . . He hath made every thing beautiful in his time."[96]

Where people have been given over to the devil, it's the season now to take them back! Establish base camps from which you and those new converts can take the world. Become an unofficial governor of those streets and make them beautiful. It's our time.

Desperate for God on the streets

In 1857, a slave named Thomas Lewis Johnson was in a state of desperation, walking the streets of Richmond, Virginia. His despair was deeper than his condition of slavery. He had a yearning inside for real

---

[96] Ecclesiastes 3:1, 11 KJV.

contact with God. He wrote of his anxiety in his autobiography *Twenty Eight Years a Slave*:

> *"Matters came to such a pass that during the day I could scarcely speak to anyone; instead of being lively, and cheerful I was gloomy and nervous, and my master wanted to know what was wrong, and even threatened to send me to Georgia. But I had made up my mind that wherever I went I would not stop seeking religion until I found peace."[97]*

Lord, have mercy, for Jesus' sake!

As he was walking, he met another Black man who told him how to find Jesus. The words changed his life. He wrote:

> *"In the year 1857 there was a great revival in America. The coloured people thought the Judgment Day was coming. Everywhere we heard of great meetings and of thousands of souls being converted. In the Richmond tobacco factories, which employed many thousands of slaves, there were many converts daily. First one and then another of my friends would set out to 'seek religion.'...*

> *"One day I met a coloured man in the street, named Stephney Brown. He was a Christian, and quite an intelligent man. He explained to me the simple Gospel. He told me to go to God, and say:*

> *"'Lord, have mercy upon me, a hell-deserving sinner, for Jesus' sake; set me out your way and not my way, for Jesus' sake.'*
> . . .

> *"As soon as my work was done for that night, and all was quiet, I resolved that, if I lived for a thousand years, I would never stop praying 'for Jesus' sake.' I went into the dining room, fell down upon my knees, and said: 'O Lord have mercy upon me, a hell-deserving sinner, for Jesus' sake.'*

> *"Then I became very happy. I got up and went into the porch. Everything appeared to be different to me. The very stars in the heaven seemed brighter, and I was feeling brighter and so very happy. I did not see any great sights, but there was an inward*

---

[97] Thomas Lewis Johnson, *Twenty Eight Years a Slave*, pp. 14-16. Online at https://archive.org/details/twentyeightyears00johnrich.

rejoicing. I had not done anything—I could not do anything—to merit this any more than the thief upon the cross, but my blessed Jesus had done it all; there was nothing for me to do."[98]

America awakened, but that didn't end slavery

The 1857 Revival that Johnson mentions began in New York City as a businessmen's prayer movement started by Jeremiah Lanphier. It started with six men on their lunch break and soon spread across the nation. Entire cities would stop for prayer. Thousands were saved. Churches were filled with new members. The press covered it extensively. Famous preachers like abolitionist Henry Ward Beecher addressed the prayer meetings.

However, not enough people awakened to the judgment of God that was about to hit America because of slavery. They were praying and getting saved, but they did not apply their faith to putting a stop to our great national sin, so God had to send a great Civil War less than four years later, in April 1861, to free the slaves.

What new judgment is about to hit America this time? We have not had eyes to see it coming in the midst of our revivals. Some of it relates to the inner cities and the heart condition of our nation. Slavery has ended, but God still has issues with this nation's treatment of Black Americans.

Becoming Accountable for the Inner Cities

The lives of many inner-city Blacks demonstrate in visible terms the results of a curse against our nation because of the sins of slavery, segregation, and racism. Each year the statistics seem to grow worse. From abortion to AIDS, from drug dealing to unwed pregnancies, growing rates of death and destruction in the Black community are everywhere.

The people of God are the only ones who can answer the cry for love in the hearts of people in the inner city. God must have a people who represent Him. Would Jesus discriminate against Black people or have enmity against Whites? We are so unlike Him. We must repent. We must cry out to Him for answers.

---

[98] Ibid.

Few Whites and affluent Blacks in leadership positions, especially in the Church, are willing to accept responsibility for resolving the crisis that exists today in the inner cities. Stricter laws and putting more Black men behind bars will not solve the problem. For real change to come, there must be a spiritual awakening.

VISION FOR BLACK AMERICA:

THEY WILL RECEIVE THE COMFORT OF THE HOLY SPIRIT'S TRUTH.

Jesus said, "And I will pray the Father, and he shall give you another Comforter, that he may abide with you for ever; Even the Spirit of truth."

John 14:16-17 KJV

In the book of Ecclesiastes Solomon wrote:

"So I returned, and considered all the oppressions that are done under the sun: and behold the tears of such as were oppressed, and they had no comforter; and on the side of their oppressors there was power; but they had no comforter."[99]

Those who ponder slavery with an honest heart cannot help becoming uncomfortable, whether Black or White.

Unresolved issues related to slavery continue to affect the descendants of both oppressor and oppressed. Until America deals with it biblically, there will be no revival in our nation's inner cities. Until Black and White turn to God and to one another, they will remain bound by its curse. Only one Comforter, the Holy Spirit, can set them all free.

God's mighty power

Looking at the seemingly impossible conditions in the inner cities, we have to remember that God's mighty power goes to work inside of someone as soon as he is born again. The reality of that power should drive us to get more troubled people saved so that we can take them to a place in God where they can access His power forever. God's power is more than we could ever hope for.

---

[99] Ecclesiastes 4:1 KJV.

The primary reason for hopelessness and lack of vision in the inner cities is that they don't know Jesus so they can't receive His power and see His vision for their lives. The people keep sinning and seem helpless to bring about change because there is no voice of the Holy Spirit in their hearts. Christians can change that by refocusing their efforts on evangelism in the inner cities.

VISION FOR BLACK AMERICA:

THEY WILL EXPERIENCE GOD'S MIGHTY POWER AND RECEIVE HOPE.

"By his mighty power at work within us, he is able to accomplish infinitely more than we would ever dare to ask or hope."

Ephesians 3:20 NLT

Refocusing on *salvation* change more than social change

We need to refocus our efforts in Black America from social change to salvation change. When people get saved, it has an immediate, ongoing ripple effect on their personal lives, their families, and their community.

Salvation change drives social change that lasts.

It improves their ability to get an education and keep a job. It gives them creativity and the willingness to take a risk like starting a business. Here's a reminder of the changes that take place when someone is born again and begins a new life in Christ:

Character qualities of Christ. When revival hits the inner cities, the new converts will walk in love and mercy. Others will want to touch their lives and become like them. They will develop in the character qualities of Christ. The churches they attend will experience a restoration of the zeal of the Lord. Strife will cease because they refuse to criticize one another or blame White people for their problems. Crime and poverty will be non-issues, because they are a voice crying in the wilderness, "Prepare the way of the Lord!" [100]

---

[100] See Isaiah 40:3 and Matthew 3:3.

Hope in a world of hopelessness. Hope is God's gift to a world lost in hopelessness, and Christians are the vessels God has chosen to carry this message. When people believe in the resurrection, they know that just as Jesus was raised from the dead, others can be raised from the dead, too—both spiritually and naturally. They carry this hope of new life in Christ to their families, churches, and communities.

Knowing that God hears prayer. Christians know that when they pray they are actually coming before the Father. God is listening. He is building them into a temple for His glory as they literally go up before God and the heavenly host, the spirits of just men made perfect, the cherubim and seraphim, and the angelic host. They

VISION FOR BLACK AMERICA:

THEY WILL KNOW THAT GOD HEARS AND ANSWERS PRAYER.

"The LORD hears his people when they call to him for help. He rescues them from all their troubles.

Psalm 34:17 NLT

can go in prayer to the place of the Lamb Slain from the foundation of the world[101] and enter His presence.

Changing the Environment of the Inner City

Every year I speak in churches around the country and I am sometimes asked to return to certain cities on a regular basis. One of the churches that I visit often is Cathedral of Faith in San Jose, California, pastored by my good friends Pastors Kenny and Ken Foreman.

I remember walking in from the parking lot to the foyer right after they had installed new carpet. I didn't know they were undergoing a renovation process, and it caught my attention. Pastor Ken told me, "We are renovating to create an environment that says to the new generation that God is definitely not closed in His creative ability. He knows how to break out so that you can be won over!"

A new environment in the inner cities will demonstrate to this generation God's greatness and creative ability. Revival will change both the natural realm and the spiritual realm. Sometimes natural things like carpet and paint give people a signal that God is at work. The Bible says

---

[101] See Revelation 13:8.

that when we see things in the natural realm we can often see more clearly what is true in the spiritual realm.

> *"Howbeit that was not first which is spiritual,*
> *but that which is natural;*
> *and afterward that which is spiritual."* [102]

When revival comes, America's cities will look like new. They will gleam with God's grace and beauty, like heaven on earth. I'm not talking about urban renewal. I'm talking about revival. The song "America the Beautiful" by Katharine Lee Bates includes this prophetic vision of beautiful cities under God:

> *"O beautiful for patriot dream*
> *That sees beyond the years*
> *Thine alabaster cities gleam,*
> *Undimm'd by human tears!*
> *America! America!*
> *God shed His grace on thee*
> *And crown thy good with brotherhood*
> *From sea to shining sea!"* [103]

Regeneration of Black America

The vision of gleaming cities is not physical changes alone but also miraculous changes in the hearts of Black Americans as exemplified in the story mentioned earlier of Thomas Lewis Johnson's conversion. After he was saved he said, "Everything appeared to be different to me. The very stars in the heaven seemed brighter." Isn't that what we want for people?

After the Civil War, Johnson became a missionary to Africa after going to England and studying in a Bible school founded by Charles Spurgeon. Tragically, his wife died on the mission field, but he trusted in God and didn't give up. He eventually remarried and became a pastor and public speaker. Later in life he was confined to a wheelchair, but he still pressed on. He rode around the streets of Bournemouth, England, sharing the Gospel. Many of the people had never met a Black man before, so he became famous for staying on the light side of racism by saying, "Shake hands—the black won't come off!" He stayed faithful to Christ for the rest of his life. He had moved from a mission field to a missionary.

---

[102] 1 Corinthians 15:46 KJV.
[103] Katharine Lee Bates, "America the Beautiful." Online at Library of Congress site http://lcweb2.loc.gov/diglib/ihas/loc.natlib.ihas.100010520/lyrics.html.

Regeneration of notorious sinners

Regeneration is a theological word for the miraculous change that occurs after someone is born again. The change is much greater than anything human efforts can accomplish or even imagine. Notorious sinners are not beyond the reach of regeneration. Jesus reached out to them.

He was full of mercy. He knew He had been sent to call sinners to repentance. He knew that His death on the cross would satisfy His Father's standard of righteousness for those lost souls.

> *"That night Matthew invited Jesus and his disciples to be his dinner guests, along with his fellow tax collectors and many other notorious sinners. The Pharisees were indignant. 'Why does your teacher eat with such scum?' they asked his disciples.*

> *"When he heard this, Jesus replied, 'Healthy people don't need a doctor—sick people do.' Then he added, 'Now go and learn the meaning of this Scripture: "I want you to be merciful; I don't want your sacrifices." For I have come to call sinners, not those who think they are already good enough.'"[104]*

God was satisfied with Jesus' sacrifice on the cross.

> *"He shall see of the travail of his soul, and shall be satisfied: by his knowledge shall my righteous servant justify many; for he shall bear their iniquities."[105]*

That sacrifice covers those who live in sin all the time just as much as those who sin only occasionally. Jesus' blood is enough to bring us all to salvation. Without Jesus, all of us are lost. With Him, we are saved.

---

[104] Matthew 9:10-13 NLT.
[105] Isaiah 53:11 KJV.

87

What Do Blacks Want, Anyway?

In the 1960s, there was an avalanche of racial tension in America. At the time, we thought the cry of Blacks came from a desire to meet legitimate social needs, but all along it was the result of a God-shaped vacuum that has not been filled. I have had good Christian men ask me in genuine puzzlement, "What do Blacks want?" They see Black leaders continually trying to shake down society for a few more concessions to criminals or a few more dollars that they claim are being denied to them, but that old line won't solve the problem.

It's time to meet *God's* needs

There is a hole in the heart of this nation that only Jesus can fill. We have missed that since the 1960s, so inner-city problems have refused to go away. When the Church focuses on itself, consumed with personal needs, angry Black leaders continue to propose outdated solutions. Black against White, they demand, "Meet my needs!" Now God is saying, "It's time for *My needs* to be met. It's time for the church to put on Christ."

What is God's greatest need for the inner cities? Win people to Christ and disciple the new converts to change their lives and the lives of those around them, and then send them as missionaries to this nation and the nations of the world. As Jesus' Great Commission says,

> *"Jesus came and told his disciples, 'I have been given complete authority in heaven and on earth. Therefore, go and make disciples of all the nations, baptizing them in the name of the Father and the Son and the Holy Spirit. Teach these new disciples to obey all the commands I have given you. And be sure of this: I am with you always, even to the end of the age.'"*[106]

---

[106] Matthew 28:18-20 NLT.

REGENERATION—SPIRITUAL REBIRTH FOR THE INNER CITY

> *"Not by works of righteousness which we have done, but according to his mercy he saved us, by the washing of regeneration, and renewing of the Holy Ghost; Which he shed on us abundantly through Jesus Christ our Saviour."* [107]

God's initiative. God initiates regeneration in an individual. It is his spiritual renovation plan. He enters the heart, and the person responds to God by faith.

New capacity for spiritual change. God causes a change in a person's sinful nature so that he is able to respond to the Holy Spirit's call to him in faith.

Second birth, or being born again. The first birth was in the flesh. The second birth is regeneration by the Holy Spirit. Jesus said that no one can enter the Kingdom of God without being born again.[108]

Radical change of character. Regeneration is a change from self-centeredness to Christ-centeredness that makes a dramatic difference in a person's character. When someone is born again, even before he has had time to change his behavior by discipline and training, his heart has already changed inside supernaturally. He is no longer a slave of sin.[109] He wants to please God.

Awakening of the mind. Sin brings dullness of thought, word, and deed but Scripture tells us how to think. Regeneration brings enlightenment because the person has a new nature that affects everything.

Resurrection from sin to a new life. Regeneration is an act of God through the Holy Spirit that results in resurrection to a new life in Jesus Christ.

> *". . . if anyone is in Christ, he is a new creation; old things have passed away; behold, all things have become new."* [110]

Messianic restoration of the world. Jesus said that regeneration was not only for individual Christians, but also for the world when His people will reign with Him in righteousness. We are being born again not only to live a better life now, or to stop crime in the streets, but to be prepared to lead in the kingdom that is to come in the future.

> *"I assure you that when I, the Son of Man, sit upon my glorious throne in the Kingdom, you who have been my followers will also sit on twelve thrones, judging the twelve tribes of Israel."* [111]

---

[107] Titus 3:5-6 KJV.
[108] See John 3:3.
[109] See John 8:34.
[110] 2 Corinthians 5:17 NKJV.
[111] Matthew 19:28 NLT.

***Our desires are changed from evil to good when we are restored to
a right relationship with God through Jesus Christ.***

*"Since you have been raised to new life with Christ, set your
sights on the realities of heaven, where Christ sits in the place of
honor at God's right hand. Think about the things of heaven, not
the things of earth. For you died to this life, and your real life is
hidden with Christ in God."[112]*

Dying to Self and Living to Rescue Others

Harriet Tubman was a field slave on Maryland's Eastern Shore when she escaped to freedom in 1849. From the time she had been a child, she had been frequently whipped, and she made up her mind to do two things: (1) wear extra layers of clothes underneath and then pretend that the whippings hurt, and (2) "I prayed to God to make me strong and able to fight and that's what I've allers prayed for ever since."

When she escaped, neither her husband (a free colored man) nor any of her family members were willing to go with her, so she went alone, calling on God to make her strong. She would eventually fight her way to freedom, and return to rescue them all.

The slaves kept a secret from the time that they were children. If they ever escaped, they should head north at night, following the North Star (Polaris), the brightest star in the Little Dipper constellation. Some sang a secret song with coded instructions called "Follow the Drinking Gourd." By walking at night and hiding by day, Harriet miraculously made her journey North to freedom in Pennsylvania, where slavery had been abolished.

Returning to rescue others

In Pennsylvania, Harriet met members of the Underground Railroad—mostly Quakers and other Christians. She knew that she must return to rescue others, so she made liaisons for future rescue missions back to the South. To earn money for the return journey, she found work in Philadelphia as a cook, laundress, and scrub woman, and saved all she could.

---

[112] Colossians 3:1-3 NLT.

In 1850, she went to Baltimore, where her sister and children were about to be sold, and brought them to freedom—the first of approximately 300 slaves that she personally escorted to safety in 19 daring journeys. She became so notorious to the slave owners that a price of $40,000 was put on her head, but she was never caught, and she never lost a single escaping slave.

She rescued her six brothers, their wives and fiancées, nieces, nephews, and in 1857 she rescued her elderly parents, who had to be transported at great risk by wagon, because they could not walk on the long journey to freedom. Her husband refused to leave the South. He had married someone else after her escape. She was under constant pressure to stop doing what she believed was right, including her own fears, but she kept looking up—not only at the North Star but also toward heaven.

Crucified with Christ, no fear of death

When you have been crucified with Christ, fear has no power over you. You are already dead, so you are not afraid to rescue people from the slave plantations, the inner cities, or the uttermost parts of the earth. You have resurrection life inside that no man can take away from you. You are connected to God in a true and living way, so you are willing to lay down your life for others, just like Jesus. Paul said:

> *"Our old sinful selves were crucified with Christ so that sin might lose its power in our lives. We are no longer slaves to sin. For when we died with Christ we were set free from the power of sin. And since we died with Christ, we know we will also share his new life. We are sure of this because Christ rose from the dead, and he will never die again. Death no longer has any power over him. He died once to defeat sin, and now he lives for the glory of God. So you should consider yourselves dead to sin and able to live for the glory of God through Christ Jesus."[113]*

Attacking the Gates of Hell

We need an end-of-the-age mentality. We have got to get back to snatching souls from hell and making disciples. Some time ago the leaders of a seeker-sensitive church movement repented for spending millions of

---

[113] Romans 6:6-11 NLT.

dollars to keep members busy with programs that never resulted in significant spiritual growth. I commend them for their honesty. While churches have been distracted with their own activities, sinners like Thomas Lewis Johnson are wandering the streets of the cities looking for just one person to tell them, "You can call on Jesus, and He will get your life straight."

Paul said it this way:

"I know very well how foolish the message of the cross sounds to those who are on the road to destruction. But we who are being saved recognize this message as the very power of God. As the Scriptures say,

"'I will destroy human wisdom and discard their most brilliant ideas.'

"So where does this leave the philosophers, the scholars, and the world's brilliant debaters? God has made them all look foolish and has shown their wisdom to be useless nonsense." [114]

American Christianity has lost its competitive edge against the devil and hell. Ungodliness reigns, from the inner cities to the marketplace to the halls of government. It's time out for passivity. It's time to invade hell with the message of the cross. I'm not talking about the demonic burning crosses of the KKK, either. This is a spiritual war for true Christians who have died to self, not those who glorify themselves and their race at the expense of others.

VISION FOR BLACK AMERICA:

CHRIST WILL LIVE IN THEM.

""I have been crucified with Christ. I myself no longer live, but Christ lives in me."

Galatians 2:19-20 NLT

Taking authority over hell

During our nation's previous wars, Black Americans always fought bravely. They had to endure discrimination in the ranks, but like Harriet Tubman they seemed to have a spiritual sense that they had a higher

---

[114] 1 Corinthians 1:18-20 NLT.

calling. They understood the principle of dying to self before they ever reached the front lines.

Jesus said that hell was not a worthy foe for the Church. The gates of hell would not be able prevail when His Church decided to attack it and break down the doors.

> *"I will build my church; and the*
> *gates of hell shall not prevail against it."* [115]

Most cities in America still have a few places that look like hell, so that must mean that the Church still needs to knock down the gates to rescue the sinners inside. Whenever the Church leaves people alone in the inner cities, the devil is only too willing to be there to destroy them.

> *Most Christians don't take authority and act on the*
> *command that Jesus gave us to march into hell, even*
> *during times of spiritual renewal. Most of the revivals and*
> *renewals in recent years have taken place inside the walls*
> *of a church. Christians—even newly awakened ones—have*
> *not challenged Satan's authority over the streets.*

It doesn't matter why those sinners are living in sin. Jesus' blood can save them forever if they will repent and turn their lives over to Him.

> *"But if we walk in the light as He is in the light, we have*
> *fellowship with one another, and the blood of Jesus Christ*
> *His Son cleanses us from all sin."* [116]

Go in there and pull them out of the fire!

> *"And of some have compassion, making a difference: And*
> *others save with fear, pulling them out of the fire; hating*
> *even the garment spotted by the flesh."* [117]

All of these people are worth saving. You can't judge them by the outward appearance. God sees their hearts. He sees their potential to become great missionaries if they are saved.

---

[115] Matthew 16:18 KJV.
[116] 1 John 1:7 NKJV.
[117] Jude 22-23 KJV.

"And the LORD said to Satan, 'I, the LORD, reject your
accusations, Satan. Yes, the LORD, who has chosen
Jerusalem, rebukes you. This man is like a burning stick
that has been snatched from a fire.'"[118]

Rescuing sinners on the streets

I can go back to Richmond, the same city where Johnson was
saved, and see men hanging out on the streets who look as if they are still
in bondage. I can go a few blocks away from the state Capitol and see
Jackson Ward in one direction and Church Hill in the other. On those
streets are dry bones—dead men walking. A few miles away are projects
like Gilpin Court and Creighton Court where Black women and children
live in dingy apartments and guys slip through on weekends to have sex,
then slip away again, leaving the women to have abortions or illegitimate
babies to raise alone.

Sinners are responsible for their own sin before God, but Jesus
didn't tell Christians to point judgmental fingers at them and leave them in
their sin. He didn't tell us to build projects to keep them away from self-
righteous people. He told us to go after sinners and rescue them, drive the
devil away, and build them into holy temples who hold the Spirit of the
living God.

The Bible uses action words for Christians. "Go." "Preach." "Tell."
You won't find a sit-in-church-on-Sunday mentality anywhere in the New
Testament to describe the Christian life. When the inner cities are full of
dead men's bones, the Church is acting dead, too. Christians, arise!

Reconciling and Unifying to Win Souls

We need to come together to fulfill God's purposes, as Jesus said.
The Church is weak when divided but strong when unified.

"My prayer for all of them is that they will be one, just as
you and I are one, Father—that just as you are in me and I
am in you, so they will be in us, and the world will believe
you sent me."[119]

---

[118] Zechariah 3:2 NLT.
[119] John 17:21 NLT.

*"If two of you agree down here on earth concerning
anything you ask, my Father in heaven will do it for you.
For where two or three gather together because they are
mine, I am there among them."*[120]

Racial division and lack of unity in the Church hurt the inner cities. The devil has no right to hinder us, so in the Name of the Lord, I cancel every assignment against unity among pastors. The Holy Ghost has full reign to cause the Father's will to come to pass in their lives. Jesus spoiled principalities and powers and made a show of them openly. Now He lives inside them. Wherever the devil shows his head, Jesus will spoil him again.

Suburban pastors helping inner-city pastors

I would like to see leaders of suburban churches unifying with inner-city pastors, sharing resources to win the battle for souls together. Some inner-city pastors may not have beautiful buildings and unlimited Sunday school materials, but they have the Spirit of God in great measure.

As the Bible says, the poor are rich in faith.[121] They know they can't do anything in their own power, so they have to rely on God for their dedication and commitment.

Evangelicals honoring Pentecostals

There will come a day when evangelical Christians no longer criticize inner-city Pentecostal pastors for prophesying and speaking in tongues. They will see them as godly men and women who are staying in the war zone, faithful in prayer until God comes on them and they have the power to cast out devils in His name.

Years ago when David Wilkerson launched Teen Challenge, he discovered that the best way to take drug addicts through withdrawal was to get them saved and baptized in the Holy Ghost. In the Bible, again and again you see that when the Holy Spirit came on people in a supernatural way, miraculous changes took place.

---

[120] Matthew 18:19-20 NLT.
[121] See James 2:5.

When Joshua asked Moses to stop some brothers from prophesying, Moses asked him, "Are you jealous for my sake? I wish that all the LORD's people were prophets, and that the LORD would put his Spirit upon them all!" [122] And then the Bible says that Moses went back into the camp to find those elders. It was as if he were saying, "They've got something going on! We better get back in there. I know I have the call. I know I have the title, but these men have my spirit. Maybe if I'm walking outside the camp I'm walking away from God. They are still prophesying while I have stopped prophesying. I'm going back in there. We're all going back in there."

VISION FOR BLACK AMERICA:

THEY WILL SEE THE CHURCH UNITE ACROSS ALL THE DIVIDING LINES.

"Let love be your highest goal, but also desire the special abilities the Spirit gives, especially the gift of prophecy."

1 Corinthians 14:1-2 NLT

> *"Two men, Eldad and Medad, were still in the camp when the Spirit rested upon them. They were listed among the leaders but had not gone out to the Tabernacle, so they prophesied there in the camp. A young man ran and reported to Moses, 'Eldad and Medad are prophesying in the camp!' Joshua son of Nun, who had been Moses' personal assistant since his youth, protested, 'Moses, my master, make them stop!'*
>
> *"But Moses replied, 'Are you jealous for my sake? I wish that all the LORD's people were prophets, and that the LORD would put his Spirit upon them all!' Then Moses returned to the camp with the leaders of Israel."* [123]

Moses said, "I wish that all the LORD's people were prophets, and that the LORD would put his Spirit upon them all!"[124] God wants every one of us to be used mightily, to the fullest extent of the Holy Spirit's power. The Bible says that the 70 with Moses eventually stopped prophesying, but Eldad and Medad didn't. They stayed in there with God so much that they provoked even Joshua to jealousy, but Moses said, "They are going for God at another level. You don't want to go for God like that, so you want

---

[122] Numbers 11:29 NLT.
[123] Numbers 11:26-30 NLT.
[124] Numbers 11:29 NLT.

to shut them up. Those men who are prophesying were able to bring out the truth about where you really are in your heart. They provoked you to envy. You have the position, but they have the possession."

"So, dear brothers and sisters, be eager to prophesy, and don't forbid speaking in tongues. But be sure that everything is done properly and in order."[125]

Pentecostals respecting Evangelicals

I have a great deal of respect for the evangelical churches that have been faithfully preaching the Gospel to sinners, even those like the Southern Baptists who were founded on the basis of slavery. Those who come from another environment such as the Pentecostals need to be sure to honor others. They may not know the others' songs or follow the same style of service, but they deserve the utmost respect. Whichever group of Christians initiates respect and reconciliation toward the other groups will be the most like Christ and the most pleasing in the eyes of the Father.

"Go into all the world and preach the Good News to everyone, everywhere. Anyone who believes and is baptized will be saved. But anyone who refuses to believe will be condemned. These signs will accompany those who believe: They will cast out demons in my name, and they will speak new languages. They will be able to handle snakes with safety, and if they drink anything poisonous, it won't hurt them. They will be able to place their hands on the sick and heal them."[126]

Multicultural shepherds for the sheep

When Christians come together in unity today like those 120 people after Jesus' resurrection, preachers like Peter will convert multi-cultural multitudes as on the day of Pentecost. It will be a unified spiritual revolution that changes the hearts of destitute human beings right where they are, and when they are transformed they will transform their environment because of their revival.

---

[125] 1 Corinthians 14:39-40 NLT
[126] Mark 16:15-18 NLT.

Workers coming from everywhere to reap the harvest

A great harvest of souls is coming to the inner cities. Jesus said to pray for more workers for the fields. I'm praying for you.

> *"Jesus traveled through all the cities and villages of that area, teaching in the synagogues and announcing the Good News about the Kingdom. And wherever he went, he healed people of every sort of disease and illness. He felt great pity for the crowds that came, because their problems were so great and they didn't know where to go for help. They were like sheep without a shepherd. He said to his disciples, 'The harvest is so great, but the workers are so few. So pray to the Lord who is in charge of the harvest; ask him to send out more workers for his fields."[127]*

National Movement of City-Wide Prayer

As I have mentioned several times, we need a national movement of city-wide prayer gatherings characterized by reconciliation and unity that targets the needs of the inner cities. I believe it is the only way to touch the heart of the nation. When people see a miraculous transformation of the inner city because of the regeneration of Black Americans, only the most hardened hearts will deny that Jesus is real. They will want to know how they can have the same Jesus and the same miracle-working power in their own lives. A unified prayer movement will help Blacks to stop fighting one another and start a systematic attack on Satan's kingdom.

Leadership by apostles and pastors

In the next prayer movement for inner-city revival, I would like to see apostles and pastors, not lay people, take the lead. When church leaders reach out to one another in unity and reconciliation, members will follow.

---

[127] Matthew 9:35-38 NLT.

FIVEFOLD MINISTRY STABILIZING CHURCH AND CITY

"[Christ] is the one who gave these gifts to the church: the apostles, the prophets, the evangelists, and the pastors and teachers.

"Their responsibility is to equip God's people to do his work and build up the church, the body of Christ, until we come to such unity in our faith and knowledge of God's Son that we will be mature and full grown in the Lord, measuring up to the full stature of Christ.

"Then we will no longer be like children, forever changing our minds about what we believe because someone has told us something different or because someone has cleverly lied to us and made the lie sound like the truth. Instead, we will hold to the truth in love, becoming more and more in every way like Christ, who is the head of his body, the church. Under his direction, the whole body is fitted together perfectly. As each part does its own special work, it helps the other parts grow, so that the whole body is healthy and growing and full of love." [128]

Intercessors and parachurch leaders have launched prayer movements in recent years that God has used, but in order to build lasting momentum for change we need the leadership of apostles whom God has called to oversee cities and nations and pastors who are able to father new converts. It's time to restore respect for the fivefold ministry of church leaders[129] because that is the biblical model that God gave us. It is the basis for the discipleship and spiritual fathering needed in the inner cities today.

City-wide prayer meetings

In the past, individual churches and ministries have brought forth fruit more for themselves than for their cities. It is time for us to come together to bear corporate fruit that benefits all of our neighbors.

I recommend the following structure for each locality:

City leaders—apostles. An apostle who has a burden for the condition of his city and is supported by an apostolic team and other church leaders should head the prayer movement. In the past I have recommended that a pastor take this role, but I believe that the apostle is the most

---

[128] Ephesians 4:11-16 NLT.
[129] See Ephesians 4.

appropriate one to take city-wide spiritual leadership. The potential influence of one city's prayer movement can be worldwide.

Prayer committee of church and business leaders. Local church and business leaders meet together to seek God for the direction of the movement, set dates and locations for meetings, offer their buildings and also find others.

Personal and corporate commitments to increase prayer. Make a commitment to increase the effectiveness of your prayer life.

As an individual by:

- Focusing your personal prayer on city-wide issues
- Dealing with your own heart attitudes
- Being open and repentant toward other leaders

As a group by:

- Organizing a corporate prayer movement
- Covering the city with prayer meetings everywhere, in all the sovereign spheres—families, churches, business and industry, civil government, education, sports and entertainment, etc.
- Working together to bring change
- Meeting practical needs of your community

Specialized committees to develop focuses for prayer. Pastors, men, women, youth, and other intercessors develop areas of focus to be included in the city-wide prayer effort and lead prayer in that area at meetings. These should include sins outside the church including crime, poverty, corporate corruption, city and local government.

Historical perspective on the city. Research the history of your locality, looking for gateways of sin where Satan has gained a foothold. Acknowledge foundations of the city that were godly and biblical and admit the church's responsibility in allowing that foundation to crumble.

Monthly meetings for church and business leaders. Meetings for city leaders should be held once or twice a month and publicized by means of a mailing list, media contacts, etc. Hold these meetings at a variety of local churches, preferably in the inner city, to promote reconciliation.

Quarterly meetings for the entire city, not just leaders. Mass meetings should be well publicized, then directed under the guidance of the Holy Spirit by the Prayer Committee, allowing for participation by individuals. When necessary, the leaders can graciously correct those who wander off point or dominate the available time, but some flexibility will make this truly a city-wide effort. A time limit on each person may be useful. These meetings can be held at church locations until they require a major city facility to contain all the people.

Prayer focus for each meeting. From the first meeting, spend most of the time in repentance and heartfelt prayer, not preaching. Focus on a specific emphasis during the meeting, so that there can be agreement while you are praying. Afterwards, evaluate the effectiveness of your prayer by following news stories in the city.

Solemn Assemblies

*"I will gather them that are
sorrowful for the solemn assembly."*[130]

We can achieve city-by-city goals in a national prayer movement of repentance and prayer characterized by local solemn assemblies.

Repentance for the sins of the Church. Christians need to take an honest look at the condition of the Church today. In the Old Testament, God called for solemn assemblies where Israel would examine itself and repent first before it spent time rejoicing. You haven't enjoyed true praise and worship until you have first wept and acknowledged where you have failed, pleading with God for His forgiveness. When our hearts are burdened by sin and shortcomings in the Church, God can speak to us in our brokenness and give us power to storm the gates of hell to save sinners.

*"I will save the lame, And gather those who were driven out;
I will appoint them for praise and fame
In every land where they were put to shame."*[131]

Repentance for our nation's sins. We accept responsibility for the impact of generational sins against God and repent, like Nehemiah, who repented not only for himself and his family but also for Israel.

*"Please remember what you told your servant Moses:
'If you sin, I will scatter you among the nations. But if you
return to me and obey my commands . . .*

---

[130] Zephaniah 3:18 KJV.
[131] Zephaniah 3:19 NKJV.

*I will bring you back to the place I have chosen for my
name to be honored.*'"[132]

The U.S. Senate's apology for lynching stated it so well when it said that "only by coming to terms with history can the United States effectively champion human rights abroad."

The Senate admitted that developing nations reject America's attempts to interfere in disputes in their countries and we are ineffective globally with conflict resolution because we have not completely dealt with the sins of our ancestors.

This issue should be confronted by the Church, beginning with the sins of the city and then encompassing the sins of the nation.

"

REPENTING LOCALLY FOR NATIONAL SINS

- Lack of holiness and neglect of obedience toward God
- Slavery and unresolved sins of racism by Whites against Blacks
- Bitterness, hatred, and blaming by Blacks against Whites
- Respect of persons, based on color and status
- Prayerlessness toward the inner cities
- Insensitivity to the lost and ignorance of their potential once they are saved
- Cooperation with the enemies of God

Recommitment to seek transformation of the inner man. We admit that we need to yield to God more fully so that He might manifest His Son in us. We need to fulfill the name of "Christian"—being like Christ—and we need to bring others into that reality.

*"God knew his people in advance, and he chose them to
become like his Son, so that his Son would be the firstborn,
with many brothers and sisters. And having chosen them,
he called them to come to him. And he gave them right
standing with himself, and he promised them his glory."*[133]

---

[132] Nehemiah 1:8-9 NLT.
[133] Romans 8:29-30 NLT.

Corporate responsibility for society. We acknowledge personal and corporate responsibility for the condition of society that reflects our lack of reconciliation with God and man, and ask God to heal our relationships as He heals our land.

> *"Then if my people who are called by my name will humble themselves and pray and seek my face and turn from their wicked ways, I will hear from heaven and will forgive their sins and heal their land."* [134]

Racial oneness. We may be ethnically conscious, but we refuse to be ethnically controlled. We recognize the oneness of all people groups as one human race before God. We need one another.

> *"And He has made from one blood every nation of men to dwell on all the face of the earth, and has determined their preappointed times and the boundaries of their dwellings, so that they should seek the Lord."* [135]

Church unity. We acknowledge sectarianism and denominationalism and replace them with Christian unity based on biblical absolutes and commitment to the same Lord Jesus Christ.

> *"When the Day of Pentecost had fully come, they were all with one accord in one place."* [136]

Discontinuity and divine intervention. We acknowledge that we cannot change the inner cities without divine intervention from God. They are in deep trouble, so we are calling on God.

> *"But in their time of trouble they cried to you, and you heard them from heaven. In great mercy, you sent them deliverers who rescued them from their enemies."* [137]

Revival. We call for a return of the biblical and historical precedent of sparking a widespread revival through prayer.

> *"Won't you revive us again, so your people can rejoice in you? Show us your unfailing love, O LORD, and grant us your salvation."* [138]

---

[134] 2 Chronicles 7:14 NLT.
[135] Acts 17:26-27 NKJV.
[136] Acts 2:1 NKJV.
[137] Nehemiah 9:27 NLT.
[138] Psalm 85:6-7 NLT.

CHAPTER 3. REVIVAL IN THE INNER CITIES

Spiritual warfare. We challenge the church to fight in the right arena and use its weapons against the right enemy—Satan and his hosts. They are already defeated foes. We must do nothing to make the world think those enemies are right, and everything to take a stand against evil, regardless of public pressure or persecution.

> *"Having disarmed principalities and powers,*
> *[Jesus] made a public spectacle of them,*
> *triumphing over them in it.* "[139]

Social change. We take responsibility for the condition of society. The Church must become the predominant agent of social change in America, following the command of Jesus.

> *"Don't hide your light under a basket! Instead, put it on a*
> *stand and let it shine for all. In the same way, let your*
> *good deeds shine out for all to see, so that everyone will*
> *praise your heavenly Father."* [140]

Restoring the streets to livability. We restore the desolations of former generations and bring healing to the inner cities as we rebuild the streets according to God's standards. This includes law and order and collaboration with police to make the streets safe for all.

> *"Those from among you*
> *Shall build the old waste places;*
> *You shall raise up the foundations of many generations;*
> *And you shall be called the Repairer of the Breach,*
> *The Restorer of Streets to Dwell In."*[141]

Intercessors Birthing Inner-City Revival

The streets of the inner city represent a nation. The rebirth of this "nation" will require a prayer gestation process that takes time, but when the fullness of time comes, the new nation can be born in a day.

> *"Who has ever seen or heard of anything as strange as*
> *this? Has a nation ever been born in a single day? Has a*
> *country ever come forth in a mere moment? But by the*
> *time Jerusalem's birth pains begin, the baby will*

---

[139] Colossians 2:15 NKJV.
[140] Matthew 5:15-16 NLT.
[141] Isaiah 58:12 NKJV.

be born; the nation will come forth. Would I ever bring
this nation to the point of birth and then not deliver it?'
asks the LORD. 'No! I would never keep this nation from
being born,' says your God."[142]

Impregnated and enlarged with vision from the Holy Ghost

When you go into your private prayer closet with Christ, you become impregnated by the Holy Ghost with the unsaved children of the world. You become enlarged with vision. You get fatter and fatter as you feel the quickening of the Spirit of God within.

During your spiritual pregnancy, you experience discomforts that try to distract you from your calling to birth God's vision into reality, so you try to see every trial and the hard times you are experiencing as the baby of that vision kicking in your womb.

"All around us we observe a pregnant creation. The
difficult times of pain throughout the world are simply
birth pangs. But it's not only around us; it's within us. The
Spirit of God is arousing us within. We're also feeling the
birth pangs. These sterile and barren bodies of ours are
yearning for full deliverance. That is why waiting does not
diminish us, any more than waiting diminishes a pregnant
mother. We are enlarged in the waiting. We, of course,
don't see what is enlarging us. But the longer we wait, the
larger we become, and the more joyful our expectancy."[143]

Ready to birth something glorious

Creation itself is expecting a glorious move of God.

"The created world itself can hardly wait for what's
coming next. Everything in creation is being more or less
held back. God reins it in until both creation and all the
creatures are ready and can be released at the same
moment into the glorious times ahead. Meanwhile, the
joyful anticipation deepens."[144]

---

[142] Isaiah 66:8-9 NLT.
[143] Romans 8:22-25 *The Message.*
[144] Romans 8: 18-21 *The Message.*

Pressed in the birth canal

The inner cities entering the birth canal will be pressed and squeezed until they come forth in new life. Jesus is praying for them, and we join Him in praying for their breakthrough.

> *"But Jesus remains a priest forever; his priesthood will never end. Therefore he is able, once and forever, to save everyone who comes to God through him. He lives forever to plead with God on their behalf. He is the kind of high priest we need because he is holy and blameless, unstained by sin."[145]*

Everything that is happening to them can work for their good when God is for them. *"If God is for us, who can ever be against us?"[146]*

Spiritual birth coach

God doesn't expect you to give up when you get tired of waiting for the vision to manifest. He says when you get tired in the waiting, the Holy Spirit comes alongside to help you along. He is your spiritual birth coach, there in the labor room with you.

> *"Meanwhile, the moment we get tired in the waiting, God's Spirit is right alongside helping us along."[147]*

A woman in labor may not have enough focus to pray the right words, but someone can pray for her. The Bible says it doesn't matter if you don't know how or what to pray because the Holy Spirit is with you.

> *"If we don't know how or what to pray, it doesn't matter. He does our praying in and for us, making prayer out of our wordless sighs, our aching groans."[148]*

You travail in pain and the Holy Ghost turns your sighs and groans into prayers. He takes your unspoken and unknown desires and turns them into specific words of intercession to the Father on behalf of those you are birthing.

---

[145] Hebrews 7:24-26 NLT.
[146] Romans 8:31 NLT.
[147] Romans 8:26 *The Message.*
[148] Romans 8:26-28 *The Message.*

*"My little children, of whom I travail in birth again until
Christ be formed in you."[149]*

The Holy Spirit stands with you. He is bringing the baby of
potential to birth.

*"He does our praying in and for us, making prayer out of
our wordless sighs, our aching groans. He knows us far
better than we know ourselves, knows our pregnant
condition, and keeps us present before God. That's why we
can be so sure that every detail in our lives of love for God
is worked into something good."[150]*

It is not too late to save the heart of the nation's cities. God has
given us a plan. May we be able to say with the apostle Paul, "I was not
disobedient to the heavenly vision."[151]

*The vision is great.
The call is great.
But we are a great people.*

Spiritual Fathering on the Streets

Some of the people most vital to the success of the inner-city
revival will be spiritual fathers. Since fathers are missing in action in the
Black community, in the coming revival they must be everywhere!

A group of ministers that I call the Street Revs *(see next chapter)*
father the men on the streets, and they also have spiritual fathers
themselves. When they model out the example of submitting to a spiritual
father, the men in the inner cities will have one more reason to see that
sonship is a valuable relationship that they want to develop. Ultimately,
God wants every man to develop the maturity and mentality to become a
good father to his own children and a spiritual father to others. God intends
to give you your own offspring who have the right spirit, just like you.
Christians raise up an eternal legacy that God gives them. Your heart is
good ground for that.

---

[149] Galatians 4:19 KJV.
[150] Romans 8:26-28 *The Message.*
[151] Acts 26:19 NKJV.

Transformational fathering

Your life is a valuable life. Your mission is a powerful mission in God. God wants to use you to touch people's lives for Him.

> *"The LORD replied, 'Take Joshua son of Nun, who has the Spirit in him, and lay your hands on him. Present him to Eleazar the priest before the whole community, and publicly commission him with the responsibility of leading the people. Transfer your authority to him so the whole community of Israel will obey him. When direction from the LORD is needed, Joshua will stand before Eleazar the priest, who will determine the LORD's will by means of sacred lots. This is how Joshua and the rest of the community of Israel will discover what they should do."[152]*

God told Moses to touch the life of Joshua, the man whom He had chosen to lead the people of Israel in his place. He said, "Take Joshua son of Nun, who has the Spirit in him, and lay your hands on him."[153] Moses was not representing himself when he laid his hands on Joshua. He was representing God, the Father. When we touch someone's life, we touch them for God. We restore a sense of God's reality to their being. When Moses imparted his spirit to Joshua, he passed on the ability to lead the people. He passed on the discernment to handle the hard cases, and the ability to delegate authority.

Jesus' model of discipleship and fathering

Everything you get from Jesus you will be able to pass on.

- Help sons discover their personal call.
- Rebuke when needed for correction.
- Remain above them like a father.
- Teach them from the Scriptures.
- Get them involved with helping needy people.
- Remain transparent about your relationships.
- Meet alone with disciples and take them with you to minister.

---

[152] Numbers 27:18-21 NLT.
[153] Numbers 27:18 NLT.

Christianity is not so much a hierarchy as it is a patriarchy

FUNCTIONS OF A SPIRITUAL FATHER

Some spiritual fathers may be younger than their sons, but they have the maturity to father them into their next level. They may not be related by blood, but they are committed by covenant.

Loves his son and makes a long-term commitment for life. He vows not to let the young man down on his watch.

Teaches his son about consecration and the Christian life. Teaches the young man based on his own relationship with God, the Bible, and his life experiences.

Covers his son's back, is there for him in time of need. There is no question that the daddy will help the young man if any crisis arises with his friends and family, or if he backslides and has to come back. He will keep expressing his belief in his spiritual son.

Keeps sons out of trouble. Strong fathers make a difference not only in the quality of life of their children but also by giving their sons vision and a good conscience to know what is right and wrong. Studies show that boys without fathers have a greater chance of ending up in jail, regardless of income, race, or the educational level of the parents.[154]

Teaches his sons to get along with people. He uses man-to-man relationships to teach godly character and develop life-long habits of building quality relationships. He helps them learn to handle their emotions in productive ways, to repent for sins and also to forgive others. He shows them when they are too dominated by their friends' lack of values and not taking a stand for their own.

Counsels them about godly relationships with young women. A father sets standards of purity for his sons that include no kissing or risky dating practices and definitely no sex before marriage. He teaches them about friendship and courtship as a holy man of God.

Takes them to church and teaches them to respect the pastor. The sons participate in activities, even those that require sacrifice, such as early morning and late night prayer meetings. They learn to sacrifice their time without complaint and conform to the length and order of the service as determined by the pastors and elders.

---

[154] Maggie Gallagher, "Fatherless Boys Grow Up Into Dangerous Men" (*Wall Street Journal,* December 1, 1998). Report of a study by the University of California's Cynthia Harper and Princeton's Sara McLanahan. Referenced online at http://www.fathermag.com/news/2770-WSJ81201.shtml.

Street Revs submitting to Street Pastors and Street Bishops

Street Revs are people with the zeal of the Lord to get people saved and show them how to change their lives. Street Revs need fathers to teach and train them and to be there for them when things get complicated. When their converts backslide or they stop coming around, or when the Street Revs say something that causes offense, they need an older and wiser man to cover them with prayer and share his wisdom for the situation. They need reminders to be like Christ, because they are Christ's ambassadors.

Spiritual daddy adds depth to his sons' lives

Christianity is grandfathers, fathers and sons helping each generation to grow up and come of age in the family. Without a strong father, you have chaos and crime, just like the inner city. When fathers are present, they are a stabilizing force. They grow into their role as men of God for their families. It is the same with spiritual fathers. People who choose churches based on the best preaching and music and the least accountability are missing one of the most important features of the true church—spiritual fathering.

> *"Look, I am sending you the prophet Elijah before the great and dreadful day of the LORD arrives. His preaching will turn the hearts of fathers to their children, and the hearts of children to their fathers. Otherwise I will come and strike the land with a curse."*[155]

Pastors fathering others to become spiritual fathers

The best pastors want to be fathers who add depth to their children, not administrators who spend all of their time in church tasks, preparing one sermon a week, arguing with deacons, and counseling rebels. That is not the biblical model. By teaching Street Revs to father the men and also submit to Street Pastors and Street Bishops we will establish a fathering link that will transfer all the way down to the people in the streets who must be fathered lest they die.

---

[155] Malachi 4:5-6 NLT.

It's the only model that will save them. Even before the
street guys are converted and become good fathers, we can
fill the streets with fathers from the churches who launch
the fathering movement.

When a spiritual father helps you to recognize your own areas of immaturity and you seek God for your change, you are learning how to become qualified to become a spiritual parent to others. Instead of staying at the level of a babe focusing your prayers on what you want, you can be there for your brother. You press through to be a better husband not only for the sake of your wife but also so you can be an example to your brothers who are struggling with their marriages. You see yourself as a parent taking spiritual responsibility for other men, and even for the generation. You are more than a mentor. You are a father.

"The Spirit of the LORD is upon Me,
Because He has anointed Me
To preach the gospel to the poor;
He has sent Me to heal the brokenhearted,
To proclaim liberty to the captives
And recovery of sight to the blind,
To set at liberty those who are oppressed;
To proclaim the acceptable year of the LORD."[156]

Why men don't want to be fathers

- Never had a father and no one has taught them how to do it
- Focused on pleasure more than responsibility
- Don't want to get married, because they don't understand it
- Unwilling to spend their money on anyone but themselves
- Unwilling to take the low road
- Following a model in the media of lazy, macho, irresponsible men
- Reacting with their pride and hormones to women who chase them
- Have been put down and mis-defined, so they adopt the faulty description that was spoken over them

---

[156] Luke 4:18-19 NKJV.

How fatherhood helps men become successful everywhere

- Fulfills creative order
- Models Jesus and His Father, Jesus and His parents in the temple
- Teaches humility and responsibility
- Blesses his wife with love
- Nurtures and strengthens his children
- Learns how to deal kindly with people
- Enjoys seeing his children succeed
- Fulfills God's vision for the family line through his children
- Has standards based on biblical principles
- Creates a coat of arms for his family
- Learns humility and servant leadership
- Honors God as the true head of the family
- Speaks from the perspective of God's will for himself and others
- Leads with love

Multicultural Fathering[157]

The inner cities need both Black and White spiritual fathers. Most White people want to empower *me* to go to the inner cities, but I tell them *they* need to go. Some Blacks will not feel that they are released from the curse of racism until they are released by members of the White race that enslaved them. They want to be blessed by those who cursed them.

As a pastor, as a father, I pray for people as I carry them to the next level. My prayer is that they will someday carry others. I have had Black people get angry with me because I father White people as well as Black, but I am not limited by my race. I have White babies in my spirit. I don't believe that you have to be White to win Whites or be Black to win Blacks. That is man's thinking. That is not God.

Where would Black America be now if White Christians had not become abolitionists and then gone on to win slaves and freedmen to Christ, then teach and train them not only in the Bible but also in academic subjects and practical work skills?

Where would the White Pentecostal movement be today if Black preachers like William Seymour and C.H. Mason hadn't shared their experience with Whites and empowered them to reach the world with an inward experience of the baptism in the Holy Ghost?

---

[157] See also Chapters 4 and 6.

Don't just go after people of the same race. Have a kingdom spirit, not a cultural spirit. A cultural mindset cuts you off from your brothers of another mother. It's all right to be culturally conscious, but it's not all right to be culturally controlled. We need to get past cultural consciousness, even if that gets some people mad.

What good is consciousness of color going to do for the kingdom of God? Only kingdom consciousness accomplishes anything. You might be thinking of the Word from a cultural consciousness when God wants you to take the Gospel to another nation.

You can't be bound into thinking about yourself and your race. My spirit gets enlarged when I see White people, so they receive me because they see that I can father them. I talk to Whites in the same way that I talk to Blacks. They don't think I am talking to them as White people. I don't get behind their backs and say, "Look at those White people over there."

"Nursing Fathers"

God needs unbiased people as instruments of revival. Moses was God's instrument for Israel. He argued with God that he had not conceived the people, that he was not a "nursing father."[158]

But God said that he was like God to them. God was saying, "If you don't carry them like a father, Moses, who will?"

PRAYER

Father, give us the sense that You will use us to change the inner cities by revival and fathering in the power of your Word. If the devil can have people following him, how much more can we with the Holy Ghost have people follow us because we will lead them straight into the kingdom. You have proven that You can keep people pure. You can keep them going for You. Now You are going to begin the work for which we have prayed so long. Now You are going to move. Thank You for including us as instruments in this next move of God.

Thank you for the weight of the anointing of the Holy Spirit upon those who are yours. Give us the power and authority to speak to those who seem to be the furthest away from you. Grip their hearts as you gripped ours when You came upon us, Lord Jesus. Let the women know

---

[158] Numbers 11:12 KJV.

they're married to you. Let the men know they're married to you. Help them to know that they are one with You. Teach them Your ways. Bring them up to the next level.

Help Black Americans to become such a people of God that the world will say, "We never heard anyone speak like this," because Jesus is so real in their lives. Let them do such wonderful works in this coming revival that only You can receive the glory for it because it's so awesome. Let every sinner repent for his sins. Let every person who has divorced you and every backslider be restored in this coming revival. Let every sick person be healed because with your stripes they are healed. Let every poor person be restored to health and wealth by coming into the kingdom of God. Oh God, let not one person be condemned but let them be encouraged as they hear the Good News. Then use them mightily. In Jesus' name, I pray. Amen.

CHAPTER 4

STREET REVS

"But ye that make mention of the Lord, keep not silence. Move heaven with your prayers, and earth with your cries. Cry aloud, spare not, lift up your voice like a trumpet! Diligence, prudence, courage, perseverance. You will care for every circuit, every society, every preacher, every family, and every soul in your charge. You will be planning continually to extend and establish the Church of God in your section. You will be eyes, ears, mouth, and wisdom, from us to the people; and from the people to us. You will be in our stead, to supply our absence. 'Tis order, 'tis system, under God, that hath kept us from schism, and heresy, and division."[159]

Letter from Bishop Francis Asbury to James Quinn

INTRODUCTION TO CHAPTER 4

The closest geographical location where we can start a new spiritual awakening is the inner cities of America.

Revival can be as simple as driving to a neighborhood, getting out and walking, praying as you walk the streets. You carry Bibles, start conversations, stir up interest, and get a sense of the neighborhood. Open your heart to the people with such great needs.

On the inner-city streets is a vast unchurched population of sinners in need of Christian brothers. In some inner cities you can find churches on almost every street corner, but after Sunday morning when they all go home, the drug dealers use the church steps to sell drugs.

This chapter is about what some people would call friendship evangelism, but it targets the inner cities. Those who go to the streets are "Street Revs." That is their jurisdiction. They talk to the guys, watch sports, start storefront churches—whatever it takes to change the

---

[159] Francis Asbury, "Letter to James Quinn" (a Methodist preacher for nearly 50 years). Wesley Center for Applied Theology. Online at http://wesley.nnu.edu/holiness_tradition/asbury_journal/vol_II/ch13.htm.

environment from sin to holiness. They work with pastors and churches that are there, and offer something new.

When Jesus called His disciples, they dropped everything they were doing. James and John left their fishing nets and their father's business. Matthew left his tax collector's table. Dr. Luke gave his medical practice to Jesus. Today when people get saved they are often not challenged to leave anything to serve God.

Street Revs can still maintain their day jobs and care for their families, but they can carve out time to be revolutionaries. They are reaching desperate people and turning their lives around.

Some can do tent-making on the side like Paul. Whatever it takes to speed up the pace where churches are turning out ministers, that's what we have to do.

Not everyone will want to go to the streets, but if only some men from each church would go regularly, regeneration would begin and it would be the start of a revolution.

I n the days of the American frontier, there were not enough preachers for all of the outlying rural communities. Therefore, a movement of preachers was created who became known as the Methodist circuit riders. Francis Asbury (1745-1816), an early national leader of the Methodist Episcopal Church in America, pioneered the circuit rider system for preachers so that one man could cover several churches and spread the joy of Christ's salvation to the multitudes.

> *"So also was Christ, the Saviour, joyously preached—*
> *preached in the fullness of his grace and the pathos of his*
> *love. The salvation offered in his name was free and full,*
> *and realizable in a present assurance and joyous*
> *experience."*[160]

As a result of these circuit riders, the number of Methodists in America grew during Asbury's lifetime from 1,200 people to 214,000 members with 700 ordained preachers.[161]

---

[160]Ezra Squier Tipple, *Francis Asbury: The Prophet of the Long Road* (New York, Cincinnati: The Methodist Book Concern, 1916). Public domain. Available online at www.Archive.org.
[161]Source of statistics—Asbury University website, www.asbury.edu.

Inner-city circuit riders—Street Revs

We need that passionate outreach mentality of the Methodist circuit riders for the inner cities today.

I call the inner-city circuit riders "Street Revs." They minister outside the church walls.
Wherever they go, they change the environment.
They raise up other men to be just like them.

Instead of waiting for a few sinners to wander into inner-city churches and storefronts, we send out Street Revs on inner-city circuits. Street Revs are Christian men who ride into inner-city neighborhoods, get out of their cars or off their bicycles, and walk the streets spreading the Gospel. They are committed to winning, discipling, and training men in a variety of friendly but noncompromising ways.

Street Revs reach guys on the street. They are marketplace ministers. They make house calls.

They are backed by Street Pastors and Street Bishops who also carry their burden for souls.

Asbury was White but he spoke out against slavery. He also empowered Blacks. He ordained the first Black Methodist minister, Richard Allen, founder of the African Methodist Episcopal Church.

For 45 years of faithful ministry, in spite of danger, fatigue, and sickness, Asbury rode an average of 6,000 miles a year—an estimated quarter of a million miles. That means that about every four years he would have circled the entire earth at the equator, which is 24,901.55 miles.

During the time he was sitting on horseback from town to town, he prayed and studied the Bible and other books he carried in his saddlebags. He preached anywhere people would listen—open fields, courthouses, tobacco houses, squares, and homes. In addition to preaching, he had the ability to recruit, train, and organize circuit riders to cover the mostly rural countryside with him. Look at the level of dedication!

Many of the circuit riders had little formal education but their conversions had been so dramatic that they had a driving passion for winning souls to Christ.

The Methodist book of *Doctrines and Discipline* provided biblical principles from the most important Scripture texts. They built their sermons and lesson plans for discipleship classes based on that manual so even relatively new converts could lead other people to the Lord.

Church services were called "meetings." In addition to the meetings, the circuit riders or "saddlebag preachers" also taught Bible classes and then quizzed the members to determine what they were learning from Scripture. Sunday schools for children were organized where they taught academic subjects in addition to the Bible.

What Street Revs do

The same concept of circuit riders could work for supplying itinerant preachers for the inner cities.

Could you be one of the Street Revs who brings a spiritual awakening to the inner cities? Here's a description of what you can do:

- Build a Street Rev's handbook of foundation doctrines for evangelism, training, code of character and conduct. Include the time-honored creeds. Study and understand Christian history and the history of the times.

- Chart out your visional strategy according to the SAM principle— Specific, Achievable, Measurable goals and a timeline.

- Walk the streets and meet people in person. Stay humble but be strong inside from a dedicated prayer life.

- Build good relationships with other pastors and ministries

- Fellowship with unsaved men in friendship evangelism.

- Recruit and sign up followers whom you can train, license, and oversee.

- Carry a Bible. Read it aloud or quote portions of it to the men, staying cheerful and humble. For familiar quotes, the King James Version is still the most well-known version to Black Americans, but the New Living Translation helps communicate in modern language the Bible's practical and piercing truths.

- Talk about Jesus, sports, other things the guys want to talk about.

- Get a uniform for head-to-toe recognition. (Be marketplace and culturally relevant.)

- Tell them from the Bible how to be born again. Keep it as natural as if you were discussing last night's football game. Assume they want to know how to be saved. Assume they have a grandmother praying for them and telling them about getting back to God.

- Work out in the gym. Play sports. Join leagues, political groups, men, women, youth, prison ministries, college outreaches.

SCRIPTURES ABOUT SALVATION IN JESUS CHRIST

These Scriptures say a lot about salvation (these are from the King James Version).

Romans 3:23. "For all have sinned, and come short of the glory of God."

Romans 5:8. "While we were yet sinners, Christ died for us."

John 3:16. "For God so loved the world, that he gave his only begotten Son, that whosoever believeth in him should not perish, but have everlasting life."

1 John 1:9. "If we confess our sins, he is faithful and just to forgive us our sins, and to cleanse us from all unrighteousness."

- Pray with the guys to be saved.

- Ask if they or anyone they know needs prayer. Pray on the spot.

- Tell the guys where to find storefront churches and local churches that are street-friendly.

- Invite them to hang out with you at a location with something set up.

- Give them street-friendly newsletters or literature on your programs and meeting places, with addresses and directions.

- Buy or rent a general headquarters for offices and training.

- Provide phone numbers for 24-hour call lines, such as pro-life pregnancy centers that prevent abortions.

- Give them a number for your own 24-hour call line if you have one established. If you don't have one, talk to the Street Pastors about setting one up with an 800 number that you can forward to whoever is on call.

- Don't promise anything you can't deliver.

- Set up 24-hour prayer teams.

Focusing on Men Before Reaching Women

Why do we make men the first priority for evangelism and discipleship instead of women and children?

1. It follows the creative order. God created men first.

2. Jesus came, as we know in the redemptive story, and He chose disciples who were men first, before the women came.

3. Research and study has shown, and the men's movement Promise Keepers also discovered, that when the father in a family gets saved, the likelihood that the rest of the family will be saved is much higher than when the woman is saved first, because he is the God-given leader of the home and family.

4. Also, the spiritual condition of the men is usually the worst and they are the most resistant to the Gospel.

Men have the potential to be converted and bring life instead of death to the cities and nations. Women carry most churches right now, while men in the inner cities may be so far from God that they are causing death not only to themselves but also to those their lives touch.

James said that "he who turns a sinner from the error of his way will save a soul from death and cover a multitude of sins." [162]

Some Black men are in a mess, but Jesus loves them, and when they are saved they will lead many to righteousness.

"Those who are wise will shine as bright as the sky, and those who turn many to righteousness will shine like stars forever." [163]

---

[162] James 5:20 NKJV.
[163] Daniel 12:3 NLT.

> ## THESE MEN CAN BE REACHED FOR JESUS
>
> - Young Black men—teens to adults, dropping out of school, unable to find work, idle, getting in trouble, looking for some excitement
>
> - Immigrants
>
> - Homeless
>
> - Orphans
>
> - Prisoners and gang leaders
>
> - Athletes and entertainers
>
> - Men who were raised to respect the church but have fallen away
>
> - College students led away from God by professors and peers
>
> - Businessmen and entrepreneurs
>
> - Educators
>
> - Anyone whom God has called

In the second wave of inner-city revival, we will have evangelism and fellowship programs for women and children because their change will be dramatic after the men get their lives right. We will have Street Sisters and Street Mothers. Righteous mothers, grandmothers, and sisters are already praying for these guys. We want to be an answer to their prayers.

Qualifications for Men Who Are Street Revs

Every Christian man who is disciplined, developing in Christ-likeness, submitted to a spiritual father, being changed, and becoming more like God can become a Street Rev. The first ones will be men.

Sound doctrine for Street Revs. The circuit riders were called "saddlebag preachers" because they carried their belongings and books in their saddlebags. The Methodist Church provided each circuit rider with a book of *Doctrines and Discipline* with information on what the church believed so that the preacher would preach sound doctrine and have a guide for his personal devotional life. Preachers have the same need today.

A Street Rev prays and reads the Bible daily and studies his Street Rev's Manual. He is gaining insight from Scripture that helps him to become more like Jesus. He is a source of light so He can carry light to the darkness. He is not alive just to survive. He is affecting peoples' lives. He believes that people will want his insight when he tells them what happened to him after he met Jesus.

Standards for Street Revs

- Saved (born again)

- Believing the Bible as the inerrant Word of God

- Under the authority of a pastor and attending church weekly, respecting other pastors

- Keeping a humble attitude, taking the low road

- Burdened for the souls of men

- Understanding issues related to Black genocide and self-genocide

- Willing to make sacrifices, including finances

- If married, staying married, taking care of wife and children

- No sex outside of marriage

- No pornography, drugs, smoking, drinking alcohol, or other questionable practices that Jesus wouldn't do

- Disciplined, trying to live a holy life to become more like Christ

- Managing personal health and finances

- Endeavoring to be debt-free

- Being discipled and discipling others

- Reading the Bible and praying daily for others' needs, not just his own

- Maintaining personal study of the Bible and other subjects

- Participating in regular team outreaches.
  - o Joining home and foreign missions, temporary and permanent
  - o Participating in disaster relief in storms, fires, and other opportunities to win to the Lord those who need Him desperately.
  - o Visiting hospitals and nursing homes.

- Willing to be accountable in writing and verbal reporting, including attending conferences called by those in authority over them.

- Willing to give away money to someone who asks.

Don't flash big wallets or lots of cash. They will watch what you take out of your pocket. Some people would never give money to a man if they thought he would misuse it or that everyone else would expect to get money, too. However, sometimes it gives you a release to step away from your judgmental self and just give to someone without restrictions, as unto the Lord. He gives us a lot of blessings that we don't deserve. It's your release to give money to someone just like Jesus said.

Jesus said, "Give to those who ask, and don't turn away from those who want to borrow." [164]

Knowledge base for Street Revs

- Foundation doctrines and Street Revs manual

- Salvation Scripture verses and Sinner's Prayer

- Explanation of key Scripture passages always ready to share

- FAQ (Frequently Asked Questions) street guys may ask and argue about including STDs, AIDS, health, criminal justice, the news

- Christian terminology

- Black American terminology

- Terms in Spanish and languages of immigrants in your area

- How to talk to people conversationally, focusing on them and not you

- How to pray for people, in genuine contact with God

- Some knowledge of sports—play a sport and/or understand sports language and read the sports page to be able to discuss the games

- Some knowledge of Black entertainers—actors, singers, TV personalities, Black media such as magazines, newspapers

- Understanding Black history and its impact today

---

[164] Matthew 5:42 NLT.

Street journals and cell phones

- Street Revs keep a journal. Some guys can do this on a cell phone. Others may want to use paper or even record their own audio notes. They use these notes for reports to their overseer or street pastor so they can learn from those above them how to be more effective.

   o   Notes on different neighborhoods
   o   Names of guys they meet
   o   What they need to take with them next time

- Cell phones give Street Revs the ability to communicate, share information, or even to get assistance in an emergency. They may want to have someone monitoring them at a home base if they are in a dangerous area. Have 911 programmed in and any other emergency numbers on speed dial or voice dial.

- Extensive training in the use of technology

Street wear

- Identifiable T-shirts, jackets, sweat shirts, hats, pants, shoes (clean tennis shoes and polished regular shoes)—*quality and stylish*

- Bible that looks like a Bible

- Extra small Bibles or New Testaments to give away

Quick Start for Street Circuits

On the inner-city streets is a vast unchurched population of sinners in need of Christian brothers. In some inner cities you can find churches on almost every street corner, but after Sunday morning when they all go home, some drug dealers use the church steps to sell drugs. Street Revs don't criticize those pastors and churches. They just come along to do something extra. Hopefully before long they will all be working together to clean up the streets.

No more than three to six months training. We train zealous Christian men to go to the streets and start making a difference as quickly as possible. In three to six months *or less* they will be out there winning souls and talking sense on the streets. They can take a crash course in evangelism with a strong focus on consecration, fasting and prayer, sound doctrine, evangelism, and discipleship. They can submit to spiritual fathers. But we must get them out there.

Aggressive fund-raising. The goal is full time support for Street Revs. Churches need to see this as a worthy benevolence.

Street Revs everywhere—quickly!

It was said of the saddlebag preachers, "They are everywhere!" That's what I want to hear about the Street Revs, and I want to hear it quickly. "Quickly" was a word Jesus used in this passage about going to the streets and inviting people to come to Him.

> "'Go quickly into the streets and alleys of the city and invite the poor, the crippled, the lame, and the blind.' After the servant had done this, he reported, 'There is still room for more.' So his master said, 'Go out into the country lanes and behind the hedges and urge anyone you find to come, so that the house will be full.'"[165]

Street Revs' transportation

Cars, trucks, buses, vans, bicycles, and motorcycles will be needed to get them to their people and sometimes to take the people to places where they can be changed and grow.

Quick start steps

- *Start a team.* A Street Rev and at least one other team member decide to go to the streets together. You are committed to praying and working together and watching one another's backs. Different partners may go out together at different times. One of the Street Revs is developing a permanent commitment to one or more locations.

- *Meet with your pastor or other spiritual father.* Tell him about your desire and allow him to give input and oversight. Get his blessing before you start. A Street Rev who is submitted to a spiritual overseer teaches those in his care to submit to him, also, as a spiritual father. Jesus said to make *disciples.*

---

[165] Luke 14:21-23 NLT.

You will be able to start inner-city outreaches quickly if the ministers starting storefront churches or hang-outs are eager and aggressive but also have wise spiritual fathers who provide accountability.

The Methodist circuit riders were responsible, dedicated men, but they weren't loners. They were appointed to their charge by a bishop who would visit the churches under his jurisdiction at least once a year. The bishop might also start new churches and then appoint pastors. The circuit riders attended annual conferences where they met with their bishops and might be appointed to new areas of responsibility.

- *Drive to a neighborhood and start walking.* A Street Rev and a team member drive to a local area where young Blacks live and hang out, park in a secure location, and then start praying as they walk the streets. They are carrying Bibles, starting conversations, stirring up interest, getting a sense of the neighborhood, making friends, sharing the Word, praying aloud for guys with obvious needs. Even some hard-core guys will melt when some genuine Christian offers to pray for them. They instinctively know if you are there for them.

- *Look for a future meeting place where you can hang out with the guys.* Find a temporary meeting place where you can invite the guys to spend time with you. They may tell you they are coming but not keep their word, but eventually, if you are consistent, they will come.

- *See what churches are in the area that you can work with.* Make notes about local churches in the area and report to your Street Pastor so that he can check back with those pastors later.

Street Revs who go to a new neighborhood need to observe what churches are in the area, then go back to meet with the pastors and courteously share their vision. The overseers of the Street Revs may make the first contact. They develop a partnership in reaching the streets, and are not in competition. This attitude will have to be communicated frequently and also lived out. Some misunderstandings may develop, but the Lord will resolve them and guys will be reached.

- *Develop a consistent presence.* Over a period of weeks, build a relationship with the neighborhood people. The men may have seen bad guys come to set up the drug trade—a "shirt-and-tie man"—or Black Muslims, or even some street preachers who never came back. They will be checking you out. Since the Street Revs are circuit riders, they go to different neighborhoods during the month to see where there is a witness from the Holy Spirit that they should start a work there.

- *Look for a permanent storefront church location.* Identify potential places where you and your Street Pastor can set up storefront churches without a storefront mentality.

- *Set up a budget and a source of funds.* Plan ahead and develop a budget for some permanent meeting places for the churches and informal hang-outs. At first you may be paying your own expenses out of your own pocket. The sacrifice teaches you to rely on God.

- *Reach out to athletic facilities or build athletic facilities.* Gymnasiums, baseball fields, and other sports facilities are great ways to reach people. The YMCA started by building places where people wanted to come.

Christian Hangouts for Men

The barbershop is the Black man's "country club." That's where the guys can hang out with other men and get the news at the same time. It's the great leveler of social class distinctions—to the lowest common denominator.

Christians need to create places that are just as open as the neighborhood barbershop where guys can come and play pool or watch sports on TV, but while they are there they get saved and grow up in Christ. Neighborhoods need both churches for Sunday morning and also places to hang out during the week—day and night.

In some inner-city neighborhoods, after dark is the time when you see the most people on the streets. They need to do something other than go to drug dealers and prostitutes, like coming to your meeting place to get Christian fellowship and discipleship at the same time as they are having fun. They get vision for themselves and their future, including education and new job skills. They understand what it means to be morally responsible and raise a family. They can be introduced to good health practices and better nutrition in the course of casual conversations or in street-friendly classes.

As you start walking the streets, scout out some temporary meeting places in the area that can serve as hangouts where you can invite guys to come after things start moving and they show some interest. Until momentum is built and storefront churches and more permanent meeting places are in place, start having meetings anywhere, even if the locations change from time to time. That way, you can get the guys together with you somewhere in the neighborhood on a regular basis so they will see that you are serious about befriending them.

Finding temporary meeting places

- Talk to local pastors, or ask the Street Pastor to talk to them, if more appropriate. If they are open to what you are doing, ask them for suggestions for local hangouts. They may offer space in their church or have a good sense where guys might like to go. Build a team effort with them whenever possible. You need each other.

- Local pastors may allow another pastor to baptize new street converts. Baptism by immersion will help identify an important turning point in the lives of the men when they died to their old selves and were resurrected to new life. Some may also have been raised in churches where baptism by immersion was practiced.

- Drive around the area and see where men are gathering. Then walk the same area and pray for discernment about what place to use.

- Begin to talk up some location options and see if the guys seem interested or turned off.

Getting the guys to come and hang out

- Provide some incentives for the guys to come such as a basketball game on TV, some gadget or game to show them, something to give away.

- Free food will be a draw, but you don't want to start something you can't finish or that could become a financial burden and hinder the work. If you aren't willing to make free food a budget item, meet somewhere that the guys can buy food if they want it.

- Meet weekly or bi-weekly or monthly, in addition to your street work, getting together socially with the guys over sports and other things that interest them and that they need, always talking about Jesus and the Bible and their salvation and consecration.

- Don't be stiff, but look for opportunities everywhere. If necessary, *make opportunities*, but don't neglect this part. That's what you're about— revival!

Temporary places where you can hang out

- Barbershops
- Church basements or other meeting rooms
- Convenience stores
- Pool, bowling, and other sports hangouts
- Colleges and universities
- Athletic facilities
- Park buildings
- YMCA, Salvation Army
- Malls and mini-malls
- Local fast food or other restaurants
- Public library meeting rooms
- Basketball courts
- Fitness centers

Permanent locations

- Creatively designed locations that you decorate and open
- Homes rented or purchased for the purpose
- A designated area of your storefront church

What's going on at the hangouts

- *Street Revs and other ministers* making things happen for Christ

- *Entrepreneurship training and incubators for new businesses, real estate and other investments.* Black Americans were strong business owners in cities across America until changes after the Civil Rights Movement.[166]

- *Financial empowerment* for existing businesses, proper management of bank accounts and budgets

- *Volunteers with the right motives and commitment* who are on fire to change lives, always looking for ways to help

- *People willing to teach classes, serve food, talk* about sports, keep guys out of jail and on jobs—love them into success

- *Emphasis on change*—getting saved, sanctified, filled with the Holy Ghost, becoming future ministers, pastors, Christian leaders, businessmen, scholars, artists, and missionaries

- *Growth in Christ and fulfillment of God's destiny*

- *Finding out how they are really doing in life.*

- *Sports and other shows on TV,* computers and video games

- *Movies that you approve and that can start discussions,* formal or informal, to get their minds working on something challenging

- *Literacy, help with getting GEDs, STEM classes* for jobs in technology

- *Basketball, pool, ping pong,* etc. Some guys might welcome your bringing in a coach to help improve their skill. You can also find ways to teach good sportsmanship.

- *Bibles, books, newsletters, Christian magazines* and other literature in versions they can understand; printed materials they will want to read because they are relevant and colorful

- *Christian music and teachings on CDs and DVDS* to play and/or give away, audio Bibles, iPods

- *Health and free medical help* —volunteer doctors and nurses and/or info on where to go to health clinics; trained volunteers to take blood pressures and do other screening; referrals, nutrition, health literature, in a permanent location

---

[166] See also Chapter 5, "Power Potential of Black American Leadership."

- *Referrals to social workers and hospitals* for people needing detox, hospitalization, etc., for the worst cases

- *Food*—how to get food if you're hungry; free food for sociability if there is a budget, or for sale in a vending machine

- *Rest rooms*—kept clean, colorful, free from sin

Classes

- Bible classes, especially foundational truths and teachings related to living a character-based Christian life

- How to be a man of God

- How to relate to women

- Marriage and family skills

- Arts and academics

- Remedial classes, such as literacy and math

- Work etiquette, going on interviews, taking responsibility, building skills for future careers; entrepreneurship

- Computers on site and basic computer training, websites

- Distance education and programmed learning access in addition to traditional classrooms with teachers

- Personal growth, how to handle yourself in a confrontation, how to take the low road, why it takes more strength to hold back than to fight back

- Writing classes and other creative outlets. Have a purpose for learning to write, such as submitting articles and writing books. Street Revs might develop a magazine and/or newspaper for their locality. They might submit work to local Black papers that could use the men as reporters, photographers, salesmen, and distributors.

- "Reaching Your Dream." Help them do the research to find what they want to do and what is available for training materials.

- *Degrees.* If they want to go to a community college or get a GED, etc., help them with the admissions paperwork, finances, homework assignments, staying on a schedule, and finishing!

Praying and Fasting for Revival

Revival isn't a secular operation. You need to hold regular prayer meetings and encourage seasons of consecration with fasting and prayer at your location.

In the beginning, your attendees may be mostly from outside the neighborhood—pastors and other people who want to pray for revival in the inner cities. However, as local people get saved or at least sensitive to the Lord, they will start to come to prayer meetings.

They may not know how to pray, but they will be driven by the good feelings they get from being touched by God. Give them a chance to grow by letting them pray, but also father them with some gentle instruction.

Challenge them to participate in times of fasting and prayer. You'll be surprised at how well they will respond because their hearts are being made tender by the Lord. They may never have been presented with a challenge like consecration, and it makes them feel good to accomplish something with spiritual value.

Interactive Education

The inner cities are suffering the most from America's declining educational system. Black Americans had a higher level of literacy 50 years after slavery than they do today.

Many Black men who end up in prison are either illiterate or limited in their education and understanding of basic information. They are usually fatherless.

Kids in the inner city drop out of high school at an alarming rate. This is a result of a combination of factors, but local Christian hangouts can reverse these factors before they fail if you give them the proper attention and create an environment for positive change.

Phonics and interactive learning models are available that could greatly improve their level of literacy. The ability to read will have a positive impact on everything else they do in life. The first incentive that drove the freed slaves to learn to read was a desire to read the Bible. God can stir that same desire in Black men today as soon as they are saved.

Some corporations are willing to provide computers if you can create a computer lab in your churches or hangouts. Teach basic computer and writing skills, how to use the Internet, how to use Microsoft Office, financial software, and creative software for photos and graphic design. These skills will also help them build resumes and get jobs.

Health and nutrition

Health concerns in the Black community are staggering. People need friendly places to go where they don't feel as if they are in a hospital environment. "Universal health care" in the inner cities could mean using the churches and Christian hang-outs to help people with their health!

• Recruit professional medical personnel as volunteers.

• Provide education for volunteers, such as that given to nurses' aides.

• Create confidential ways to help with pregnancy and sexually transmitted diseases that don't push them toward abortion and immorality. Make it righteous health. Teach abstinence and marriage of one man and one woman.

• Develop health opportunities in churches, even monthly clinics. Take blood pressure, get weight, test for blood sugar, have diabetics bring in equipment to talk to someone who can teach them about monitoring and managing their disease with the goal of complete recovery.

• Mention health and nutrition from the pulpit or podium or standing on the street, interspersed with Scripture, because your body is the temple of the Holy Ghost.

• Provide literature and books with healthy diets and foods that Black people want to eat. Develop local diets based on taste preferences among the people you are reaching.

Entrepreneurship and starting businesses

Black men know how to run a business. Some Black men on the streets know how to operate inside the drug trade. We just have to redirect their abilities to something legitimate. You can help men start businesses, like the model of Tuskegee Institute where students coming out of slavery were taught discipline and job skills in the context of the Bible. You can start out small and expand later. There is new interest in the Christian business community about assisting with this. Honesty and integrity are absolutely essential, as well as safeguards for the money, but it can be done. It has been done before in Black America with great success.

- Cooking and selling food (with the proper licenses), even something simple like cookies and cakes. Include healthy food sales and restaurants that help people lose weight and enjoy it.

- Publishing—newsletters, books, magazines, poetry, art, photos. Print-on-demand helps keep investment in book inventory small.

- Bookstores, used book stores, Bibles, new and used CD, DVD, MP3, and games

- Clothing—new and used, even high-end merchandise, including bright and oversize clothes for women; new products like tennis shoes that you can buy at a discount and sell at a profit

- Fashion shows with clothing for sale from department stores. This can be an opportunity to teach the men how to dress for success. Give them a vision for something professional instead of hoodies and it will change their attitude about themselves and what they can accomplish.

- Financial investing that is safe for new investors

- Car washes and simple repairs and maintenance such as oil changes and changing tires

- Performances that charge admission. Put on shows that set standards of holiness, including shows for children in the neighborhood that charge a small fee. You might get sponsors to provide food to sell or give away.

- Real estate—fix up buildings and sell them for a profit, which will also improve the appearance of the neighborhood. Investigate the "tiny house" option for vacant lots.

- Day care—be extremely trustworthy and tutor the children so that their grades improve; give them vision for a bright future

- Franchises and direct marketing (with proper oversight to maintain integrity, such as spiritual fathers and pastors)

- Convenience stores

- Mini-malls that you build from the ground up and make the ghetto look like the cleanest areas of suburbia

Storefront Churches
(Men, Women, and Children)

The most important structures that developed after slavery were the churches. The church was the center of everything because God and the Bible were at the center of their lives. The pastor was the biggest man in town. The church building was the center of activity.

Attractive storefront churches and Christian hang-outs springing up everywhere in the inner cities will be a physical indication that God is on the move. Existing churches can also be repaired and renovated. Work with them to make everybody look better. There is no competition.

Godly men in the neighborhood and places where Christian activities are going on day and night will make men more open to embrace Christ and the Christian life. They will have more reminders to quit sinning and become godly. The faithful pastors who have been plowing in the cold for years will even be energized, if you respect and honor them.

Unlike the hangouts, the churches are not just for men. However, since women are usually farther ahead spiritually than the men, pastors need to be careful to keep focusing their messages on the men and not just the women. Preach to the men about how to grow up in God. Show the ladies how to be Kingmakers who build up the men, good mothers, and single career ladies developing their own interests and careers before marriage. Give everyone something that is better than sex outside of marriage and drugs—"living God's way."

Storefront churches without a storefront mentality

Unfortunately, some Christians who go to the inner city to start churches have such a low budget that their storefront churches look bad. Storefront churches that look like the slum neighborhoods around them won't give people any hope for change. In this new move we need storefront churches without a storefront mentality.

City governments sometimes get inspired to start revitalization efforts to repair homes and other buildings. They give benefits in enterprise zones so that businesses can provide jobs. Those are all vitally important.

However, that is not the most important change needed. Every inner city needs more storefront churches and Christian meeting places where street guys can get help to overcome their sin-life. They need Street

Revs who not only love them but also father them into the transforming power of God.

The time is approaching when Jesus will say that our time is up for persuading people to get right with Him. We may be saved, but we will have their souls weighing heavily on our hearts because we should have done more. Jesus said:

> *"But while they were gone to buy oil, the bridegroom come, and those who were ready went in with him to the marriage feast, and the door was locked. Later, when the other five bridesmaids returned, they stood outside, calling, 'Sir, open the door for us!'*
>
> *But he called back, 'I don't know you!'*
>
> *"So stay awake and be prepared, because you do not know the day or hour of my return."* [167]

A few years ago a McDonald's restaurant opened on Hull Street in a poor section of Richmond. It stood out like a city on a hill. The building looked brand new. Everything glistened. The parking lot was paved and well lighted. The staff members were well dressed and courteous. Security was unobtrusive but known. That's what an inner-city church should look like. I mean, become the new standard of light for a community!

Multiple storefront churches for one Street Pastor

The storefront churches may be pastored by someone other than the Street Revs, if they do not have the training or experience for that level of responsibility. The Street Revs should be there to participate in services and may become pastors later on, but in the beginning it will speed up the process of getting to the streets if there can be spiritual partnerships with more experienced pastors leading services. They don't always have to be held on Sunday, either. The pastor can be a circuit rider with other church responsibilities.

On the American frontier, one Methodist circuit rider served two or more meeting places. That same model could work for inner-city hang-outs if the pastors stay consistent wherever they go. The circuit riders built relationships with the people that they could depend on. The bishop might

---

[167] Matthew 25:10-13 NLT.

change the pastor's circuit at the annual conference, but usually he would have at least a year or more in that one place.

Soul-power

Soul power—the power that comes from saving souls—will be dynamite for the inner-city services and Bible studies. They can be adapted to people on the streets if they are friendly and informal and provide ample opportunity for discussion. It's important to keep a positive attitude that invites feedback without mocking the novice who asks a silly question, and yet teaches him the proper respect for the leader.

You will always meet people who try the limits, but you will also meet people who have been put down so much that they need to be lifted up. They have legitimate questions that need answers. They need to talk out what they are thinking. Some of them are very creative and have gifts that the body of Christ needs.

Street-friendly services

- Greeters are always in place to welcome everyone.

- Street Revs familiar to the guys on the street always participate in their local storefront services. They are the men's link to the speaker and the church.

- Congregation members who are volunteers from outside the area are given orientation to help them to be friendly and effective.

- Content is Bible-based and includes how to be saved and live a holy and devoted life for Christ.

- Speakers are often brought in from outside to create excitement, including athletes, businessmen, musicians, artists and entertainers—people who are living godly lives

- Men are given opportunities to participate, if they are not too shy—a testimony, a song, reading a Scripture aloud if they can read and would not embarrass themselves. This is not meant to be an endorsement of them as mature Christians but simply giving them a place to express their new faith.

- Men don't have to dress up if they don't have good clothes. They are made welcome regardless of how they are dressed. However, once they feel more established, they can be encouraged to fix up what clothes they have to show the proper respect for the Lord's day. They may have learned this as children.

- Provide motivational messages and a positive atmosphere. Tell them that they can do anything with God's help. They can become a Christian leader or businessman; they can get an education, etc.

- Bibles are available. The guys are encouraged to hold one. When a reference is given in the message, you can graciously help them to find their place or let them look on with you. Give Bibles to take home, along with reading guides and other information on prayer and the Christian life. If they don't have a good mastery of reading skills, maybe they will admit it and you can help them. Assume that they are good candidates to become future Christian leaders. It can happen!

- Prayer is legitimate, not necessarily short. Keep your eyes open or designate someone else to keep watch. You don't want to give the devil an opportunity.

- Encourage the guys to pray out loud and give prayer requests. You may be surprised at their spiritual sensitivity.

- Music should be upbeat and appealing to Blacks, even if it is a recording. Some may be familiar with old hymns, some with modern Gospel. Use Christian music videos if there is a way to project them. If music is live, use amplification, if possible. Provide the words on song sheets or projector. Keep the songs short and easily understood with a strong beat and a good message. The music should be good enough to pull people off the streets.

Street Sisters and women's ministries

Black women have had generations of raising their families alone without the men. They need to learn how to adjust their self-sufficiency to bring men into the picture by trusting the Lord and finding a godly church that empowers men.

- Street Sisters and Street Mothers win and disciple women

- Virtue and abstinence for singles are restored as worthy goals, along with being a wife and mother who pleases God.

- They get enough encouragement to always say "No!" to sex outside of marriage because they have Jesus as their first love now.

- Gossip and complaining stop. Praise begins.

Children's evangelism

Churches with both on-site programs for children at the church and home Bible clubs and bus ministries can be very effective in reaching children at an age when they are forming an understanding of their faith. A seventh grade boy I'll call Joe was suspected of committing acts of vandalism against a Christian family down the street, although nothing had been proven and they had not confronted him. Without the love of Jesus, they might have given up on him, but instead, with the urging of the Holy Spirit, they invited him to a children's Bible club in their home that was part of their church's outreach ministry.

Joe wasn't always a good influence, but after a while he became interested in spite of himself. With the advantage of his age he would help some of the younger children. He could repeat key points of a Bible story. He liked playing the part of a disciple in a Bible skit, and the sincere look of understanding on his face showed that his heart was being touched.

Joe's family was not interested in going to church, but through the home Bible club he found contact with God and His Word, and eventually he was saved and stayed saved. Years later, he married a Christian and they became leaders in their church.

Bibles for everyone

The storefront churches and permanent meeting places should have a good supply of Bibles, books, and Christian literature for various ages and interests. You can also have Bible computer programs and handheld electronic Bibles. Some of this will disappear, so don't put out anything you are not willing to lose or get damaged.

Bible budget. Put Bibles in your budget. Let people take them home with them. You can buy inexpensive Bibles in many places, including the American Bible Society and Christian Book Distributors. Try not to get the cheapest ones. Give them respect.

Bible studies. The Methodist book of *Doctrines and Discipline* gave the circuit riders study guides they could use in teaching and discussion groups at each location. He wouldn't always be there to lead the Bible studies or even the Sunday service, so by necessity he had to train the people to be lay leaders even before they were ordained. Every member needed to learn what he knew. There could not be a pew mentality in the wilderness—or the inner city.

Ideally, you are in the Word yourself and seeing lessons that you can create based on a theme or a book of the Bible, building on foundational Scriptures. If you need a jump start, go shopping online or in Christian stores or even discount stores to find something you can use as a guide and share with others.

PRAYER

Father, I pray that you will open the eyes of men in the Church to go to the streets to find new brothers, lead them to the Lord, and help them to find their destiny. Open their ears that they might hear. Cause their hearts to be tender that they might understand what you have declared and predestinated for them. Don't let a single one of these lost men die without your will being fulfilled in our lives. Do mighty things through them as they become men of God. Defeat the devil. Destroy every work of the enemy. Raise up your righteous standard and let us see your will with a new intensity. Where men are discouraged, where they have been defeated, where they don't have the victory, do something new to bring the change. In Jesus' name, I pray. Amen.

CHAPTER 5

POWER POTENTIAL OF BLACK AMERICAN WORLD LEADERSHIP

"For ye see your calling, brethren, how that not many wise men after the flesh, not many mighty, not many noble, are called: But God hath chosen the foolish things of the world to confound the wise; and God hath chosen the weak things of the world to confound the things which are mighty; And base things of the world, and things which are despised, hath God chosen, yea, and things which are not, to bring to nought [nothing] things that are: That no flesh should glory in his presence."[168]

"We have surmounted all the perils and endured all the agonies of the past. We shall . . . prevail over the dangers and problems of the future, withhold no sacrifice, grudge no toil, seek no sordid gain, fear no foe. All will be well. We have, I believe, within us, the life-strength and guiding light by which the tormented world around us may find the harbour of safety, after a storm-beaten voyage."[169]

Winston Churchill, "Withhold No Sacrifice"

INTRODUCTION TO CHAPTER 5

Something miraculous is about to happen. The people group in America that seems like the least likely to succeed is about to ascend to greatness—finally realizing the potential of the power that God has given them to serve Him and fulfill His will. Black America has been down, but they are not out. They are about to wake up from their spiritual slumber and realize that the devil and some of their own leaders have been tricking them into becoming their own worst enemy. Not only that, too many of them have become a burden to America when they should have been a blessing.

---

[168] 1 Corinthians 1:26-29 KJV.
[169] Winston Churchill, "Withhold No Sacrifice." Chateau Laurier, Ottawa, 9 November 1954. Online at http://www.winstonchurchill.org/resources/quotations/499-famous-quotations-and-stories. Accessed October 2016.

The problems that have been stopping Black Americans from recognizing the plan that God has for them are about to be reversed. Blacks are going to lead the way for America to fulfill its destiny as one nation, under God, indivisible—a blessing to the world.

I have a vision for Black Americans becoming so transformed from an encounter with Jesus that the eyes of the world are upon them, and people everywhere want to become just like them, but first they need to be willing to look honestly at their own sin. They need to look with an unwavering gaze on the way that God judges unrighteousness even before they call on Him to bless them with strength to lead the world.

The world wants to make excuses for Black America's sins so that they can excuse their own. Politicians go out of their way to show favor to lifestyles that are killing Blacks. They provide funding for doctors to heal their diseases instead of telling them that they are sin-sick and need the Great Physician to straighten out their lives.

The Bible says that Christians are a holy nation, God's chosen people. Christians don't have to stumble in sin like other people. Their lives reveal righteousness as they walk erect in the light of God's favor. That is the kind of people Blacks are called to be—not only for themselves, but also to demonstrate the reality of God to the world.

"But you are a chosen generation, a royal priesthood, a holy nation, His own special people." [170]

W hen the late Nelson Mandela, the future leader of South Africa, was nine years old, his father died and he went to live with his father's relative, who was the acting regent of the Thembu people of the Xhosa tribe.

This chief was a Christian, like Mandela's mother. In addition to attending church and completing chores, Mandela waited on tables at important tribal gatherings and observed how the chief conducted himself at meetings.

---

[170] 1 Peter 2:9 NKJV.

Carrying ourselves as kings

In later years, people noticed a regality about Mandela. His walk, his posture, even his dress were kingly. He had learned how to carry himself from constantly observing the chief. He noticed how the chief listened to what everyone else had to say before he gave his input. That was an exercise in self-control that Mandela later used as president, and it served him well in the tangled political situation that he inherited when he went from prison to president of South Africa.

Black Americans need to think of themselves as kings and statesmen, as Mandela did, even as children. They must look at their stumbling blocks as stepping stones that will empower them for greatness. Black men with droopy pants, dreadlocks, and earrings in their ears don't look like future world leaders. Start looking like what you're about to become. You will either be entrapped by your past or empowered by your past. People who have suffered great tragedies don't overcome them by dwelling on them or becoming arrogant rebels. They overcome them by moving on. Moses had humble beginnings as the son of a slave, but God made him a leader who delivered millions. Joseph and David persevered through trials before ascending to leadership. Blacks can, too.

Discrediting the Myth That Black Men Can't Lead

In 1966 an unlikely basketball team from the mining town of El Paso, Texas, won an upset victory in the NCAA national basketball championship against the University of Kentucky. The Disney movie *Glory Road* captured the racial conflict of the final game as an all-Black team from Texas Western College (now the University of Texas at El Paso) defeated an all-White Kentucky team lead by Hall-of-Fame Coach Adolph Rupp, while fans waved huge Confederate flags from the stands. It's hard to believe today after the way that Black players have come to dominate basketball, but until Texas Coach Don Haskins, who was White, recruited, trained, and led this multiracial Texas college team to victory, Blacks had been primarily relegated to the bench, if they were recruited at all.

In that final NCAA game, Haskins used only his Black players, and the team won an upset victory. It has been called one of the most important games in the history of basketball. It opened a door to Black leadership and accomplishment in sports that most of White America had not imagined was possible.

Glory Road, which is based on the true story of the Texas team's rise, includes a theme exposing what many White people of that day thought—*Blacks can't lead.* Apparently many still believe that today. I have been saying for years that you will know that God has moved when you see Southern mega churches with predominantly White membership submitted to a Black pastor!

Unlikely spiritual leaders will emerge to lead the charge

With increasing frequency, prophetic words are coming forth that the next great revival will come out of Black America. Looking at today's statistics, Blacks seem like the most unlikely people group with the character to lead a spiritual movement. That's why Blacks need prayer. Blacks need the focus of the Church on the restoration of Black America. I pray that not only will you come to believe that Blacks can lead the next great awakening, but also you will want to do everything in your power to participate in making that prophetic word become a reality. With God, nothing is impossible.[172]

VISION FOR BLACK AMERICA:

THEY WILL OVERCOME THE PAST TO CHAMPION HUMAN RIGHTS AT HOME AND ABROAD.

". . . only by coming to terms with history can the United States effectively champion human rights abroad."

U.S. Senate apology to the victims of lynching[171]

After slavery, Black America was rising. In spite of segregation, discrimination, and Jim Crow laws, Blacks had churches where they developed godly leaders. They found ways to get educated and most of them became literate. They started successful businesses among themselves. Their families were together. Responsible fathers were in the home, raising godly children.

What went wrong?

---

[171] 109th CONGRESS, 1st Session, S. RES. 39, "Apologizing to the victims of lynching and the descendants of those victims for the failure of the Senate to enact anti-lynching legislation." Online at http://thomas.loc.gov/bss/109search.html. Enter search using text from above title.

[172] See Luke 1:37.

Objectively Looking at Their Problems

Blacks will become great leaders if they identify and overcome the problems that keep them from fulfilling their destiny. Here are some reasons why Black America is not producing enough great leaders.

INTERNAL REASONS FOR LACK OF BLACK LEADERS

1. Religion substituted for true Christian faith

2. Sanger's attack on Black men and promotion of inordinate sex

3. Breakdown of the Black family and loss of respect for parents

4. Financial income that requires subservience

5. Disunity within their own race

6. Anger and unforgiveness toward White people

7. Belonging to only one political party

8. Disdain for education and a strong work ethic

9. Alcohol, drugs, and the wine of the world

10. Loss of vision to become world leaders

---

1. Religion substituted for true Christian faith

Most Christians talk about Jesus only when they are around people with whom they feel comfortable because they know they won't get into confrontations. Wouldn't a little of that kind of confrontation liven up the political scene? Once you have a real relationship with God, you don't care what that other person thinks. That's when you have moved past religion into a true relationship with God. You know that once that other person meets Jesus, it's over. You can't hold office as a Christian if you keep looking over your shoulder to

VISION FOR BLACK AMERICA:

THEY WILL NOT BE AFRAID TO OBEY GOD PUBLICLY.

"But Peter and the apostles replied, 'We must obey God rather than human authority.'"

Acts 5:29-30 NLT

see if the media is blasting you and people still like you and still want to vote for you. You have to set the agenda. You represent a new move. Be willing to be a one-term office-holder if that's what it takes to keep your integrity.

The Harlem Renaissance replaced Christian faith with Renaissance man's faith—secular man's greatness instead of God's greatness. Literature became antagonistic. Gospel music went from spiritual worship to just a good, foot-stomping beat that happened to have words from the Bible. Preachers who could get people in the aisles on Sunday had been drinking and having sex outside of marriage on Saturday night. Not everybody was like that, but in some circles there was too much hypocrisy and too little holiness.

The Civil Rights Movement was birthed in the Church and carried by ministers but some of them were not living the life. Behind closed doors they battled among themselves. Sexual sin was joked about and excused—by ministers. At the end of this chapter is a description of the kind of Black church that could lead this charge to clean up America's families, finances, and political activities, but first they will have to clean their own house.

When atheists want to take God's name out of the pledge of allegiance and remove public displays of crosses and the Ten Commandments, Blacks should be leading the charge against them. Blacks should dominate over these Goliaths in the name of God and with the spirit of David. Defeating their cause is saving our nation. If no one else will stand against them, they will pick up whatever they have at hand and sling it and knock them down. They are not fighting just for themselves. They represent the godly remnant that is not afraid of the taunts of unbelievers. They have already defeated the lion and the bear on the backside of the mountain. Before

VISION FOR BLACK AMERICA:

THEY WILL RAISE UP DAVIDS WILLING TO FIGHT THE PAGANS WHO DEFY GOD.

"As soon as the Israelite army saw him, they began to run away in fright. David . . . asked them. "Who is this pagan Philistine anyway, that he is allowed to defy the armies of the living God?"

1 Samuel 17:24, 26 NLT

America can become one nation, under God, indivisible, with liberty and justice for all, Black America must come to its senses and be reborn as a new nation within a nation qualified to lead others.

2. Sanger's attack on Black men and promotion of inordinate sex

Planned Parenthood was birthed out of a demonic attempt to destroy Black America as a race—not only by reducing the population of a "disfavored" race, but also by destroying the dignity of Black men by inciting in women strong rebellion against men. The family is the foundation of society. Slavery tried to destroy the Black family, and it was just recovering when it hit Margaret Sanger's *Woman Rebel* and her philosophy that sex for its own sake with birth control was the "Pivot of Civilization." The Black family stayed together until Planned Parenthood's ultimate weapon won court approval—abortion, the final blow. Reversing the attack on Black men will be a major step in their recovery.

> *"Behold, I will send you Elijah the prophet*
> *Before the coming of the great and dreadful day of the*
> *LORD. And he will turn the hearts of the fathers to the*
> *children, And the hearts of the children to their fathers,*
> *Lest I come and strike the earth with a curse."* [173]

When God restores the hearts of fathers to their children, and the hearts of children to their fathers, Blacks can become blessed again.

3. Breakdown of the Black family and loss of respect for parents

The level of immorality and abandonment of marriage in the Black community undermines the ability of Blacks to be strong leaders. Strong marriages and families build strong leaders. The Bible makes it a requirement for bishops. When a Black minister or other public figure either lives in sin or rushes into divorce, he is not being a godly example of someone who can lead the world.

Someday soon, Black America will have the best record in the world for lasting marriages. They have it in them to be loyal and committed to one mate for life, and to give their children the security of parents who stay in covenant for life. Blacks have a history of strong families. Until about 40 years ago, the majority of Black homes enjoyed the traditional family structure where children lived with two parents.[174] One of the ways that Blacks will develop more strong leaders will be the restoration of the family through the involvement of the Church.

---

[173] Malachi 4:5-6 NKJV.
[174] U.S. Bureau of the Census, "Living Arrangements of Black Children Under 18 Years Old" (1960-2005). Online at http://www.census.gov/population/socdemo/hh-fam/ch3.pdf.

HISTORICAL RECORD OF STRONG BLACK FAMILIES

The single-parent family in Black America is a recent change.

1960: 67% lived with two parents.

1968: 59% lived with two parents

1970: 58.5% lived with two parents

1971. 54.4% lived with two parents

1975. 49.4% (first year less than half Black Children living with two parents)

2005. 32% lived with two parents[175]

2012. 26.7% children under 18 lived with two parents (married parents, 8.4%; unmarried parents 18.3%)[176]

2014. Only 17% of Black teenagers aged 15-17 lived with both parents[177]

Growing up in the Black community in the past, you not only respected your own parents but also respected your friends' parents. They could rebuke you just like your own momma and daddy if they wanted to, and you just had to take it. My momma made sure that I respected her. She wasn't afraid of being accused of child abuse. My mother represents all of the Black women who stand in the gap for fatherless children so that they will grow up to become great men and women of God and future leaders. When I went through a time of backsliding, I would look my mom in the face and say, "Show me there is a God. Prove to me there is a God." She had to be a Kingmaker mom.

During slavery, Blacks were not given the legal rights and protection of marriage laws. Husbands and wives were sold apart. Yet to their everlasting credit they honored their marriages as Christians, regardless of the lack of civil protection. In 1897, AME Bishop W.J. Gaines wrote this about his parents, who were former slaves:

---

[175] Ibid.

[176] Jonathan Vespa, Jamie M. Lewis, and Rose M. Kreider, "America's Families and Living Arrangements: 2012" Online at https://www.census.gov/prod/2013pubs/p20-570.pdf. Accessed November 2016.

[177] Patrick F. Fagan and Christina Hadford, "The Fifth Annual Index of Family Belonging and Rejection. Family Research Council Marriage and Religion Research Institute, February 12, 2015. Online at http://downloads.frc.org/EF/EF15B28.pdf. Accessed October 2016.

*"The negro had no civil rights under the codes of the
Southern States. It was often the case, it is true, that the
marriage ceremony was performed and thousands of
couples regarded it and observed it as of binding force,
and were as true to each other as if they had been lawfully
married. . . . The colored people generally held their
marriage (if such unauthorized union may be called
marriage) sacred, even while they were yet slaves. . . . .*

*My own father and mother lived together for over sixty
years. I am the fourteenth child of that union, and I can
truthfully affirm that no marriage, however made sacred
by the sanction of law, was ever more congenial and
beautiful. Thousands of like instances might be cited to the
same effect."* [178]

Children were torn from their parents, or they were terrified as they
saw and heard their parents being whipped in agony. Women were not
spared. It was a great comfort to the Christian slave in the story below to
know that after his mother whom he deeply respected passed away she had
a new life in heaven with no night or sorrow, nor anyone to oppress her.

A BELOVED SLAVE MOTHER'S BURIAL

"Not a prayer was said nor a hymn sung for the white folks seemed to feel that
the sooner the matter was over the more time the slaves would have for work,
and the slaves—well they were not supposed to feel at all, they were only cattle.
Nevertheless the form that now lies in that unmarked grave, far in the sunny
south, was that of my mother, and my mother was just as dear to me, kind
reader, as your mother is to you; and though she died a slave, and lies buried
where I may never visit her grave, I hope by the grace of Him who died that we
might live, to meet her in that land where all shall be free, and where there shall
be no night nor any sorrow, and where there shall be none to oppress." [179]

[178] Gaines, W. J. (Wesley John) (1840-1912), *The Negro and the White Man* (Philadelphia:
AME Publishing House, 1897), pp. 143-144. Electronic Edition online at
http://docsouth.unc.edu/church/gaines/gaines.html. Gaines was a Bishop in the African
Methodist Episcopal Church and a co-founder of Morris Brown College in Atlanta. He also
served as vice president of Payne Theological Seminary.
[179] Allen Parker, *Recollections of Slavery Times* (Worcester, Mass.: Chas. W. Burbank &
Co., 1895), Chapter 7. Online at http://docsouth.unc.edu/neh/parker/menu.html.

4. Financial income that requires subservience

Blacks have been hard working people ever since slavery. After the Civil War slavery was ended, but former masters developed diabolical schemes to keep Blacks in financial bondage to them. Blacks struggled to make a living in a nation that despised them, or at best saw them as second class citizens. When government handouts began during the administration of Franklin Roosevelt, America was in the midst of a Great Depression and most of the nation was in need. Blacks, as a people group, were hit especially hard. What could be wrong with a little financial blessing? The harm didn't come with the first public assistance The problem arose when Blacks learned to depend on those handouts. White people found out they could justify segregating Blacks if they gave them public housing. Now Blacks don't want to let go of those benefits or shut down the projects, regardless of what those things have done to ruin their initiative and destroy their families and communities. They can't oversee nations if that small amount of benefits can become their god.

VISION FOR BLACK AMERICA:

THEY WILL NO LONGER BE POOR AND RULED BY THE RICH AND LENDERS.

"The rich ruleth over the poor, and the borrower is servant to the lender."

Proverbs 22:7 KJV

5. Disunity within the Black race

When Blacks come together in unity instead of putting one another down, you will know that God has moved. Unity builds power. In the first generation after slavery, Blacks were coming together and people were cheering them on, but then cracks developed in the foundation. W.E.B. DuBois initially praised Booker T. Washington after a speech at the Atlanta Exposition on September 18, 1895. Later, he attacked the same speech as an accommodation with Whites.

Today's Black historians often give more recognition to DuBois than to Washington, because collaboration with Whites is one hated label that sticks. Washington's work at Tuskegee and his favor with wealthy White benefactors is still bearing fruit today. Yet division in Black America is so strong that it's almost impossible to give Washington credit for anything because of that divisive mindset.

6. Anger and unforgiveness toward White people

If Blacks keep waiting for Whites to give them respect so that they can fulfill their destiny, they will be like the man sitting beside the pool of Bethesda to whom Jesus said, "Do you want to be made whole?" [180] The man made lame excuses about no one being there to carry him into the water. That man might have been lazy and maybe he had gotten used to being sick. But maybe he was just disillusioned from years of waiting and watching for the right moment, only to have somebody stronger get into the water first. Maybe he was too weak to keep the faith in the midst of unfulfilled expectations. All the time, Jesus was getting ready to come on the scene and release him.

BE A MAN! GET UP AND WALK!

"One of the men lying there had been sick for thirty-eight years. When Jesus saw him and knew how long he had been ill, he asked him, 'Would you like to get well?'

" 'I can't, sir,' the sick man said, 'for I have no one to help me into the pool when the water is stirred up. While I am trying to get there, someone else always gets in ahead of me.'

"Jesus told him, 'Stand up, pick up your sleeping mat, and walk!'

"Instantly, the man was healed! He rolled up the mat and began walking!" [181]

A Black man or woman whom God has destined to be a leader in this generation will rise up when he hears Jesus say straight up: "Stand up, pick up your bed, and walk!" [182] They may hear Jesus speak through one of us. Maybe through you.

When I get discouraged by the delays, I refuse to quit because I don't want God to say to me in that great day, "Just as I was ready to bless you, you quit."

---

[180] See John 5:6 KJV.
[181] John 5:5-9 NLT.
[182] See John 5:8.

Prejudice is still a reality, but unforgiveness will stop the recovery of the Black race every time. When Black leaders try to keep Black people angry, it gets them nowhere with God. They want Blacks to be angry with Whites, angry with Republicans, angry with this senator or that president.

Where is God in all of that? Anger and unforgiveness cause God to reject them and make people reject them, too.

I can't tell you how many times I have laid out my vision to White Christian consultants who charged thousands of dollars and left me worse off than before. They didn't discern that they should help me in a way that was best for me. They didn't enter my world except to present their program and collect the check. They never tried to understand how Blacks functioned so that they could provide their services accordingly, because they could only operate according to their pre-programmed methodology from the White world. Even when someone White volunteers, most of the time he is not going to find out what Blacks are doing and where they are coming from. He will make a decision based on minimal information, interpret it from his familiar perspective, and then go away satisfied that he understands.

VISION FOR BLACK AMERICA:

PEOPLE WHO HELP THEM WILL DISCERN WHAT THEY NEED AND PROVIDE HELP AS TO MATURE MEN OF GOD.

"But strong meat belongeth to them that are of full age, even those who by reason of use have their senses exercised to discern both good and evil."

Hebrews 5:14 KJV

However, if I carried the memory of those experiences with anger I would release God's anger—not against them but against me! Blacks don't have to maintain arrogance and anger to win the day. They win if they have God's backing and they talk like gentlemen.

After Hurricane Katrina you didn't hear many Black leaders say, "Don't worry about it. We've got this covered. We've been raising money for years for just such a crisis." What did they do? Rush to the scene—not to bring aid but to complain! What are they still doing? Whining from the bench! They hardly ever get in the game with anything of substance.

They complain to the press because somebody else didn't give money or didn't recognize the need.

If Blacks don't develop their own resources and build leaders with the character of statesmen, they will always be takers, and no one will respect them. When they are treated unfairly, they should refuse to hold a grudge.

7. Belonging to only one political party

Every time the Democrats have a party, they know who will be there to dance to the tune—Black folks. Blacks'-loyalty doesn't make people respect them. Some Democrats think they own them and some Republicans think they are hopeless and give up. Blacks should give both parties the benefit of their wisdom and insight, and make both parties more godly. Instead of complaining about the President of the United States, Blacks should find out how they can become the President.

This is not the day to hate the President.
This is the day to become the President—and a
godly President, at that.

It is important to not only study the history of racism in American history but also to develop a strategy for Black leadership beyond rousing a crowd to its feet. God expects us to examine the heart of a man and learn what issues he stands for. That is how He will ultimately judge us.

Unless Blacks overrule their emotions and make decisions by righteous judgment and the mind of Christ that comes from God, He will desert them and give them the government they deserve.

8. Disdain for education and a strong work ethic

Blacks will become self-sufficient and self-sustaining when they return to the biblical ethic that the ability to create wealth comes from God and is developed by study and hard work. Blacks need to fight a mindset among Black youth that calls good evil and evil good. They put pressure on one another to fail and call that success. They would rather quit and do something menial than stay in school and learn how to do something they love. God will turn that around.

*"Always remember that it is the L*ORD *your God who gives you power to become rich, and he does it to fulfill the covenant he made with your ancestors."*[183]

9. Alcohol, drugs, and the wine of the world

You can't become a leader when your mind is blown with alcohol and drugs. The speakeasy liquor in the Roaring Twenties wasn't the only kind that caused Black America's downfall. It was also the wine of the world.

"Lest our hearts, drunk with the wine of the world, we forget Thee."

James Weldon Johnson, "Lift Every Voice and Sing"

10. Loss of vision that they can become world leaders

Black American Christians should live with a sense of divine agitation because they are so easily distracted from having an impact on the world. They should take it personally. When you look around, how many people's lives are being changed because of your influence? How many cities have felt your influence? Have you done anything for America, or are you always asking what America can do for you? What does Jesus want you to do to change your world?

Let's not get into self-deception. Most Black American Christians are mostly ineffective at reaching people on a worldwide scale. Most of the world hasn't heard from the majority of Black Americans. Why are they unknown? The little bit of penlight they have is enough to light up the darkness. So why aren't they anxious to take the light

VISION FOR BLACK AMERICA:

THEY WILL TURN FROM SATAN AND TAKE GOD'S LIGHT TO THE DARKNESS.

"I am going to send you to the Gentiles, to open their eyes so they may turn from darkness to light, and from the power of Satan to God."

Acts 26:17-18 NLT

and go there? Talking isn't enough and even praying isn't enough if it isn't followed by action.

---

[183] Deuteronomy 8:18 NLT.

God requires action commensurate with your prayers. If your obedience doesn't match your prayers, then your Christian life is just religious. It's not real. If you spend 90 percent of your time praying and only 10 percent doing, you are 90 percent religious and the Holy Spirit won't back your intentions.

God backs what you do that comes out of your praying. God wants Christians to take cities, but if you stay home, those cities are going to hell while you're praying. Prayer is great, but only if it leads somewhere. Pray there and then go there.

Jesus gave the disciples a divine commission to *go* into all the world and preach the Gospel, but most Christians are not going into the world, and they are definitely not preaching. Paul knew that the world saw preaching as foolishness, but he knew it was the key to the world's salvation. Christians need to return to the call to preach—not just in churches, but wherever they find people who need God.

VISION FOR BLACK AMERICA:

THEY WILL GO AND MAKE DISCIPLES OF NATIONS INSTEAD OF ALWAYS STAYING WHERE THEY ARE.

"Therefore, go and make disciples of all the nations, baptizing them in the name of the Father and the Son and the Holy Spirit. Teach these new disciples to obey all the commands I have given you. And be sure of this: I am with you always, even to the end of the age."

Matthew 28:19-20 NLT

"So where does this leave the philosophers, the scholars, and the world's brilliant debaters? God has made them all look foolish and has shown their wisdom to be useless nonsense. Since God in his wisdom saw to it that the world would never find him through human wisdom, he has used our foolish preaching to save all who believe." [184]

Blacks expect the world to come to them and expect them to bring something in their hand to give to them when they come. It's time for Blacks to blow the world's mind with the level of prayer, preaching, and Christian love that they are pouring out for others, not for themselves. Black Americans are going to get off the bench and into the game of life. Now is the time to help others from a position of Christ-like compassion.

---

[184] 1 Corinthians 1:20-21 NLT.

Why Black Americans Are Qualified to Lead—Vivien Thomas

When a gifted young Black man named Vivien Thomas first took a job with a White surgeon, Dr. Alfred Blalock, who was doing research at Vanderbilt University, neither of them knew that one day Thomas would help pioneer the entire field of cardiac surgery and train future world-class heart surgeons to become medical pioneers.

Thomas was originally hired in a subservient role cleaning dog pens for the animals that Dr. Blalock used in his medical research, but he was so quick to grasp the medical aspects that he soon became Blalock's valued assistant. When the surgeon obtained a position at Baltimore's Johns Hopkins University, he demanded that they bring Vivien Thomas.

Their collaboration was portrayed in the award-winning HBO film *Something the Lord Made,* including their pioneering work in developing successful surgical procedures on the so-called "blue babies," who were born with a fatal combination of four heart defects called Tetralogy of Fallot. Their work made world headlines, but because of racism Thomas received almost no recognition at the time. Thomas was not only a researcher but also a great teacher who quietly trained doctors who became giants in their field, such as Dr. Denton Cooley, world renowned cardiac surgeon, who always credited Thomas. Here is a quote from an interview:

> *"Dr. Denton Cooley has just come out of surgery, and he has 47 minutes between operations. "No, you don't need an appointment," his secretary is saying. "Dr. Cooley's right here. He wants to talk to you now."*

> *"Cooley suddenly is on the line from his Texas Heart Institute in Houston. In a slow Texas drawl he says he just loves being bothered about Vivien. And then, in 47 minutes— just about the time it takes him to do a triple bypass—he tells you about the man who taught him that kind of speed.*

> *"No, Vivien Thomas wasn't a doctor, says Cooley. He wasn't even a college graduate. He was just so smart, and so skilled, and so much his own man, that it didn't matter.*

> *"And could he operate. Even if you'd never seen surgery before, Cooley says, you could do it because Vivien made it look so simple."* [185]

---

[185] "Like Something the Lord Made." Longform Reprints. Originally published in the *Washingtonian.* Online at http://reprints.longform.org/something-the-lord-made-mccabe. Accessed September 2016.

Doctors trained by Thomas became leading surgeons and chiefs of surgical departments. Out of deep respect for his brilliant skill and servant leadership, the famous doctors commissioned an oil painting of Thomas and arranged to have it hung at Johns Hopkins next to paintings of White doctors who had previously received all the recognition. Like Vivien Thomas and biblical heroes such as Joseph, Moses, and David, Black Americans have been on the backside of the mountain, but they are about to come forward to do great deeds.

LEADERSHIP QUALITIES OF BLACK AMERICANS

1. Faith in Jesus Christ

2. Strong motivation of love

3. Prayer, fasting, and a righteous lifestyle of consecration

4. Belief in the Bible as the inerrant Word of God

5. Expecting miracles every day

6. Supernatural ability to forgive and be reconciled

7. Humility and servant leadership

8. Awareness of God's judgment on ourselves

9. Awareness of God's judgment on others

10. Restraint when given political power

11. Intelligence

12. Courage and persistence for Christ, regardless of danger

13. Trustworthiness with wealth

14. Value placed on education

15. Scientific inquiry based on Creation and spirituality

16. Awareness that eternal life begins now

When Black Americans understand their destiny and acknowledge the strengths that God has given them, they will be launched into their finest hour. They will be able to go to any nation with their heads held high—not in pride but in boldness and confidence that God backs them and so does the United States of America. They will be leaders that godly people are drawn to because they have the character of Christ.

> "... *those who turn many to righteousness*
> *will shine like stars forever.*"[186]

1. Faith in Jesus Christ

Jesus Christ is the only foundation on which to build all cultures. As Christians, we have Christ in us. In Christ, all people are united. All people have the same value. The same price was paid for all—the precious blood of Jesus. Whether or not Whites see the value of Blacks and allow them to lead, they are still winners in life and champions for Jesus Christ.

I am not one to celebrate and commemorate the pagan rituals of Africa. We are not African-Americans. We are Black Americans. Our spiritual lifestyle comes from Christ. Our ancestral home is America.

When the slaves were brought to America, they were spiritually deceived. Most of them had the wrong ideas about God because they had not yet met the true God and Savior Jesus Christ. Most of them came from parts of Africa where the Gospel had not yet penetrated. God had given them a spiritual sensitivity, but they still associated it with demonic spirits, nature, the Muslim religion of their captors, and other untruths. In this country, their adopted native land, they became one family of God characterized by a lifestyle of faith in Christ.

One of the reasons that Blacks' problems don't get solved is that they blame their problems on everything but separation from God. How many AIDS cases would exist if people believed in virginity and sexual purity instead of immoral sex and condoms? How many people would have gonorrhea and syphilis if everyone was abstinent until marriage?

If Blacks continue in their sin—not only sexual sin but the sins of lack of love for one another and the inability to speak the truth in love, even toward their enemies, they will remain under God's curse. If they repent and acknowledge that they have brought some of this on themselves with their ungodly lifestyles and their rejection of God's standards, and

---

[186] Daniel 12:3 NLT.

return to Jesus Christ as their Lord and Savior, they will experience a great deliverance. Some Blacks still have a witness inside of God's wrath. If someone will come and tell them the truth about Jesus' forgiveness, they will repent and get saved.

2. Strong motivation of love

Some Black leaders would rather talk about power than love—especially if it's Christian love—but that is what made Black America strong and that is what will make them great in the coming days when they will truly shine. That is why I believe that Black Americans will lead in the future, because they have spiritual sensitivity to Jesus' call to love everyone, even your enemies.

Christian love is real, not imaginary. Love is as necessary to the body of Christ as ligaments are to the natural body. It is a spiritual force—free, active, strong, courageous, and eternal. It values the object of its love above everything else. When we love others we most resemble our Heavenly Father.

Why are some Blacks missing that kind of love today? They don't go after it the way their forefathers did. They can't birth love when they abort each new vision. They aren't longsuffering if they give up when their feet get weary. They can't bring forth a baby if they quit when the labor pains come. The ancestors of Black America endured hardships for them. The witnesses in heaven are waiting to see what they do with this opportunity. People become strong by loving one another, especially when others are not easy to love. Think of how hard

VISION FOR BLACK AMERICA:

THEY WILL PRESS THROUGH THE PAIN TO DEVELOP CHRIST-LIKE PEOPLE.

"I feel as if I am going through labor pains for you again, and they will continue until Christ is fully developed in your lives."

Galatians 4:19-20 NLT

it must be for Jesus to love us, let alone die for us. You have to work at love and work it into your heart through prayer, meditation, and continual exercise of your faith until Christ is formed in you. Then you can become knit together with one another in the bond of love. Then you become God's delight, and it becomes His pleasure to show you off as an example to the world.

3. Prayer, fasting, and a righteous lifestyle of consecration

Before the Black preacher William Seymour (1870-1922) launched the worldwide Pentecostal awakening at Azusa Street in the early 20th Century, he went to Los Angeles where he fasted and prayed for a month. Then he began meeting temporarily in a house on Bonnie Brae Street where he and a few others received the gift of speaking in tongues. Such large crowds gathered that he had to find another location.

The small building that they found at Azusa Street had recently been used as a stable, like Jesus' birthplace. He and the small group of Blacks who were with him pitched in and cleaned it up. They called it the "Apostolic Faith Mission."

The seats were made of planks and the pulpit consisted of wooden crates, but eventually as many as 600 people of all races would crowd inside a space only 40 by 60 feet, with hundreds more outside. The walls were lined with crutches and wheelchairs no longer needed after people were healed. Thousands of people came from everywhere. For more than three years the Apostolic Faith Mission at Azusa Street met three times a day, seven days a week. The results have increased exponentially worldwide since that time.

The prayers of Black America have been carrying the people of this nation even more than their labor. They pray all night. They fast. They seek God until He comes. Before I was saved and I was still in the world, I thought nothing of staying out late on Friday night to party. Now I am more committed to staying up late to pray than I was to serve sin and the devil. The people around me are the same way. We know that prayer is the key to what is about to happen. Prayer is our personal strength and the source of our power to lead and serve others. Prayer lays the tracks. We pray there before we go there, in effect laying the tracks for revival.

> *"These were [Jesus'] instructions to them: 'The harvest is so great, but the workers are so few. Pray to the Lord who is in charge of the harvest, and ask him to send out more workers for his fields. Go now, and remember that I am sending you out as lambs among wolves.'"[187]*

---

[187] Luke 10:2-3 NLT.

Black Americans have impressed others with the sincerity of their prayers for generations. In the middle of the nineteenth century, when Harriet Beecher Stowe was writing *Uncle Tom's Cabin*, she noticed the deep prayer life of Phebe, a Black woman in the college town where she was living with her husband, a professor at Bowdoin College in Brunswick, Maine. When Phebe died, even a former governor came to pay his respects.

BLACK WOMAN HONORED FOR HER PRAYER LIFE

"In the town of Brunswick, Maine, where the writer lived when writing 'Uncle Tom's Cabin,' may now be seen the grave of an aged coloured woman, named Phebe, who was so eminent for her piety and loveliness of character, that the writer has never heard her name mentioned except with that degree of awe and respect which one would imagine due to a saint.

"The small cottage where she resided is still visited and looked upon as a sort of shrine, as the spot where old Phebe lived and prayed. Her prayers and pious exhortations were supposed to have been the cause of the conversion of many young people in the place. . . . At her funeral, the ex-governor of the State and the professors of the college officiated as pall-bearers, and a sermon was preached, in which the many excellences of her Christian character were held up as an example to the community."[188]

Harriet Beecher Stowe

When you become personally more consecrated, you increase your ability to hear God's voice and pray for others. You are listening instead of talking. Jesus could hear God because He is God. He is holy, harmless, and undefiled. When you become like Jesus, you become more holy, more harmless, and more undefiled, and you can hear God more clearly. Hearing God clearly is an inevitable result of the process of consecration. Godly Black Americans may think that they don't have the power to change society yet,

VISION FOR BLACK AMERICA:

THEY WILL FAST AS A SACRIFICE FOR OTHERS' RELEASE.

"Gather my saints together unto me; those that have made a covenant with me by sacrifice."

Psalm 50:5 KJV

---

[188] Harriet Beecher Stowe, *The Key to Uncle Tom's Cabin* (Boston: Jewett, 1854), p. 41. Online at http://jefferson.village.virginia.edu/utc/uncletom/key/kyhp.html.

but they can change themselves through their commitment to consecration. Then they can hear God when He tells them how to lead.

Jesus fasted and He expected His disciples to fast. Leaders in the early church considered fasting and prayer to be more important than some of the other duties that were consuming their ministry time. They delegated tasks to the deacons and said, "Then we can spend our time in prayer and preaching and teaching the word."[189]

Dramatic results occur in earth as in heaven through the prayer and fasting of consecrated people. Growing up in the Black Church, I saw people willing to fast for days. We have continued that tradition in my churches to this day. When people fast, they gain a sense of spiritual accomplishment and sensitivity. Jesus said that some things come out only by prayer and fasting,[190] including our unbelief.

> *"And when they had ordained them elders in every church,*
> *and had prayed with fasting, they commended them to the*
> *Lord on whom they believed."* [191]

4. Belief in the Bible as the inerrant Word of God

A few years ago, right before an important national election, I was asked by Dr. James Dobson of Focus on the Family Action to travel with his team to three key swing states to speak on the theme "We Vote the Bible." I was the only Black speaker and the crowd seemed to sense my excitement about how the Bible applies to all of life—including politics.

Other than their natural enthusiasm and ability to bring a crowd to its feet, what spiritual power do Black pastors bring to the table that adds to their presentations? Unbelievers treat Black preachers with respect, even when they are openly preaching standards from the Bible that they don't follow. I believe that is because they sense that their faith is genuine. They can tell that they believe the Bible.

> *"But we see Jesus, who was made a little lower than the*
> *angels for the suffering of death, crowned with glory and*
> *honour; that he by the grace of God should taste death for*
> *every man."* [192]

---

[189] Acts 6:4 NLT.
[190] See Matthew 17:21 KJV.
[191] Acts 14:23 KJV.
[192] Hebrews 2:9 KJV.

SLAVE BORN AGAIN BY BELIEVING THE BIBLE

"I was wonderfully impressed, too, with the use which the preacher made of the last words of the text, *'for every man.'*

"He said the death of Christ was not designed for the benefit of a select few only, but for the salvation of the world, for the bond as well as the free; and he dwelt on the glad tidings of the Gospel to the poor, the persecuted, and the distressed, its deliverance to the captive, and the liberty wherewith Christ has made us free, till my heart burned within me, and I was in a state of the greatest excitement at the thought that such a being as Jesus Christ had been described should have died for me—for me among the rest, a poor, despised, abused slave."

Life of Josiah Henson[193]

Harriet Beecher Stowe used some of Henson's real-life experiences in slavery as a model for Uncle Tom in *Uncle Tom's Cabin.*

5. Expecting miracles every day

Many Black pastors I know pray for miracles and healings almost every time they meet. Sometimes it happens in regular Sunday services.

Blacks in history saw the God of miracles clearly at work at the time of the Emancipation Proclamation, just as the Israelites saw Him working as they were freed from Egypt.

From then on Blacks set aside annual times to commemorate God's release from slavery, just like the Jews.

One of those celebrations occurs in many Black churches every year on New Year's Eve as they remember God's miracle of deliverance.

---

[193] Josiah Henson (1789-1883), *The Life of Josiah Henson, Formerly a Slave Now an Inhabitant of Canada, as Narrated by Himself:*. Online at https://archive.org/details/lifeofjosiahhens00hens.

DID YOU KNOW? New Year's Eve Watch Night Services

On January 1, 1808, the international slave trade officially ended in the United States. Although the domestic slave trade continued in some states until the end of the Civil War and the ratification of Amendments to the U.S. Constitution, the Black Church considered this date so significant that many Black pastors began to preach New Year's sermons every year to thank God for what had been accomplished and to pray for a final end to slavery. This practice decreased over time until a new tradition began.

On December 31, 1862, Blacks gathered in homes and churches awaiting the news that the Emancipation Proclamation was now the law of the land. At midnight, January 1, 1863, all slaves in the states under rebellion (the Confederacy) were declared free by President Abraham Lincoln. People fell on their knees to pray, sing, shout and praise the Lord for delivering His people from bondage.

The Civil War would not end for two more years, but that night in history was such a dramatic breakthrough for Blacks that it is still honored to this day.

From then on, many Black churches on New Year's Eve hosted "Watch Night Services" that recalled the prayer gatherings on "Freedom's Eve."

6. Humility and servant leadership

I want to ask every person with aspirations to lead this nation, will you become a humble leader after God's own heart? Will you restore the respect for leaders that your ancestors understood? If you go down and are broken, God can raise you up. You can't walk on people and criticize them and expect God to be pleased. You have to be walked on to bridge the gap between the lost and God, between unrighteousness and righteousness.

When you become a servant leader like Jesus, you become a bridge for people to walk on to get to God. When Jesus is carrying you, you can carry others. When you are submitted to the One who carries the government on His shoulders, you can carry it on your shoulders. God's Word is the foundation that upholds the world.

DID YOU KNOW? Heroic Slave, Humble Congressman Smalls

Robert Smalls, a former slave, served in the U.S. Congress as a representative from South Carolina during Reconstruction, between 1875 and 1886. That was 13 years after he had made a daring escape as a slave to pilot the Confederate ship *Planter* out of Charleston harbor and into Union territory while the ship's captain and White crew members were ashore. He picked up his wife and three children, also slaves, then sailed away with eight Black crew members, praying:

> *"Oh Lord, we entrust ourselves into thy hands.*
> *Like thou didst for the Israelites in Egypt,*
> *Please stand over us to our promised land of freedom."* [194]

Smalls knew the right signals to pass out of the port right under the noses of the Confederate sentries. At daybreak, safely out of reach, he raised the Stars and Stripes and surrendered himself and the ship into Union hands. Smalls provided the Union with invaluable intelligence concerning Confederate forts and encampments and was later chosen to pilot the ship.

> *". . . at the election in 1872 he was elected [state senator from*
> *South Carolina], defeating General W. J. Whipper. His record*
> *here was brilliant, consistent, and indeed he led in all the*
> *most prominent measures. His debating qualities were tested,*
> *and he was acknowledged a superior and powerful talker. He*
> *was on the 'Committee on Finance,' chairman of the*
> *'Committee on Public Printing,' and a member of many other*
> *leading committees."* [195]

With some of the money from his reward he purchased the house where he and his mother had been slaves and moved in. One day, the wife of his former master, Mrs. McKee, came by the house that he now owned. She was elderly and somewhat confused, and still thought that it was her house. Instead of turning her away, Smalls brought her in and gave her back the bedroom that had been hers before the Civil War and then served her. [196]

He died in 1915 at the age of 76, much honored. In 2001 The Army launched a Logistics Support Vessel (LSV-8) named the *Major General Robert Smalls*, the first ship named after a Black American.

---

[194] Dennis Adams and Grace Morris, "Robert Smalls—War Hero and Legislator (1839-1915)"
(Beaufort, SC, County Library). Online at http://www.bcgov.net/bftlib/smalls.htm.
[195] William J., Simmons, *Men of Mark: Eminent, Progressive and Rising* (Cleveland, OH: Geo. M. Rewell & Co., 1887). Online: http://docsouth.unc.edu/neh/simmons/simmons.html.
[196] Robin Mazyck and Charlene Israel, "An Unlikely Hero." CBN News, April 21, 2007. Online at http://www.cbn.com/CBNnews/138685.aspx.

Where are the statesmen like those of the past who can function as leaders in the power of humility?

Blacks have been trained for centuries to become servants, and servants make the best leaders. Instead of looking at their past and despising it, or seeing their past in the context of what has hurt them, they need to look at it all redemptively. God allowed it and God can use it to take you to greatness.

7. Supernatural ability to forgive and be reconciled

In times past, Blacks were quick to forgive as a lifestyle. In recent memory, White people had an opportunity to see the level of forgiveness that is the lifestyle of Blacks as they were constantly bombarded with hate during the Civil Rights Movement. Some popular movies about those days accurately depict the incredible level of grace that Blacks have historically extended to their enemies. More recently in 2015 it was shown after Black victims at Emanuel African Methodist Episcopal Church in Charleston were killed.

VISION FOR BLACK AMERICA:

THEY WILL STAY STRONG IN THEIR ABILITY TO FORGIVE.

"Even if he wrongs you seven times a day and each time turns again and asks forgiveness, forgive him."

Luke 17:4 NLT

During the Civil War, the Black soldiers were not only courageous under fire but also noble in their forgiveness. Black historian Benjamin Brawley wrote in 1921 in *The Social History of the American Negro* how well Black soldiers treated Confederate soldiers they captured in the war. Brawley concludes that, contrary to racist propaganda, "a nation that still lynches the Negro has to remember that in all these troublous years deeds of violence against white women and girls were absolutely unknown." [197]

> *"To the credit of the men be it said that in their new position they acted with dignity and sobriety. When they picketed lines through which Southern citizens passed, they acted with courtesy at the same time that they did their duty. They captured Southern men without insulting*

---

[197] Benjamin Brawley, *A Social History of the American Negro*. Online at http://www.gutenberg.org/files/12101/12101-h/12101-h/12101-h.htm. Accessed September 2016.

them, and by their own self-respect won the respect of others. Meanwhile their brothers in the South went about the day's work, caring for the widow and the orphan; and a nation that still lynches the Negro has to remember that in all these troublous years deeds of violence against white women and girls were absolutely unknown." [198]

8. Awareness of God's judgment on ourselves

William Wells Brown, an articulate former slave, wrote an account called *The Negro in the American Rebellion* in which he described the story of bravery later presented in the Academy Award-winning movie *Glory* mentioned earlier about the colored troops of the Massachusetts 54th in the Civil War. One scene depicts a praise service on the night before a battle when they know that many of them are facing almost certain death. As they sing, "Lord, Lord, Lord," calling on Jesus, one of the characters, Sergeant Major John Rawlins, played by Morgan Freeman, prays about the "great gettin' up mornin'" and "the Judgment Day." Blacks knew that one day all would face God, and they wanted to be right.

VISION FOR BLACK AMERICA:

THEY WILL STAY RIGHT WITH GOD AND UP TO DATE ON THEIR REPENTANCE.

". . . then you will begin to say, 'We ate and drank in Your presence, and You taught in our streets.' But He will say, 'I tell you I do not know you, where you are from. Depart from Me, all you workers of iniquity.'"

Luke 13:26-28 NKJV

In my book Your *Journey with God* I encouraged every person to ask the question at the end of each day, "May I go to sleep now, Father?"

Before the old Black folks went to bed each night, they took time for introspection. They examined their day to see if they had committed any offenses against God. If there was a need for repentance, they would say, "I'm sorry, Father. Please forgive me." They wanted to be sure that if they did not awaken the next morning, they would be ready to meet God. They could stand before the Judgment Seat of Christ without fear that He would say, "Depart from me, all you workers of iniquity." [199] On Sunday when they gave their testimonies in the church service, they would say,

---

[198] Ibid.
[199] Luke 13:27 NKJV.

"I thank you, Lord, for waking me up this morning and starting me on my way." What was "on my way" to them? It's not what "on my way" means today. It meant doing the work of God, because that was why He woke you up. He didn't wake you up to have sex outside of marriage or steal money or fulfill your lusts in some perversion. He woke you up so that you could serve Him with your life. If you didn't wake up, if you had kept your life right, you would end up in heaven, not hell.

DID YOU KNOW? Christians Will Face Judgment Seat of Christ

"So our aim is to please him always, whether we are here in this body or away from this body. For we must all stand before Christ to be judged. We will each receive whatever we deserve for the good or evil we have done in our bodies. It is because we know this solemn fear of the Lord that we work so hard to persuade others."[200]

"For we must all appear before the judgment seat of Christ; that every one may receive the things done in his body, according to that he hath done, whether it be good or bad. Knowing therefore the terror of the Lord, we persuade men."[201]

In the words of this Negro spiritual, you can see that Blacks were not afraid to warn people about hell. Some of them understood about God's judgment better than we do today.

> *"And I tell you, sinner, you had better had pray . . .*
> *For hell is a dark and dismal place . . .*
> *And I tell you, sinner, and I would n't go dar ! . . .*
> *Cry holy, holy!"* [202]

Blacks would not find it so amazing that they are experiencing problems if they would look honestly at their own sin and remember that God judges unrighteousness. If they don't deal with their sins, His wrath will descend on them and they will experience His judgment. Instead of living under a blessing, they will live under a curse. From all the statistical evidence, it is obvious what choice Black Americans have made. Sin is always the wrong choice. Don't choose death. Choose life.

---

[200] 2 Corinthians 5:9-11 NLT.

[201] 2 Corinthians 5:10-11 KJV.

[202] Thomas Wentworth Higginson, "Negro Spirituals" (*Atlantic Monthly*, June 1867). Online at http://xroads.virginia.edu/~HYPER/TWH/Higg.html.

9. Awareness of God's judgment against sin in society

When historians describe the American slave rebellions, they often explain that some leaders of those revolts believed that God was calling them to be the instruments of His wrath against the sins of a society that maintained slavery.

Black Americans have historically believed that God judges sin in our society and expects His people to take a stand against it.

Nat Turner. On August 20, 1831, this intelligent and educated slave led a rebellion in Southampton County, Virginia, that resulted in the deaths of 55 White people. From childhood, he had believed that God was speaking to him, and he said he received several divine confirmations that he was to carry out this action as God's judgment against slavery. He remained at large for several weeks, but then was captured and hanged.

Julia Ward Howe wrote a Civil War song about God's judgment based on her understanding as a White woman of the terrible cost to America from the sin of slavery. Here are some of her familiar words in "The Battle Hymn of the Republic"

> *"Mine eyes have seen the glory of the coming of the Lord;*
> *He is trampling out the vintage where the grapes of wrath are stored;*
> *He hath loosed the fateful lightning of His terrible swift sword;*
> *His truth is marching on. . . .*
>
> *"He has sounded forth the trumpet that shall never call retreat;*
> *He is sifting out the hearts of men before His judgment seat;*
> *Oh, be swift, my soul, to answer Him! be jubilant, my feet;*
> *Our God is marching on.*
>
> *"Glory! Glory! Hallelujah! Glory! Glory! Hallelujah!*
> *Glory! Glory! Hallelujah! Our God is marching on."[203]*

She wrote the words to be sung to the tune of "John Brown's Body," which the Union soldiers had been singing in memory of the dead abolitionist as they marched along highways in the South to free the slaves.

---

[203] Julia Ward Howe, "Battle Hymn of the Republic." "The hymn appeared in the *Atlantic Monthly* in 1862. It was sung at the funerals of British statesman Winston Churchill, American senator Robert Kennedy, and American presidents Ronald Reagan and Richard Nixon." History and words to the song online at http://www.cyberhymnal.org/htm/b/h/bhymnotr.htm. Accessed October 2016.

DID YOU KNOW? Words about God's Judgment on Sin of Slavery

*The biblical language of God's judgment often permeated the
motives given by those—both Black and White—who repudiated
slavery. This list is not necessarily a justification for what they
did but is an example of how God's judgment was expressed.*

Nat Turner (1831). "I had seen in the heavens, it was plain to me that the
Saviour was about to lay down the yoke he had borne for the sins of men, and
the great day of judgment was at hand."[204]

John Brown (1859). "This court acknowledges, as I suppose, the validity of the
law of God. I see a book kissed here which I suppose to be the Bible, or at least
the New Testament. That teaches me that all things whatsoever I would that
men should do to me, I should do even so to them. It teaches me, further, to
'remember them that are in bonds, as bound with them.' I endeavored to act up
to that instruction."[205]

Southern Baptist Convention (1995). ". . . we lament and repudiate historic acts
of evil such as slavery from which we continue to reap a bitter harvest, and we
recognize that the racism which yet plagues our culture today is inextricably
tied to the past."[206]

Presbyterian Church in the United States (2002). "Whereas, the aftereffects of
these sins continue to be felt in the economic, cultural, and social affairs of the
communities in which we live and minister."[207]

10. Restraint when given political power

I lived in Richmond, Virginia, when the balance of power between
Blacks and Whites on the City Council finally shifted in favor of Blacks,
and there were more Black councilmen than White. What was the first
thing the Black majority did? Stepped on the Whites. They went after

---

[204] Nat Turner, *Confessions of Nat Turner* (1831). Full text online at
http://etext.virginia.edu/toc/modeng/public/TurConf.html.
[205] John Brown, "John Brown's Last Speech, November 2, 1859." Online at
http://www.iath.virginia.edu/seminar/unit4/brown3.html.
[206] Wellington Boone, *Breaking Through* (Nashville, TN: Broadman and Holman, 1996), p.
206.
[207] "Racial Reconciliation," PCA 30th General Assembly, 2002, 30-53, III, Items 14 - 16,
pp. 262 - 270. Online at http://www.pcahistory.org/pca/race.html.

things favorable to their race. They proved unqualified for Christ-like leadership. That is not the true potential of Black America.

Black political leaders in Reconstruction sought after God's heart to love their neighbor as themselves—even if their neighbor was White. When you are in training for leadership, the most important factor that determines your potential for advancement is not what you are going through, but how you are going through it. While Black America was going through suffering, they were producing men and women of character and substance. They need that today.

After coming out of slavery, most freedmen were not bitter. Rarely did the freed Black elected officials take revenge or strike back. When those Black legislators were given positions of power, they were good and honest men who tried to do good deeds during their tenure.

11. Intelligence

Benjamin Banneker was a brilliant free Black man of the 18th century who published an annual almanac from 1791 to 1802. It had information on medicines, the tides, astronomy, and eclipses.

Banneker sent a copy of his first almanac to Thomas Jefferson, and in his letter he challenged the future president's positions on slavery.

Jefferson responded, and later recommended him for the surveying team that laid out the city of Washington, DC.

Look at the intellectual level of this Black man in his letter on the next page. He was basically saying to Jefferson, "You owned slaves while you wrote the Declaration of Independence. That was a contradiction. You led a hypocritical life." That was bold.

DID YOU KNOW? Benjamin Banneker and Thomas Jefferson

Banneker was a highly intelligent free Black man in Maryland who "successfully forecast a 1789 solar eclipse. His correct prediction contradicted those of better-known mathematicians and astronomers." [208] He wrote this letter to Thomas Jefferson, brilliantly challenging the inconsistency of the future U.S. President's position on slavery.

"Sir, how pitiable is it to reflect, that although you were so fully convinced of the benevolence of the Father of Mankind, and of his equal and impartial distribution of these rights and privileges, which he hath conferred upon them, that you should at the same time counteract his mercies, in detaining by fraud and violence so numerous a part of my brethren, under groaning captivity and cruel oppression."[209]

In Banneker's day, Black American intellectuals, including free Blacks and former slaves, helped lead the abolitionist movement. Other Blacks at a later time held office during Reconstruction, giving articulate speeches and creating compelling writings.

They were people of faith and intelligence, even those who had once been slaves, like Frederick Douglass and Booker T. Washington. These people defied the misconceptions that slaves were ignorant. Their lives were a testimony of the truth.

"A recently reprinted memoir by Frederick Douglass has footnotes explaining what words like 'arraigned,' 'curried' and 'exculpate' meant, and explaining who Job was. In other words, this man who was born a slave and never went to school educated himself to the point where his words now have to be explained."

Thomas Sowell[210]

---

[208] "Mathematician and Astronomer Benjamin Banneker Was Born November 9, 1731." America's Story. Library of Congress. Online at http://www.americaslibrary.gov/cgi-bin/page.cgi/jb/colonial/banneker_2.
[209] "Copy of a Letter from Benjamin Banneker, &c. Maryland, Baltimore County, August 19, 1791." Online at http://etext.virginia.edu/readex/24073.html.
[210] Thomas Sowell, "Random Thoughts" (Townhall.com, Thursday, June 24, 2004). Online at http://www.townhall.com/columnists/ThomasSowell/2004/06/24/random_thoughts.

12. Courage and persistence for Christ regardless of danger

I would like to see White church historians begin to acknowledge the martyrdom of American slaves and Black freedmen who stood for the principles of the Bible. During segregation, Southern Black pastors had no right to vote or participate in the community, yet they shepherded their flock each day according to the Bible. They lived under the daily threat of violence and death, and the testimony of these men and women of God rings true to these words in Scripture.

> *"But others trusted God and were tortured, preferring to die rather than turn from God and be free. They placed their hope in the resurrection to a better life. Some were mocked, and their backs were cut open with whips. Others were chained in dungeons. Some died by stoning, and some were sawed in half; others were killed with the sword. Some went about in skins of sheep and goats, hungry and oppressed and mistreated. They were too good for this world. They wandered over deserts and mountains, hiding in caves and holes in the ground.*

> *"All of these people we have mentioned received God's approval because of their faith, yet none of them received all that God had promised. For God had far better things in mind for us that would also benefit them, for they can't receive the prize at the end of the race until we finish the race."* [211]

DID YOU KNOW? Slave Rescues 100 Passengers from Fire (1845)

Slave won his freedom for going into the flames of a burning bridge.

"Ransom Montgomery . . . was the second person of color who possessed a share in Atlanta's soil. He obtained his freedom by a noble act of his life. This act was the saving of the lives of more than one hundred passengers during the burning of the bridge over the Chattahoochee river while a passenger train was crossing it. By this act the State of Georgia unloosed the chains of slavery which bound Ransom, made him a free man, and gave him all that land lying near and around the Macon round-house and along where the Milner spring used to be."[212]

---

[211] Hebrews 11:35-40 NLT.
[212] E.R. Carter, *The black side: a partial history of the business, religious and educational side of the Negro in Atlanta, Ga.* Online at http://fax.libs.uga.edu/E185x93xG4xC323/#/.

13. Trustworthiness with wealth

After Booker T. Washington was freed from slavery as a child, he went to work at the age of nine in a salt furnace and then a coal mine in West Virginia to help his family. Driven by the desire for education, at the age of 16 he worked his way across 500 miles to reach Hampton Institute[213] in Virginia. Then he worked his way through school as a janitor and graduated in 1872. He later returned to teach, and by that time had made such an impression on General Samuel Chapman Armstrong, founder of Hampton, that in 1881 Armstrong recommended Washington as the principal to develop Tuskegee Institute in Alabama as a school for Blacks. Armstrong told the search committee that he knew no White person who could do a better job.

When Washington arrived at Tuskegee, as he wrote in his autobiography *Up from Slavery*, he found almost no buildings but "hundreds of hungry, earnest souls who wanted to secure knowledge."[214] Within a short time he had taught them not only basic academic subjects but also how to make bricks and construct the buildings that became the school. They learned industrial and agricultural skills with which to earn a living and become productive.

Washington drew the attention of wealthy White benefactors who not only became involved in Tuskegee but also came to rely on his advice for their other financial grants to help Blacks.

George Eastman, founder of the Eastman Kodak Company, wrote to Washington in 1902, "I have just been re-reading your book *Up From Slavery*, and have come to the conclusion that I cannot dispose of five thousand dollars to any better advantage than to send it to you for your Institute."[215]

In 1911, Julius Rosenwald, head of Sears and Roebuck, agreed to raise $50,000 for Tuskegee. A year later, he made a commitment to donate $25,000 to every Black community recommended by Washington where the people wanted to build a public school and were willing to raise a specified amount of matching funds. At the time of Rosenwald's death in 1932, he had subsidized schools for more than one out of four Black children in the United States. Some of those 5,000 schools still stand.

---

[213] Now called Hampton University, it is designated as one of the Historically Black Colleges and Universities.
[214] Booker T. Washington, *Up from Slavery*. Chapter VII, "Early Days at Tuskegee." E-text online at http://xroads.virginia.edu/~HYPER/WASHINGTON/ch07.html.
[215] Booker T. Washington Papers, University of Illinois. Online at http://www.historycooperative.org/btw/Vol.6/html/370.html.

DID YOU KNOW? Black Business Districts Thrived in These Cities

Atlanta, Georgia	Sweet Auburn Avenue
Birmingham, Alabama	Scratch Ankle, 4th Avenue Historic District
Chicago, Illinois	Bronzeville
Columbia, Missouri	Sharp End
Durham, North Carolina	Hayti District and Parrish Street
Houston, Texas	Fourth Ward
Jackson, Mississippi	Farish Street
Kansas City, Missouri	18th and Vine
Los Angeles, California	Central Avenue
Louisville, Kentucky	Walnut Street
Meridian, Mississippi	Merrehope
Miami, Florida	Overtown
Nashville, Tennessee	Jefferson Street, Fisk U
Richmond, Virginia	Jackson Ward
St. Louis, Missouri	The Ville
Tulsa, Oklahoma	Greenwood
Washington, DC	Greater U Street Historic District, Howard U

14. Value placed on education

After slavery ended, thousands of White missionaries from the North, many associated with the American Missionary Association, went to the South to teach the illiterate former slaves to read. Before the war, most Blacks were prevented by law from receiving an education. Afterwards, reading the Bible became their greatest incentive to learn.

Black schools often had poor conditions and lacked basic equipment, but Blacks of all ages threw themselves into their studies. Teachers gave the Blacks dignity by enforcing strict standards of English grammar, and the freedmen met those standards. In reports back home, the missionaries marveled at the ability of the former slaves to grasp difficult concepts. Some students had to walk five miles to the nearest school.

DID YOU KNOW? Slaves to Superstars—The Fisk Jubilee Singers

In 1871, only four years after the American Missionary Association had founded Nashville's Fisk University for freed slaves, the school faced a financial crisis. University treasurer George White had been organizing small groups of Blacks to sing Negro Spirituals, so he suggested a fund-raising tour in the North. On tour, the students faced curiosity and some hostility for performing like professional musicians and not like a minstrel show.

The students were selfless Christians. They gave one of their first badly needed offerings to victims of the Chicago fire instead of keeping it for themselves. In Columbus, Ohio, after a night of thanksgiving and prayer, George White named them "The Jubilee Singers" from the biblical reference used often by the freed slaves from Leviticus 25. It was "the Lord's release."

The young people persevered, and before long they were receiving standing ovations and upbeat reviews. They began sending money home. In 1872 they sang for President Ulysses S. Grant at the White House, and in 1873 toured Europe, raising enough money for the school's first building, appropriately called Jubilee Hall. England's Queen Victoria was so impressed by the humble singers with the beautiful spirits that she commissioned a giant floor-to-ceiling portrait of the original singers that still hangs at the school.[216]

From being illiterate, Black Americans became almost 75 percent literate within 50 years. It was a miraculous turnaround that has not been seen before or since.

15. Scientific inquiry based on Creation and spirituality

George Washington Carver (1864-1943), a former slave, became the world's foremost expert on peanuts and sweet potatoes. He had many offers after college, but chose to become a faculty member and agricultural researcher at Tuskegee Institute.

Carver became famous not only for his research but also for his openness about crediting "Mr. Creator" for all of his discoveries. He told a New York City audience, "I never have to grope for methods. The method is revealed at the moment I am inspired to create something new. . . Without God to draw aside the curtain I would be helpless." [217] The *New York Times* published an editorial called "Men of Science Never Talk that

---

[216] Fisk Jubilee Singers history online at http://www.fiskjubileesingers.org/our_history.html.
[217] "Quotes from Dr. Carver." George Washington Carver National Monument. Online at http://www.nps.gov/archive/gwca/expanded/quotes.htm

Way" criticizing Carver for referencing God instead of evolution. However, he didn't back down. He quoted Scripture.

> *"I regret exceedingly that such a gross misunderstanding should arise as to what was meant by 'Divine inspiration.' Inspiration is never at variance with information; in fact, the more information one has, the greater will be the inspiration."*[218]
>
> George Washington Carver, Former slave, famous scientist

The George Washington Carver National Monument was established by an act of Congress in July 1943 after his death. It includes 210 acres of the original farm where he was once a slave. He was only the third American honored in that way up to that time.

God does not promote principles that crowd Him out. He created the earth and people of all cultures. Today's global economy is characterized by rapid change because of new technology and world travel, but people on earth also need a rapid change in global *spirituality*. We need another spiritual awakening.

16. Awareness that eternal life that begins now

Christians are called to bring glory to God both now and in eternity. What you think and say now is preparing you for what is to come. Christians don't expect a soft life, obsessed with self-love and personal comforts. This is earth, not heaven. Things will be all right over there, but on earth there will always be trouble. However, God can create such an environment of heaven inside of you that you think as He thinks and sense what He senses and feel what He feels. Even while you are on earth you prepare for eternal life now.

Sometimes Blacks bring glory to God by how they handle sickness. Sometimes God is honored by the way that they survive privation. They bring glory to God by how they handle lack of money and how they maintain an attitude of virtue while finding a wife or a husband. Your inside life can become an impenetrable space that is off limits to the powers of darkness. You are responsible for what goes on inside. You don't listen to the devil's lies that you can't make it. You don't think that you're just an old dishrag. You know inside that God has called you to be a tree of righteousness that brings glory to God.[219] That is what God has ordained for you.

---

[218] William J. Federer, *George Washington Carver: His Life & Faith in His Own Words* (St. Louis: Amerisearch, 2003), p. 54.
[219] See Isaiah 61:3.

Why Black Leadership Will Come from the Church

Historically the Black Church has been the birthplace of Black leaders and I am convinced that this pattern will continue. Black self-genocide will not be reversed by secular solutions alone. We will need the intervention of God and the backing of God's people.

Here are some reasons that I believe the Black Church has this potential and why this nation should focus its energies on the resurgence of the Black Church as a powerful force for change in Black America.

LEADERSHIP QUALITIES IN THE BLACK CHURCH

1. Respect for pastors and leaders

2. Commitment to the church family

3. No limits on time spent in church

4. Youth learning leadership in the church

5. Christian brotherhood

6. Spiritual sensitivity and power

7. Hunger for revival

---

1. Respect for pastors and leaders

Black pastors are treated with the utmost respect in the Black Community. They were the leaders of the community from the time of slavery and Emancipation. On the plantations, they might have to lead a meeting crowded into a slave cabin or sneak away to the woods, but those preachers helped their "congregations" to endure everything for Christ, because Jesus was real to them all day long.

VISION FOR BLACK AMERICA:

THEY WILL BE AN EXAMPLE OF THE RESPECT DUE TO A MAN OF GOD.

"Dear brothers and sisters, honor those who are your leaders in the Lord's work. They work hard among you and warn you against all that is wrong. Think highly of them and give them your wholehearted love because of their work."

1 Thessalonians 5:12-13 NLT

In today's world, when White pastors approach Black pastors with the intent of initiating reconciliation, sometimes they are unsuccessful because of their unwitting disrespect. Whites may make a single call or send a single letter and think that will start the dialogue. They may try to host multicultural meetings, but usually Blacks don't come—even if they say they will—and Whites wonder why.

Some Black pastors have titles that have been used in their religious tradition for years. If the Whites don't use titles in their own circles or are suspicious of titles like "bishop," they don't think they should have to use any titles. They either call the Black pastor by his first or last name immediately, or rudely ask if they can just use his first name, because in their environments they are called by their first names.

I am always careful not to take offense or demand respect, but it is still true that those conversations show me a lack of sensitivity toward the Black community. What is the Black pastor to say? Should he demand that the person asking use his title regardless of his usual habits? Centuries of history would have to be explained, and most decide it is not worth it.

The respect that Black Americans give to their pastors will be an invaluable asset in the awakening to come as pastors lead people forward into victory in the coming spiritual battles.

2. Commitment to the church family

We used to have a saying when things went wrong—"Sunday's coming!" We knew that every week we could go to church to sing and praise God and talk about His goodness. Church wasn't optional. It wasn't inconvenient. It was a privilege and an opportunity and we all looked forward to it. The church was the place where you could find acceptance, even if you were considered inferior by the majority culture. You could develop your leadership potential in church. The whole family went. After slavery, the

VISION FOR BLACK AMERICA:

THEY WILL BE LEADERS IN A NEW MOVEMENT FOR CHRISTIANS TO RESPECT THE CHURCH.

". . . and upon this rock I will build my church; and the gates of hell shall not prevail against it. And I will give unto thee the keys of the kingdom of heaven: and whatsoever thou shalt bind on earth shall be bound in heaven: and whatsoever thou shalt loose on earth shall be loosed in heaven."

Matthew 16:18-19 KJV

pastor would give direct input into the family, especially to the husband if the pastor suspected he wasn't keeping up his responsibilities. White slave masters were ignorant of the impact of the Christian faith on their slaves so they made dire predictions of slave uprisings that never came to pass.

The church was the place where people dreamed dreams and developed business ideas. They talked about how to handle themselves as Christians in the marketplace. When they were blocked by prejudice, they received mutual support from their brothers and sisters for whatever they were going through. They prospered spiritually regardless of adversity.

3. No limits on time spent in church

When we went to church, we didn't give God an hour and then expect the pastor to dismiss us so we could go home and eat fried chicken. We planned the day around church. Sometimes we would take food to the church for afterwards, but we were never in a hurry. God might have something to say to us through the songs of praise, or the testimonies, or the pastor. What could be more important than that?

The rest of your life can be affected by what happens in church—on Sunday or any other day of the week.

I remember when I was a child going to church. If we had a service on a school night, I took my homework with me and finished it in the back of the church. When my homework was done, one of the old mothers would call me up front and someone would ask me, "Son, are you saved?"

I would say, "Yes, ma'am."

Someone else would ask, "Do you have the Holy Ghost?"

Then I would say, "Umm, I'm not sure, I don't think so."

Then someone would say, "No, you don't have it. You need the Holy Ghost. These are dark and evil days."

Sometimes people would tarry all night praying for the Holy Ghost. When the manifestation of the Holy Ghost came they would know it was God and they would be so excited they would shout out, "He's real! I know He's real!"

4. Youth learning leadership in the church

My mother lived a life of sin until I was about ten years old, and then she was miraculously saved. I went from never going to church a day in my life to going almost every night. In the Black tradition, it was not unusual for children to preach and lead worship at a young age. They could also play instruments by ear under the anointing of the Holy Spirit. With a commitment to Jesus Christ and being discipled under a program of faith, spiritual fathering, discipline, and Bible-based leadership training, Black children can grow up to lead our nation.

5. Christian brotherhood

Black men call one another "Bro" or what sounds like "brah" (brother) because they learned brotherhood in the church. They have in common their relationship with Jesus and that makes everyone part of one family. Their family of faith kept them when all else failed. The expression of their faith as brothers still sets Blacks apart from many other groups. Christ is their cultural identity.

"Friendship" in the Bible is a covenant word. Jesus calls us "friends" because a friend will lay down his life for you. When most Americans talk about friends, they don't usually mean that they are dedicated to another person to the point of life or death. They don't mean that they would give them anything they asked if they had a need.

When you have money and your friend needs money but you don't give him anything, he has to go to every other source but you. That is not a brother.

When you do something wrong, you want your brother to have the liberty to rebuke you and let you know what you should have done it differently. I have brothers like that, and I am a friend and a father to others in the same way. Those are the kinds of relationships across racial lines that will help Blacks lead this revival.

6. Spiritual sensitivity and power

Many Blacks are most comfortable with informal church services. They talk back to the preacher. In the presence of God, they may weep or lay out on the floor because the power of God is so strong. They were already humbled from being enslaved, so when Jesus came He didn't have to break their pride. He found people willing to give Him glory freely.

Some slave masters became agitated when they saw the abandonment to God and extravagant faith after their slaves got saved. The slaves had to keep their joy under wraps except when they were with their fellow believers. They learned to disguise their enthusiasm. They sang Gospel songs as work songs, and intermingled with the lyrics were secret passwords about freedom and escaping from slavery, not to mention deliverance from sin. They loved to sing because it lifted them above their dreary world into heaven's realm. They were able to focus on eternity.

In books written by former slaves and slave narratives recorded by government workers during the Great Depression before the last slaves died out, you will find Blacks speaking in unaffected language about Jesus. Blacks talk naturally about God, and not only pastors. They have to depend on Him daily. They need Him!

The slave woman in the story below crawled all the way to her master to plead to be allowed to go to a prayer meeting. How does that compare to someone today who does not go to church at all or always arrives late and goes home to criticize the pastor?

PLEADING FOR MASTER'S PERMISSION TO SEEK GOD

"One night, I started out, and, as I came to a persimmon-tree, I felt moved to go down on my knees and ask the Lord to help me, and make Master David willing [to let me go to the church]. In a few minutes, I felt very happy. I wanted to remain on my knees, and wished I could walk on them till I could come before Master David. I tried to do so, and was almost surprised to find I could get along so well.

"At last, I reached the piazza, and was able to enter the room, where I saw him sitting; and, as I did so, I said, 'O Master, may I go to meeting?' He saw my position; and, as if 'rent by the Spirit,' he cried out: 'Well, I'll go to the devil if you ain't my match! Yes: go to meeting, and stay there.'

"After this, I had no trouble from this cause. When I was to be taken into the church, I asked him if he was willing, and he said: 'I don't care. If that's your way of getting to heaven, I don't care. I only wish you were all there.' So I was baptized, and have been trying, in my poor way ever since to serve the Lord." [220]

---

[220] *The Narrative of Bethany Veney, A Slave Woman.* Worcester, MA, 1889. Press of Geo. H. Ellis, 141 Franklin Street, Boston. Online at http://docsouth.unc.edu/fpn/veney/veney.html.

Slaves would risk being beaten by the master for attending secret prayer meetings in the woods. If they were in a cabin, they would have to whisper their prayers under a pot in the cabin to muffle the sounds of faith.

Blacks had such an inner witness of the reality of God that nothing else motivated them at that level. That is why when emancipation came they were not backward in their intellect or morals. They were the product of an independent life of faith unknown to the ruling class of Whites.

To some extent, the Blacks' experience with Jesus set them apart from the rest of America, even from the White church—not primarily because they wanted to be separate, but because there was no room for them at their inn.

7. Hunger for revival

In the early 1800s, when America's spiritual awakenings took the form of camp meetings, an energized anticipation began to dominate the faith of the slaves and free Blacks.

They were already spiritually sensitive by nature, but when they connected with the true and living God in those dynamic outdoor environments alongside Whites who were also born again, from then on they knew Jesus by experience and an inner witness.

Those who wrote about the camp meetings later described the intense energy and endurance of the Blacks who sang beautifully and fervently all night long.

When sweeping revivals have come in the past, they have come through humble people with an enduring faith in a living God who answers prayer. They have come through people willing to be broken, willing to ignore criticism and do whatever new thing God demanded of them.

That is one of the reasons that God has used humble Black men and women of God in the past and will use them again.

Wilt thou not revive us again:
that thy people may rejoice in thee?[221]

---

[221] Psalm 85:3 KJV.

183

HOW THE SLAVES MET THE REAL JESUS

Vital factors took the slaves beyond mere formal religious ceremonies to a personal relationship with Christ.

- Attending church with their masters.

- Breakout of revivals and camp meetings they were allowed to attend.

- Reality of an inner witness when they were saved.

- Availability of denominations like the Baptists and Methodists who had more emotional church services that they preferred.

- Ending of American slave trade that eliminated the disruptions that occurred each time that pagan slaves arrived from Africa.

- Opportunities to form their own "churches," even secretly during slavery (Note that the title of the book *Uncle Tom's Cabin* refers to a slave church that met in his family's humble cabin where he was the de facto spiritual leader of the slaves. In spite of laws against encouraging slave literacy, the slave master's son read the Bible to them because of his respect for Uncle Tom.)

- Limitations on the size of Black gatherings required that large churches be broken up into smaller ones. This proved to be an advantage because more "churches" were formed that practiced personal discipleship by the "pastor."

- Secret prayer and praise meetings on the plantations.

- Slave songs predominantly about Jesus as King, Moses as Deliverer, and freedom in this world and the next that became the Negro Spirituals.

- Miraculous escapes guided by God such as the Underground Railroad and people like Harriet Tubman who heard God guiding her to freedom.

- Emancipation Proclamation by Abraham Lincoln, who led the nation in repentance to God for slavery and openly relied on God to restore the Union.

A New Birth of Freedom for Black America

Black folks are just as hungry for God right now as they were then. They just need to be targeted again with the true Gospel. Who is getting to them now? It's the Black Muslims, rap artists, entertainers, and sports figures. It's also the false prosperity preachers and immoral pastors who have secret lives of sin but can preach up a storm and get them in the aisles.

They need the real Jesus again. In the words of Abraham Lincoln's Gettysburg Address, Black America needs "a new birth of freedom." They can't keep playing the game on somebody else's terms when God has given them the ability to play on their own terms and win the world.

As Americans—including Black Americans—we have a God-ordained destiny to change nations and lead people to independence from slavery to the world into liberty in Christ on a worldwide scale.

The decline of Black America is a problem that cries out for a unified movement by the Church of Jesus Christ. As soon as Blacks see that they have a God-ordained destiny and begin to function according to the eternal purposes of God, Blacks will be able to resolve their problems and will become problem-solvers for the world. They already have the seed of faith. Let's make the seed grow.

Black America's legacy as a world force for freedom in Christ has not yet been realized, but that day is coming soon. That's why I say that Blacks are not African-Americans. Blacks are Americans. Their roots go back for centuries in the greatest nation on earth.

Whatever great things the people of Africa accomplished in the past were notable, but they were small compared to the accomplishments of Black Americans. If it were possible to list all of the unsung Black heroes who built this nation but were never recognized because of prejudice, it would be incredible evidence of God's greatness. Black young people need to learn about more of those godly examples today.

In the past, many African nations lacked something that made America a great world power—our Christian base. They didn't have founders spelling out destiny for them in biblical terms. America did.

What true Americans look like—Black Americans who know Jesus

If you want to know what true Americans look like, just look at Black Americans who know Jesus. They have greatness written all over them because they have God as their Father and Jesus as their Savior. They live in the greatest nation in the world—one nation under God.

Blacks don't need pagan African holidays or African heroes to feel good about themselves. All they need to know is that God has caused them to prosper in *this* great nation. Their potential is unlimited *here* because they have God's blessing. They are able to pray in Jesus' name, "God bless America," and so God hears and answers their prayers.

The incredible untold history of Black Americans shows their endurance and leadership qualities, godly fathering, leadership within the Christian environment of the church, financial enterprises following biblical principles, and righteous acts by statesmen in civil government.

Be encouraged, and please join me in prayer that Black Americans will not only recover from the wounds of the past but will also arise to fulfill their God-given destiny. This nation and the world needs them today—leaders unashamed of the Gospel of Jesus Christ.

PRAYER

Our Father, we are asking You today to raise up champions from the Black Church who will once again bring glory to Your name. Strengthen the entire American Church as a seedbed for godly leadership that crosses all racial boundaries. Restore Black America's leadership lifestyle of faith in Christ, prayer, fasting, forgiveness, and belief in miracles. Give them an awareness of eternity and Your judgment on their sins and the sins of society. Restore their foundation of strong families. Rebuild the courage and desire for greatness that drove Black leaders of the past, in spite of obstacles. Renew their vision as deliverers for this generation who are not afraid to speak the name of Jesus. Thank you, Lord, for doing it today. In Jesus' name. Amen.

CHAPTER 6

FATHERING THE FUTURE

*"And he shall turn the heart of the fathers to the children, and
the heart of the children to their fathers,
lest I come and smite the earth with a curse."*[222]

INTRODUCTION TO CHAPTER 6

Today's Black men need a restoration of the power of vision in their lives. The Bible says that without vision people perish.[223] We give them a fresh vision of the great fathers that they can become and the great things that God still wants them to achieve as men.

In the past, men of Black America overcame impossible odds to lead their families and this nation. One example of courage is the Tuskegee Airmen, men who were willing to fight for their country in the air but had to qualify again and again before their country would see them at the level where they were. Because of their persistence, many American lives were saved in World War II. They flew aircraft escorts for bombers into the heart of the war zone, and then brought the bombers safely back.

The potential for today's Black men is even greater than it was in those glory days, but we are in a battle for their souls against the powers of darkness. The power we have as Christians is greater than the principalities and powers arrayed against them because we have God's backing, and we shall prevail. This chapter concludes with a visionary prayer list on behalf of Black men that was birthed out of a time of intercession. That prayer is a seed into an even greater prayer movement on behalf of Black men that will come forth now.

Jesus told this story: "A man had two sons. The younger son told his father, 'I want my share of your estate now, instead of waiting until you die.' So his father agreed to divide his wealth between his sons.

"A few days later this younger son packed all his belongings and took a trip to a distant land, and there he wasted all his money on wild

---

[222] Malachi 4:5-6 NLT.
[223] See Proverbs 29:18.

living. About the time his money ran out, a great famine swept over the land, and he began to starve. He persuaded a local farmer to hire him to feed his pigs. The boy became so hungry that even the pods he was feeding the pigs looked good to him. But no one gave him anything.

"When he finally came to his senses, he said to himself, 'At home even the hired men have food enough to spare, and here I am, dying of hunger! I will go home to my father and say, "Father, I have sinned against both heaven and you, and I am no longer worthy of being called your son. Please take me on as a hired man."'

"So he returned home to his father. And while he was still a long distance away, his father saw him coming. Filled with love and compassion, he ran to his son, embraced him, and kissed him. His son said to him, 'Father, I have sinned against both heaven and you, and I am no longer worthy of being called your son.'

"But his father said to the servants, 'Quick! Bring the finest robe in the house and put it on him. Get a ring for his finger, and sandals for his feet. And kill the calf we have been fattening in the pen. We must celebrate with a feast, for this son of mine was dead and has now returned to life. He was lost, but now he is found.' So the party began."[224]

Fathers who refuse to give up on their wayward children are just like God. They don't devalue them when they become an embarrassment and a source of frustration, because that is not like our Heavenly Father.

Our Heavenly Father is like the Prodigal's father. We can come to Him with a wasted life, having ruined ourselves financially and every other way, and He's just glad to see that we've come home. That's the model we need in this hour, for both spiritual and natural fathers. Once we commit ourselves to becoming like Him, this generation will begin to turn around.

God told Abraham, "I am giving all this land, as far as you can see, to you and your descendants as a permanent possession." [225] Abraham passed down his vision to Isaac, then Isaac to Jacob, then Jacob to his sons. Abraham was the father of faith. He passed down a life of faith to his sons and they passed it on to their sons. Visionless fathers transmit death and despair to their children instead of life and faith. The

---

[224] Luke 15:11-27 NLT.
[225] Genesis 30:15 NLT.

result of irresponsible fathering is spiritual death—in the fathers and in their children. The children never find out from their fathers why they are alive, so they are unable to pass down a godly heritage to the next generation after them.

About seven out of ten Black children today have no father to raise them. In the Black community, only about 30 percent of children live with two parents in the home. Some fathers raise children alone, but you may recall that in some inner-city areas the rate of single parenthood—mostly single moms—is as high as 90 percent.

Some mothers work hard to raise their children, but without a father kids miss a vital influence in their lives that God has ordained that they should have. The significance of fathers at home cannot be determined by surveys and sociology. It is determined by the Bible. The restoration of fathers in the Black community is not optional. It is required by God.

Children can't turn their hearts to a father they have never met. They can't receive from him if they don't know who he is. If he's in jail, he can't raise them. If he's dead, he can't impart family values to them. We need to recover this generation of fathers.

Fathers give identity and value to their children, and some of the best fathers in American history have been Black.

Early in American history, slave fathers valued their children so much that they were willing to risk their lives to protect them. Some escaped through the Underground Railroad so that they and their families would be free. After the Civil War, fathers were known to walk hundreds of miles searching for their lost wives and children.

Because of Black self-genocide, many Black men no longer see themselves with the kind of God-centered, generational vision that fathers need to have in order to believe that life is important, either their lives or their children's lives. Black men need to recapture the vision that they are made in God's image and God gave them their children, who are people of value with potential for greatness.

According to Malachi 4, a fatherless generation is a cursed generation. If we reach Black men and restore them to faith and vision, then teach them what it means to be a man on an adventure with God, especially as a father, we will move a lot closer to transforming the inner cities and making Black America into the kingdom of God—in earth as it is in heaven.

Faith, Vision, and Adventures with Fathering

Black men need a return to true fatherhood—men who have sex only within the covenant of marriage and take full responsibility for raising their offspring in the nurture and admonition of the Lord. Black men today need a supernatural infusion of faith, vision, and adventures with fathering.

A father imparts vision to his children—life and hope for the future. When men lose an understanding of fatherhood and abandon their natural and spiritual roles, their children never receive a life-giving generational transfer from father to child, and the fathers are not fulfilled.

FAITH, VISION, AND ADVENTURES WITH FATHERING

1. Faith to father a family

They believe that God has ordained a great future for them and their children, so they say yes to Jesus and willingly enter His training program for life.

2. Vision for a great family

They see every positive thing that God intends for their lives as fathers. Instead of believing lies of the devil that their lives are hopeless and expendable, they know that their lives have meaning. This generation needs them.

3. Adventures of fathering under God

They expect great adventures with God where they apply biblical principles and learn His ways. When they build relationships with their wives and children, they have already been preparing in the Spirit to turn them to the Lord.

3-1. Adventures in being an example
3-2. Adventures in touching people's lives
3-3. Adventures in extreme faith
3.4. Adventures in being corrected

1. Faith to father a family

Faith that is tried in the fire can withstand seasons of doubt. When you ask God for the faith to father a family, He can give you the substantial realization that you have an expected future, and it is good. Faith makes the future real in the present. Your faith brings the future into the now. If you

VISION FOR BLACK AMERICA:

THEY WILL HAVE FAITH FOR THEIR FUTURE FAMILIES.

"What is faith? It is the confident assurance that what we hope for is going to happen. It is the evidence of things we cannot yet see."

Hebrews 11:1 NLT

See yourself as a godly person like Christ now you can bring that realization to pass, because God said, "Now faith is."[226] You may have been an ungodly sinner, but it is not too late to be a mature man of God and a father to this generation. Faith makes the future real in the present. You don't have to wait until later to handle your challenges. You know you can handle anything that life dishes out to you because you know God and you know your purpose, by faith.

2. Vision for a great family

God gives you a vision of His intentions for your life as a father even before you get changed. Prayer then becomes an affirmation of your part of the agreement according to what God has revealed to you. If you pray according to the will of God, you know He hears you.[227] You can get God's vision by praying according to His will. When you pray the vision, you are saying to God that you are willfully agreeing with what He has determined for your life. You have already heard something from God by the time you ask God to fulfill it.

3. Adventures of fathering under God

An adventure with God is a happening that you don't want to miss. When you walk with Jesus, your life becomes an adventure. The whole Church is being viewed with excitement right now by a great cloud of witnesses.[228] We are a spectacle in both heaven and earth. All the host of heaven—the Lord, just men made perfect, the angels—are watching us because there is something of substance happening right where you are.

---

[226] Hebrews 11:1 KJV.
[227] See 1 John 5:14.
[228] See Hebrews 12:1.

Your family is being watched by the heavenly host, but you are also the star attraction of the demonic host. Those spirits try to disrupt the intentions of the Lord for your life and the life of your family, but they are weak compared to what is really going on in the kingdom.

There is no creativity in the world of Satan. The devil is a created being, a fallen angel. Jesus said to him in the wilderness of temptation, *"Get thee behind me, Satan."*[229] Other versions say, *"Follow behind me, Satan,"* and that is what Satan does. He follows behind the real. He imitates the real. The Bible says that the devil masquerades as an angel of light, meaning that he doesn't have true light. He only fakes it.

3.1 Adventures in being an example

The apostle Paul said, *"I sometimes think God has put us apostles on display, like prisoners of war at the end of a victor's parade, condemned to die. We have become a spectacle to the entire world--to people and angels alike."*[230] In other words, there are no better examples of how to be a father than examples in the Church. Jesus goes so far as to say in Matthew 5, *"You are the light of the world. You are the salt of the earth."* The only significant things happening on the earth are in the church.

3.2. Adventures in touching people's lives

God encourages us to go to Him and bother Him with anything that keeps us from becoming more like Him. The Bible says, *"Men ought always to pray."*[231] When your life is an adventure under God, people want to come to your house. You draw a crowd. When your children come home, they know you are the greatest man in town. People love to call you their friend, and they watch your life to learn how to live theirs.

3.3. Adventures in extreme faith

You can become a great father by trusting God in extreme faith. Paul said, "I have been crucified with Christ. I myself no longer live, but Christ lives in me. So I live my life in this earthly body by trusting in the Son of God, who loved me and gave himself for me."[232] "What this means is that those who become Christians become new persons. They are not the same anymore, for the old

---

[229] See Luke 4:8.
[230] 1 Corinthians 4:9 NLT.
[231] See Luke 18:1.
[232] Galatians 2:19-20 NLT.

192

life is gone. A new life has begun!"[233] That is an adventure statement. Freshness comes through adventures with God.

3.4. Adventures in being corrected

What tough times are you going through right now? Is God working something out through your trials, or have you missed God and you're suffering the consequences? Do you have a pastor or a spiritual father who teaches you to be a man so that you in turn can father others? If you were in training to be an Air Force pilot, you would have many "opportunities" to get rebuked so that you could become a specialist who could be depended upon in battle. Your life is a learning adventure when you can take rebuke in the right way, as the Bible says.

> *"As many as I love, I rebuke and chasten: be zealous therefore, and repent. Behold, I stand at the door, and knock: if any man hear my voice, and open the door, I will come in to him, and will sup with him, and he with me. To him that overcometh will I grant to sit with me in my throne, even as I also overcame, and am set down with my Father on his throne."*[234]

Back to the Basics of Fathering

On the next page are some important statistics that relate to fatherless families. When you see what has happened to fathering in the Black community, you can see why the degeneration of the family has brought such a crisis to this population.

Black America needs to get back to the basics, which means getting back to God and His definition of the family and fatherhood. They need preachers with the authority and calling of John the Baptist. The angel told John's father before he was born that John would prepare the way for Jesus and turn the hearts of the fathers to their children. He would prepare those who were disobedient to accept the wisdom of a father.

---

[233] 2 Corinthians 5:17 NLT.
[234] Revelation 3:19-21 KJV.

HOW FATHERLESS FAMILIES HURT BLACK AMERICA

- Only 34% of Black children under 18 live with both parents who are married to each other (Whites 70.7%).[235] 49% live with a mother who is alone for various reasons. 34 percent live with a mother who has never married.[236]

  > *"Boys raised outside of an intact nuclear family are more than twice as likely as other boys to end up in prison, even [taking into account] a range of social and economic factors."* [237]

  > *"Children who grew up in a single parent home are twice as likely to get divorced than children who grew up in a two-parent biological family."* [238]

- 38 percent of Black children live in poverty. "Black children were almost four times as likely as white or Asian children to be living in poverty in 2013, and significantly more likely than Hispanic children."[239]

  > *"Children who grow up in a household with only one biological parent are worse off, on average, than children who grow up in a household with both of their biological parents, regardless of the parents' race or educational background, regardless of whether the parents are married when the child is born, and regardless of whether the resident parent remarries."* [240]

---

[235] U.S. Census Bureau, C3. Living Arrangements of Children Under 18 Years1 and Marital Status of Parents, by Age, Sex, Race, and Hispanic Origin2 and Selected Characteristics of the Child for All Children: 2015. Online at http://www.census.gov/hhes/families/data/cps2015C.html. Accessed October 2016.
[236] Ibid.
[237] Cynthia C. Harper and Sara S. McLanahan. "Father Absence and Youth Incarceration." Annual Meeting of the American Sociological Association (San Francisco). 1998. Referenced online at http://www.smartmarriages.com/factsheet.html.
[238] Larry L. Bumpass and James A. Sweet. 1995. "Cohabitation, Marriage and Union Stability: Preliminary Findings from NSFH2." NSFH Working Paper No. 65. Center for Demography and Ecology: University of Wisconsin-Madison. Referenced online at http://www.smartmarriages.com/factsheet.html.
[239] Eileen Patten and Jens Manuel Krogstad, "Black child poverty rate holds steady, even as other groups see declines." Pew Research Center (July 14, 2015). Online at http://www.pewresearch.org/fact-tank/2015/07/14/black-child-poverty-rate-holds-steady-even-as-other-groups-see-declines/. Accessed October 2016.
[240] Sara McLanahan and Gary Sandefur. 1994. Growing Up with a Single Parent: What Hurts, What Helps. Cambridge: Harvard University Press. Referenced online at http://www.smartmarriages.com/factsheet.html.

"And he will persuade many Israelites to turn to the Lord their God. He will be a man with the spirit and power of Elijah, the prophet of old. He will precede the coming of the Lord, preparing the people for his arrival. He will turn the hearts of the fathers to their children, and he will change disobedient minds to accept godly wisdom." [241]

Fathers prepare you to face the future

Fathers help you to develop godly character. A child doesn't say, "I will always be undeveloped in my character. I won't control my lusts." That's why he needs a father.

"Children raised apart from a biological parent are disadvantaged in numerous ways. They are more likely to drop out of high school, less likely to attend college, and less likely to graduate from college than children raised by both biological parents. . . . Boys who grow up without their fathers are more likely to have trouble finding (and keeping) a job in young adulthood. Young adult men and women from one-parent families tend to work at low-paying jobs."

Sara McLanahan
"Life without Father: What Happens to the Children?"[242]

Fathers force you to grow up. They give you vision and purpose for a greater life beyond your lusts. They give their children a sense of hope in the midst of the challenges of their background and environment. They teach them standards and principles that work.

"Children, obey your parents because you belong to the Lord, for this is the right thing to do. 'Honor your father and mother.' This is the first of the Ten Commandments that ends with a promise: And this is the promise: If you honor your father and mother, 'you will live a long life, full of blessing.'"[243]

---

[241] Luke 1:16-17 NLT.
[242] Sara McLanahan, "Life without Father, op. cit., p. 37.
[243] Ephesians 6:1-3 NLT.

CHILDREN ARE BLESSED WHO HAVE FATHERS

"Low paternal interest in children's education has a stronger negative impact on children's lack of qualifications than contact with the police, poverty, family type, social class, housing tenure and child's personality."[244]

Positive influences that a father has on his children

- Personal faith in God

- Self-esteem and self-confidence

- Character traits of discipline and obedience

- Normal relationships with family and friends

- Compassion toward those who are weak

- Good behavior in home and school

- Higher educational achievement

- Less tendency for delinquency or substance abuse

- Positive attitude toward everyday life and the future

- Creativity and willingness to take risks in new areas

- Higher socio-economic level than single-parent homes

- Better career success

- Higher rate of abstinence before marriage

- Healthy relationships with the opposite sex

- Infrequent same-sex tendencies

- Good marriages and strong parenting skills as adults

---

[244] Jo Blanden, "'Bucking the trend:' What enables those who are disadvantaged in childhood to succeed later in life?" Working Paper No 31 Corporate Document Services. London: Department for Work and Pensions. Online at http://dera.ioe.ac.uk/7729/1/WP31.pdf. Accessed October 2016.

The Father's Blessing

One of the ways that Black men can get a heart for fathering is to remember that children are a blessing from the Lord. Children give fathers the privilege of blessing them with their words and their dedication to their children's success. The population control and eugenics lobby has been promoting a negative message about the birth of Black children for more than a century and it is wearing people down, but the truth is stronger than a lie. They need to resurrect the truth. Regardless of where children came from or what is wrong with them, they have a right to live and a right to receive the father's blessing.

VISION FOR BLACK AMERICA:

THEY WILL LOVE THEIR CHILDREN.

"Children born to a young man are like sharp arrows in a warrior's hands. How happy is the man whose quiver is full of them!"

Psalm 127:4-5 NLT

TYPES OF FATHERS' BLESSINGS IN THE BIBLE

- Loved his son (Genesis 37:4).

- Showed kindness (Jesus addressed His Father as "Abba" in Mark 14:36, which is from the Greek word *"aabah,"* which means "to show kindness").

- Taught his children about God continually—in the house, when walking, when lying down or rising up "that your days may be multiplied, and the days of your children . . . as the days of heaven upon the earth" (Deuteronomy 11:18-21 KJV).

- Gave spiritual direction to "his sons and their families to keep the way of the LORD and do what is right and just" (Genesis 18:19 NLT).

- Made decisions about a son's future wife (Genesis 28:1-2).

- Received honor from his son (Malachi 1:6).

- Chose the son who would inherit his property (Galatians 4:23).

- Disciplined his children with fairness and restraint. (Ephesians 6:4).

- Nurtured and corrected his children in the Lord (Ephesians 6:4)

Every father in the Bible whom we call a patriarch spoke blessings over his children. Men can use their mouths to speak blessings over their families. On a consistent basis they should lay hands on their children.

They should seek God for fatherly insight and speak that insight over their children. A father's blessing on his children reflects his vision for them. In order to bless somebody, you have to see them with eyes of revelation. Blessing and vision go together.

When you are raised with the praise and affirmation of a father, it does something good for you that can last a lifetime. Fathers give words of commendation and learn to speak good things about their children instead of looking at what is wrong.

Children do what their daddies do and follow what their daddies say. When you have renegade daddies who have reneged on their responsibilities, you have a generation of children who have lost hope and who are irresponsible because their daddies were that way. Curses follow down from parents, but the reverse works also. If you're blessed, the next generation will be blessed and be a blessing.

One of the greatest contributions that the church can make to society and especially the Black community is to restore the father's father's blessing. We need to get the young men saved and take them to a level of consecration where they want to please God as fathers and raise their families for God. Waiting for sex until marriage becomes the obvious choice because that is what God would want. Then we can teach them how to be good fathers and good citizens.

VISION FOR BLACK AMERICA:

ALL THE NATIONS OF THE WORLD WILL BE BLESSED BECAUSE THEY OBEYED GOD.

". . . blessing I will bless you, and multiplying I will multiply your descendants as the stars of the heaven and as the sand which is on the seashore; and your descendants shall possess the gate of their enemies. In your seed all the nations of the earth shall be blessed, because you have obeyed My voice."

Genesis 22:17-18 NKJV

First, you receive a father's blessing.
Then you walk in a father's blessing.
Then you impart a father's blessing.

I have heard White business leaders and educators on the boards where I happen to be a member start talking about "those ghetto people." Then they look at me and say, "You're not like them."

So I tell them, "I know you just haven't heard my testimony. I may enunciate my words more clearly now than I used to, but I'm ghetto and gutter. I'm a visible manifestation that God can save anybody and get him straight." I never had a father, but somehow I always thought that I could be somebody. It was not based on anything that anybody said to me. It was just a gift from God.

Stealing the Rights of Fatherhood

Ever since the Supreme Court's *Roe v. Wade* abortion decision in 1973, the law has taken the life of an unborn child out of the hands of his father and placed it solely in the hands of his mother. When a man and woman conceive a child, under abortion law the man loses all jurisdiction over his child's life. The mother has absolute control over whether the child lives or dies. Whether she is single or married, fatherhood is irrelevant. The father can't stop her from going to an abortionist and killing his child. That's the law.

That is not the biblical model. The Bible would never condone a mother's murder of her unborn child, which is called feticide. The Bible also teaches that fathers have a vital role in a child's life from the time of conception. God created the father first. The woman came from Adam's side, not the reverse. God created conception of children as a parenting process, not a female dominated process. Fathers deserve honor.

> *"Honor your father and mother, as the LORD your God commanded you. Then you will live a long, full life in the land the LORD your God will give you."* [245]

The male sperm is the vehicle for determining the gender of a child. The female has the XX chromosome, but the male has the XY chromosome. Whatever gender the child becomes is determined by whether the X or Y chromosome unites with the woman's egg. The family DNA is transmitted through the seed of the man.

How Women Were Taught to Devalue Men

The devaluation of men and the attack on fatherhood began in slavery, was developed in the era of segregation, lynching, and White false accusations of rape, but it has been perpetuated and expanded in the past

---

[245] Deuteronomy 5:16 NLT. See also Ten Commandments in Exodus 20:12; Leviticus 19:2-3.

century through the birth control movement of Margaret Sanger, founder of Planned Parenthood.[246] She was a widely published author on two main themes—eugenics (there were lower races of human beings and they should not be allowed to reproduce, which will be covered in the next chapter) and women's rebellion against men.

Because of her rebellion against a man's ability to make a woman pregnant, she promoted birth control to allow women to have unlimited sex. She taught women to maintain an adversarial relationship with men regarding pregnancy. She taught them to devalue men as spoilers of their sexual fun because pregnancy could result. She persuaded women to dominate men and rebel against men in the arena of sex and conception.

SANGER INCITED WOMEN TO REBEL AGAINST MEN

"Birth Control places in the hands of women the only effective instrument whereby they may reestablish the balance in society, and assert, not only theoretically but practically as well, the primary importance of the woman and the child in civilization." [247]

Woman Rebel: No God's. No Masters—*her publication for women*
Margaret Sanger, Founder of Planned Parenthood

The Bible teaches that sex and conception are a blessing from God and a vital part of God's eternal plan and purpose for humanity. Marriage is a unifying of two people into one, and children are a blessing from the Lord that result from the oneness of a man and a woman, not just a woman. Sanger focused on a woman's reproductive rights over her body and the necessity to produce healthy children (by her definition), instead of conceiving just any children (judged by human standards for who should live and who should die).

VISION FOR BLACK AMERICA:

THEY WILL REMEMBER THAT BABIES IN THE WOMB HAVE FATHERS.

"But the angel said, 'Don't be afraid, Zechariah! For God has heard your prayer, and your wife, Elizabeth, will bear you a son! And you are to name him John. You will have great joy and gladness, and many will rejoice with you at his birth.'"

Luke 1:13-14 NLT

---

[246] See also Chapter 7, "Planned Parenthood vs. Black America."
[247] Margaret Sanger, *The Pivot of Civilization*. Online at http://www.gutenberg.org/files/1689/1689-h/1689-h.htm.

For purposes of her birth control campaign, Sanger focused on the conception of children as essentially the mother's business only. The fetus in the womb began to be described as a part of the woman's body instead of the individual person that he or she really was under God. The child was a pawn in the creation of a brave new world populated only by people whom the eugenicist Sanger considered perfect.

Sanger taught women to rebel against God and man

Most of the women having abortions today say that they are Christians. Many are Catholic, where abortion is clearly forbidden. Yet Sanger and her successors have taught women to rebel against God and the Church while the Bible clearly says that God creates every life and He is able to provide for every child conceived on the earth.

Rebellion against God was at the root of Margaret Sanger's beliefs. That's why she named her publication *Woman Rebel: No Gods. No Masters*. Rebellion against God was also at the root of the first woman's rebellion in the Garden of Eden. She believed Satan, who basically said God was a liar and she would *not* surely die if she ate from the Tree of the Knowledge of Good and Evil.

Adam told her what God had told him but she chose to rebel against his words and deny his leadership position under God as her husband. She was deceived by Satan and she acted on that deception against her husband.

Jesus said clearly that Satan is a liar and he comes to deceive. God is not a liar. God says throughout the Bible that He will provide for us. There is no shortage of resources with God. You can't exhaust His benefits by having too many children. The Bible never gives an economic restriction on the size of a family. God never tells you to kill one of your children in order to have enough money to feed the rest of them.

When you trust God for His provision, you also find His glory. You could ask God for the greatest thing you could ever imagine but your mind still couldn't even reach His level. Something that is too much for you is not too much for God.

Don't reduce God down to your human level. He is God. He is the Creator. You are the created. God is *"able to do exceedingly abundantly*

above all that we ask or think, according to the power that works in us. " [248]
His power can take you to levels that you've never even seen before if you
trust Him. With God there is never an "unintended pregnancy."

The Bible says, *"Unto him be glory in the church."* [249] The word
glory means the things that are seen, the things that are manifest. That
glory is in the church. That glory is in you. God wants the glory to be seen.
He wants to do something extravagant for you that you can't measure.

God entrusted mothers with the sacred responsibility of carrying
the fragile life of a developing child that He has brought into the world
through the union of the marriage bed between a man and a woman.

Like Satan in the Garden, Sanger taught the woman that she was
the wisest person on earth. She could not trust God or man. She must rebel.
She must demand the right to have sex without conception and insist on the
purpose of childbearing as the creation of a master race.

Because of the Internet, you can read decades of writings by
Margaret Sanger and see that she denied the biblical teachings about the
equal worth of all people and the role of God as Creator and Provider.

You can also see the results of her beliefs in the locations and
functions of Planned Parenthood clinics. These clinics have an oversized
impact on the Black family because they are mainly located near areas of
majority Black populations. Black women are stealthily provided with
services of birth control and abortion that have reduced the potential
population of the Black American race by untold millions of people.

Sanger established clinics in the ghettoes in order to limit the
population of people groups like Blacks whom she considered undesirable
and of less value to society than her race. That was a result of her belief in
eugenics.

Sangers eugenic beliefs about favored races extended beyond race
to gender. Sanger favored not only the educated, economically productive
White race over poverty-stricken minorities, but she also favored women
over men. She was a woman in control, redefining culture according to her
terms, not God's.

She made birth control an issue of women's rebellion against men.
In her book *Pivot of Civilization* she pounded home the message that sex

---

[248] Ephesians 3:20 NKJV.
[249] Ephesians 3:21 KJV.

was a woman's right to enjoy without the necessity of becoming pregnant. If the father of the child didn't like it, that was too bad.

GOD'S JUDGMENT ON WOMEN DISHONORING MEN

"I will fully repay you for all of your sins, says the Sovereign LORD. For to all your disgusting sins, you have added these lewd acts. Everyone who makes up proverbs will say of you, 'Like mother, like daughter.' For your mother loathed her husband and her children, and so do you. And you are exactly like your sisters, for they despised their husbands and their children." [250]

SANGER'S ATTACK ON PASTORS AND PRIESTS

The dire consequences that Sanger predicted for a society without birth control instead apply to society today after her policies were implemented and birth control became readily available.

"We know where we are with a man who says, `Birth Control is forbidden by God; we prefer poverty, unemployment, war, the physical, intellectual and moral degeneration of the people, and a high deathrate to any interference with the universal command to be fruitful and multiply'; but we have no patience with those who say that we can have unrestricted and unregulated propagation without those consequences."

Margaret Sanger, *Pivot of Civilization*[251]

Satan's lies about shortages

Population control philosophers such as Margaret Sanger, Thomas Malthus, Francis Galton, and others begin with the lies of the devil in the Garden. *(See also Chapter 7.)* They are based on a false presupposition that the earth does not contain enough resources to support its population unless mankind intervenes.

---

[250] Ezekiel 16:43-45 NLT.
[251] Margaret Sanger, *The Pivot of Civilization.* Entire book available online at http://www.gutenberg.org/files/1689/1689-h/1689-h.htm#2HCH0004.

Satan excited the woman, "If you eat off this tree, you will be as God, knowing good and evil."[252] He was saying, "God has not provided for you. There is something that God didn't give you when He made you. He short-changed you. If you eat off this tree you will be as God."

Listen, devil, the man was already like God by birthright. He was already in God's image. All he had to do was to function like Him. The devil was lying. He was sowing a seed of need and unbelief when God had already created everything that man would ever need before He made the man. Man was created without need except his need for God!

We were created to live on the supply side, to be fruitful, multiply and replenish the earth and subdue it. God made the earth for you and me. There is no need to kill babies in the womb to save money and preserve resources, because there are no shortages. It is all a lie of the devil.

Undermining fathers

Government-funded welfare programs intended to help widows have destroyed the Black family by providing money for unwed mothers to carry on without a man in the house.

Planned Parenthood taught women that they didn't need men and the civil government funded that rebellious vision at the rate of billions of dollars. Immature men who lived only for sex and not for fathering joined in and Sanger's anti-father bias was perpetuated. Fathers became cursed. Women became cursed. All who rejected God's creative order were no longer able to conceive and receive the blessings of fathers and mothers.

> *"There is a generation that curses its father,*
> *And does not bless its mother.*
> *There is a generation that is pure in its own eyes,*
> *Yet is not washed from its filthiness.*
> *There is a generation—oh, how lofty are their eyes!*
> *And their eyelids are lifted up.*
> *There is a generation whose teeth are like swords,*
> *And whose fangs are like knives,*
> *To devour the poor from off the earth,*
> *And the needy from among men."*[253]

---

[252] See Genesis 3:5.
[253] Proverbs 30:11-14 NKJV.

When the life or death of a child and the role of a man and woman to be a father and mother are reduced down to a woman's right to privacy, is it any wonder that a race that worships abortion has been cursed?

Men who should be raising children to perpetuate their names on the earth are falling by the wayside, feeling meaningless, especially Black men who are already weak from relentless attacks on them for centuries. We need God.

FATHER LOST RIGHT TO SAVE CHILD FROM ABORTION

Roe v. Wade (1973 U.S. Supreme Court decision) based the legality of abortion on the mother as the sole person responsible for the life or death of the unborn child. The father of the child was completely disregarded. *Roe* referred to a woman's privacy in basing its ruling on the "Due Process Clause of the Fourteenth Amendment, which protects against state action the right to privacy, including a woman's qualified right to terminate her pregnancy."[254]

Men and women in rebellion lacking substance to resist abortion

Men and women driven by sex alone don't want children. They don't have enough substance within themselves to see what God wants to accomplish through their children. They don't see the abundance of God as a reality because they are not living consecrated lives. Children are a bother instead of a fulfillment of God's destiny and purpose and God's blessing to those who become parents. Women have greater priorities than spending nine months being pregnant. Their sex life will be affected. They don't want kids around. They are too tired. They don't want to get up at night.

VISION FOR BLACK AMERICA:

THEY WILL HONOR FATHERS ONCE AGAIN.

"Honor your father and your mother, as the LORD your God has commanded you, that your days may be long, and that it may be well with you in the land which the LORD your God is giving you."

Deuteronomy 5:16 NKJV

---

[254] U.S. Supreme Court, Roe V. Wade, 410 U.S. 113 (1973), 410 U.S. 113, Roe Et Al. V. Wade, District Attorney Of Dallas County, Appeal From The United States District Court For The Northern District Of Texas. No. 70-18. Argued December 13, 1971. Reargued October 11, 1972. Decided January 22, 1973. Online at http://caselaw.lp.findlaw.com/scripts/getcase.pl?court=US&vol=410&invol=113.

They will have to take them to school. They will have to buy clothes. They can't feed them.

All of a sudden, God is broke. They have become dominated by desires that rule God out. Maybe they did not have fathers who brought them to Jesus. Maybe the man in their lives can't give them faith.

If she isn't married to the father of the child, he is no example of faith and provision. He's a renegade, but God is still in control. God has prepared the provision for that child to be taken care of regardless of the child's father or her faith. She needs to turn to God for His ever-present help, *and she must not kill that child.*

Fathers Make a Difference

The Bible makes it plain and studies confirm the fact that children raised with a father in the home do better than fatherless children in almost every area. There are always notable exceptions, and I want to be sure to give credit where it is due to the noble mothers like mine who struggle to be a mom *and* a dad because of renegade fathers. However, on the whole, fatherless kids are affected negatively by the lack of a father. They drown in a sea of worthlessness and don't even know why they develop no sense of their own value. They can't find themselves.

Remember that the Bible says that without vision the people perish. The word "vision" means sight and seeing, and indicates direction and goals. The word "perish" means a loss of motivation for living. One of the main reasons that the Black community is perishing in crime, disease, and lack of vision is the absence of fathers. Some families have been raised by a succession of single moms for generations. Three generations of single mothers and their daughters and granddaughters may live under the same roof in some ghetto project. The fathers are nowhere to be seen. They come and go like transients. They have sex on weekends and disappear.

VISION FOR BLACK AMERICA:

THEY WILL GET NEW VISION AND NO LONGER PERISH.

"Where there is no vision, the people perish."

Proverbs 29:18 KJV

Black children need the love and principles of a genuine father who stays around to raise them. Kids need love and they need standards from a father who is consistent and godly. Standards build security in children. They give them a rock they can lean on. When kids learn to respect their dad as a real man of God who stands for something, they can function much better in society.

A father has the ability to take his family to a place where they are blessed beyond measure. When he resolves to live the Word and speak it into his wife and children, it becomes real to them. They get changed by hearing from God through him, and moving on what they have heard. He lays hands on them and speaks life into them, as often as it takes to get them changed. He prophesies over them in Jesus' name. He declares that they are not going to remain where they are in God when God has ordained for them to be so much more.

God gives families a holistic picture of His plan. Fathers who go after God begin to see His plan for their own lives, and for their family, church, and society. God opens their eyes to principles and truths larger than what they are dealing with. He takes them above their self-centered thinking to the place where they think like God and they want to be a father like God.

VISION FOR BLACK AMERICA:

THEY WILL END THE CURSE THAT CAME WITH DISHONORING FATHERS.

"For God commanded, saying, 'Honor your father and your mother'; and, 'He who curses father or mother, let him be put to death.'"

Matthew 15:4 NKJV

Fatherhood is a high calling. The Black men who refuse that calling have not had this level of vision for it. I believe when they understand more of a father's role they will run to it instead of running away from it, because God will be in it.

A FATHER'S FAMILY COMMITMENT

1. The father's work is fulfilling the family vision.

2. The father's life is a living testimony of faith in God.

3. The father speaks over his wife and family what they are becoming.

4. The father affirms his children's potential.

5. The father listens to God, writes it down, and does what God says.

6. The father transmits the family virtues—their "coat of arms."

7. The father knows his wife's tendencies and favorite things.

8. The father keeps a journal to honor and record his wife's input.

9. The father takes his children into his world with him.

10. The father spends time with his children in their world.

11. The father submits to his own spiritual father.

12. The father introduces his family to cross-cultural friends.

13. The father discusses sex with his children.

14. The father maintains his sexual purity.

15. The father trains his children how to treat his wife.

---

1. The father's work is fulfilling the family vision.

He develops a long range plan for the family with his wife's input and carries the responsibility for carrying it out. The husband and wife have a divine assignment from God. They have a purpose to fulfill together. She takes her husband's name and she also takes on his destiny for the family.

2. The father's life is a living testimony of faith in God.

His wife and children know his testimony and his spiritual state at any moment. He is praying for them, sometimes all night. He is carrying them with his commitment.

3. The father speaks over his wife and family what they are becoming.

When you can see people as God sees them, you can give vision to your family. Their lives will literally change before your eyes as you speak into them their greatness and calling as God shows it to you.

4. The father affirms his children's potential.

God sent His Son not only to be a sacrifice but also to prove that He believed in us before we could ever accomplish anything to please Him. God's love and acceptance make it possible for us to please Him. Condemnation and judgment never accomplish that. That's something to remember when you are trying to figure out how to raise your children.

5. The father listens to God, writes it down, and does what God says.

God talked to Adam in Genesis 1. The devil and the woman talked in Genesis 2 and 3. You are always listening to something. What do you do with what you hear? What have you heard that you accepted or rejected?

> *"I will stand my watch And set myself on the rampart,*
> *And watch to see what He will say to me,*
> *And what I will answer when I am corrected."*[255]

6. The father transmits the family virtues—their "coat of arms."

Abraham represented a generation that had a visitation from God. Through generational transfer he modeled his relationship with God and his lifestyle down through his seed. That is why God said, "I am the God of Abraham, Isaac and Jacob." A father transmits his values (such as respect and serving), his non-negotiables (convictions about right and wrong), and his life Scriptures.

---

[255] Habakkuk 2:1 NKJV.

7. The father knows his wife's tendencies and favorite things.

The Bible says, "Husbands, love your wives, even as Christ also loved the church, and gave himself for it."[256] Marriage is a model of the relationship between Christ and the Church. A man who loves his wife as Christ loves the church pays attention to what she likes in clothes, stockings, shoes, favorite colors, vacations, hair, spa, nails. These are simple ways that he shows that he has noticed her. The children will take notice and want their marriages to be just like that.

8. The father keeps a journal to honor and record his wife's input.

Jesus said of marriage that "the two are united into one."[257] Because the husband and wife are one, what she says is important to him. When she gives input, he writes it down because he values what she says. He meditates on it and considers how to implement what she has told him.

9. The father takes his children into his world with him.

My children are grown, but they are still part of my life and ministry. Sometimes they travel with me and at other times they are functioning in my place at the home base. They have learned my ways from being with me.

10. The father spends time with his children in their world.

Whatever your children enjoy and whenever they are playing on teams in sports or performing, you make time for doing that with them, beginning in the early years.

11. The father submits to his own spiritual father.

Does anyone see you with the eyes of revelation and speak into your life? When you have a spiritual father you not only have accountability, you also want to change to please him.

---

[256] Ephesians 5:25 KJV.
[257] Mark 10:8 NLT.

12. The father introduces his family to cross-cultural friends.

When you have a heart for people of all backgrounds, then you are in agreement with God's heart. God is no respecter of persons.[258]

13. The father discusses sex and morality with his children.

A father's beliefs are more important to his children than any other information in convincing them to wait for sex until marriage.

14. The father maintains his sexual purity.

A Christian man lives by biblical standards for his own sexual purity, and his family knows that they can trust him. He wouldn't think of abusing that trust with impure thoughts, magazines, movies, or the Internet.

15. The father trains his children how to treat his wife.

When a husband backs his wife before the children, her influence increases exponentially.

Fathering, not Mentoring, Builds Men into Fathers

When I began my ministry in Richmond, Virginia, more than 40 years ago, I found a hunger in young men to have a spiritual father who would love them and hang out with them, but also one who would discipline and correct them. They got rebuked so many times that they started joking about it. One time we heard someone give a testimony but he couldn't pronounce the word rebuke.

VISION FOR BLACK AMERICA:

THEY WILL ACCEPT REBUKE AND BE ENCOURAGED.

"Patiently correct, rebuke, and encourage your people with good teaching."

2 Timothy 4:2 NLT

---

[258] See Romans 2:11.

He called it "rebuck." So from then on, that was what we called it.

I preached what we called "pure fire and brimstone," but they loved it. We developed a lot of our own terminology for the consecrated life. When we found that the Greek word *"psuche"* meant "flesh," we talked about guys who were *psuche-ing out*—in other words, they were in the flesh. They had an attitude. They were in sin.

Then we adopted Jesus' words in John 8:23, *"Ye are from beneath; I am from above: ye are of this world; I am not of this world."* We would say, "That was beneath." Or we would say, "That's a beneath life."

In those days I wasn't traveling as much as I am now, so we spent a lot of time together. We played a lot of basketball, which attracted other guys whom we won to Christ. Some pro basketball players joined the church and then we were unbeatable against other churches in town. It was a lot of fun but it had a serious impact on those guys. Many of them are leading churches and ministries today, and most are still married to their wives and going for God.

In the 1990s I started speaking at Promise Keepers in the early days of that men's movement, so I would always take some of the guys along. Many pastors and leaders I knew then didn't want to share the influence that God was giving them, but I saw it as a natural extension of fathering. To this day, most who traveled with me are still going for God.

Mentoring is not parenting

Parenting differs from the idea of mentoring, which comes from a character named Mentor in Greek literature. Mentors are teachers and coaches. A golf pro can hire a mentor, but he can also fire him. Mentors are temporary. Parents are permanent. It is said of a Hebrew father that when the eldest son becomes of age, then the daddy is ready to die. The whole goal of a Hebrew father is to bring his son to age so that he can take the place of his dad.

VISION FOR BLACK AMERICA:

THEY WILL BECOME SPIRITUAL FATHERS TEACHING OTHERS.

"And the things that thou hast heard of me among many witnesses, the same commit thou to faithful men, who shall be able to teach others also."

2 Timothy 2:1-2 KJV

God is waiting for the church to come up into Him in all things, to grow up so that the Father can put into your hands the responsibilities of a son. If you follow His example, you will always have sons coming up under you to whom you can give everything you know so that after you are gone they will achieve even more greatness.

INFLUENCE OF A GODLY GREAT GRANDFATHER

One of the most significant breakthroughs for sufferers of arthritis was the synthesis of cortisone by a 20th century Black scientist named Percy Julian, grandson of a slave. Dr. Julian also developed a flame retardant use by the Navy that saved lives during World War II.

In 1950, Dr. Julian was named Chicagoan of the Year and moved into a neighborhood called Oak Park, the first Black family in the community. However, in spite of his achievements, he and his family had to deal with racism. A few months after they moved in, on Thanksgiving Day, an arsonist set fire to their home. In June of the following year, someone in a passing car threw dynamite at the house where it exploded outside his children's window.

However, he didn't give up or get bitter. He used those experiences to give him a greater resolve. He credited his persistence to his family background and the influence of his great grandfather's faith. Here's how he described it:

"We were singing on that day a beautiful spiritual,
'There is a balm in Gilead to make the wounded whole.
There is a balm in Gilead to heal the sin-sick soul.'

"'Grandpa Cabe,' I asked, 'what's a balm in Gilead?'

"'Well, Sonny, you see, Gilead was a famous town in Israel for the manufacture of salves to heal wounds and sores,' he told me. 'And they called these salves balms. Now one day Jeremiah was having a hard time trying to lead his people the right way. Everything was going wrong for Jeremiah, and he cried out in anguish, "Is there no balm in Gilead?" You see, what he was saying was, "Ain't there no way out?" I want you to know that, Sonny, because I believe */there is always a way out.'" [259]

---

[259] "Response," in *Percy Lavon Julian, A Tribute* (Jacksonville, Illinois: MacMurray College, 1972), pp. 24-25. Quoted in Percy Lavon Julian. National Academy of Science Biographical Memoirs. Online at http://www.nap.edu/html/biomems/pjulian.html#REF1.

Spiritual fathers and elders

The equivalent of a spiritual father is an elder in a church. In 1 Timothy 1 the Bible says if any man desires to be a bishop he desires a good thing. "Bishop" is the same word for elder.

When men desire to become fathers or bishops or elders over spiritual children, that is a good thing. An elder is someone you can call on and rely upon. You don't have to be 50 years old to be an elder. You can be a young man who is mature enough to be sent out to be a pastor.

We have discovered in ministry that godly children of 9, 10 and 11 years old can take over their schools and start Bible clubs if they see the whole school as theirs. Some child is going to lead in the elementary and middle schools. Either a gang leader is going to lead, or a child of God. They become the father in that school under the authority of the teacher, the principal, and their natural and spiritual covering at home.

How a Father Teaches His Children Abstinence

A few years ago, a movement started where single young people signed pledges to stay pure until marriage. If you can believe the surveys, many of them did not keep their pledges. I believe that more children would stay pure if their parents were involved in their commitments, especially the fathers. Statistics are in their favor.

Time out together and a chastity ring

One way that a father can show his children that abstinence is important is to take his son or daughter out to dinner or do some other special thing together. While they are out together for this special time, he gives them a "chastity ring" or some other symbol to show his personal commitment to their sexual purity. This becomes a seal on something sacred. The conversation that follows can build the moment into an opportunity for practical guidelines and open the door for future conversations.

If parents make jokes about sex or buy their children contraceptives or condoms, that's like saying, "I give up!" God wouldn't give up. God cares about children's virginity very much.

CHILDREN STAYING PURE TO PLEASE DADDY

- "In survey after survey, children report that they want to talk to their parents about their sex-related questions, that it would be easier to delay sexual activity and avoid teen pregnancy if they were able to have more open, honest conversations about these topics with their parents, and that parents influence their decisions about sex more than friends do."[260]

- "Non-Hispanic black teens (54%), Hispanic teens (50%), and Non-Hispanic White teens (43%) all say parents most influence their decisions about sex."[261]

- ". . . a girl whose father leaves before she is five years old is eight times more likely to have an adolescent pregnancy than a girl whose father remains in her home."[262]

Fathers teaching sons about sexual restraint

Boys are dominated by their lusts and desires. Fathers can teach them to restrain those desires by remembering that God sees them and God wants something better for them than inordinate sex.

Today's young Black men need God and role models and spiritual fathers who can teach them to think like a man of God. They may not have earthly fathers, but they have a heavenly Father watching over them. They can learn how God thinks from prayer, the Word of God, and the good example of other men. This is a great challenge that the Church must meet.

Single men today need to restore the standard of former generations (Isaiah 61:4). Fathers can impart that vision into their sons. God expects men to set a standard. They are not creating a standard. They are restoring former standards that were established by God. In past generations Black America had that standard.

---

[260] "Tips for Parents." U.S. Department of Health and Human Services. Online at http://www.hhs.gov/ash/oah/adolescent-health-topics/reproductive-health/teen-pregnancy/tips-for-parents.html. Accessed October 2016.

[261] Bill Albert, "Who Most Influences Teens' Decisions about Sex? Parents: New Survey Findings Released" (October 4, 2016). The National Campaign to Prevent Teen and Unplanned Pregnancy. Online at https://thenationalcampaign.org/blog/who-most-influences-teens%E2%80%99-decisions-about-sex-parents-new-survey-findings-released.

[262] Rob Schwarzwalder and Natasha Tax, "Daddy's Girl: How Fatherlessness Impacts Early Sexual Activity, Teen Pregnancy, and Sexual Abuse." Family Research Council. Online at http://downloads.frc.org/EF/EF15L32.pdf. Accessed October 2016.

Fathers who teach their sons to abstain from sex are not inventing legalistic doctrines, but seeking to fulfill the mind of Christ. God does not have a double standard—one for ancient times and one for now. He has only one standard, and it is based on His holiness.

When fathers lead their sons to the Lord and carry them along in daily habits of holiness, their sons will make a difference in their generation. God expects Christians to be the manifestation of Christ on earth. Jesus dealt with the purity of the inner man, so any standard we set must have as its end result an inner change that comes out of a relationship with Him. Inner transformation leads to outer manifestation. When a young man takes a stand for celibacy, it becomes a wake-up call to others.

LIFETIME ADVANTAGES OF ABSTINENCE

"We found that men and women who were virgins at age 18, when evaluated approximately 20 years later, had about half the risk of divorce, had completed about an additional year of education and had annual incomes nearly 20 percent higher than those who were not virgins at 18. We used 18 as the cutoff age because it gave approximately equal populations of virgins and non-virgins to study." [263]

Your gender was established when you were born

God did not make a mistake when he made you a male or a female at birth. He is not confused about the gender on your birth certificate. When a father refuses to accept immoral sex outside of marriage in his children as normal but as assaults against God, he will defeat the devil's attempt to take out Black men who have the potential to be moral and spiritual leaders of this generation.

---

263 "New Study Finds Abstinence Pays Off in the Long Run." Article online at http://www.lifesite.net/ldn/2005/may/05050607.html. Study by Focus on the Family Medical Issues Analyst Reginald Finger, M.D., M.P.H.; Tonya Thelen, B.S.; John T. Vessey, Ph.D.; Joanna K. Mohn, M.D.; and Joshua R. Mann, M.D., M.P.H. Full study at Adolescent and Family Health website at http://www.afhjournal.org/toc.asp?issue=0304.

Fathers as protectors of their daughters' virtue

The biblical standard for a father's protection over his daughter was established in the Old Testament. Until she came of age, she was under the guidance and protection of her father. He placed great value on his daughter and took seriously his responsibility.

Under Old Testament law, any attacker who violated a woman's virginity had to answer to her father. The father had ultimate responsibility before God to answer for his daughter's virtue.

As a result of the breakdown of the family, especially in the Black community, daughters no longer have the protection of their fathers.

One of the privileges of a father over his daughter was the right to confirm or reject the person she wanted to marry. The young man asked the father for his permission. There was a time of courtship when the father could observe the behavior of the young man toward his daughter. The young man's restraint from having intercourse with her was used to determine his fitness as a future husband. A young man was expected to win the father, not the young woman, because the father was her covering.

Reviving the concept of courtship approved by the father

Fathers give their children an understanding of courtship—a time when a young couple who are attracted to one another should talk to their parents about how they are considering marriage. Even if the parents' marriage isn't perfect, they probably know many right principles. Involving the father in the process, if he is a man of principle, will go a long way toward keeping the couples' relationship pure.

Spiritual Fathers for the Inner Cities

As you may recall from Chapter 4, the army of godly men called Methodist Circuit Riders changed the spiritual landscape of our country in its early days. These men of God went West to newly settled areas, traveling on horseback from town to town, planting Methodist meeting groups and returning to father them as often as they could. "They were everywhere." Everywhere you turn in the inner cities in the future, I picture an army of spiritual fathers.

I have a vision of a spiritual army of men who will challenge the breakdown of society and change the inner cities of America by being spiritual fathers. It will require humility to go into the ruined neighborhoods where despair, vice, and violence have reigned and bring the spirit of a father, but I believe that God will back us, because Blacks are dealing with issues at the very core of Who God is and how He created them. The inner-city battlefield needs soldiers who will go beyond the man-centered programs that have usurped Christ-centered solutions for the family and society. Where hearts are darkened,[264] Christ in the person of Christians can bring them into the light. Jesus said,

> *"Let your light so shine before men, that they may see your good works and glorify your Father in heaven."* [265]

God wants to change this generation. No one can stop Him because there is life in His words. Jesus said, *"And the very words I have spoken to you are spirit and life."*[266] He is God. Nothing can refuse Him. He speaks and it comes to pass.

Find your spiritual father before you start your inner-city ministry

One of the most important first steps in becoming a spiritual father is to be under a father—first under God, the Father, and then under a pastor or other spiritual authority. Just as children growing up with a father have a more successful life than those who are fatherless, those who want to become ministers do best if they have been fathered.

The apostle Paul wrote to the churches in Corinth as a father bringing correction for their change.

> *"I write not these things to shame you, but as my beloved sons I warn you. For though ye have ten thousand instructors in Christ, yet have ye not many fathers: for in Christ Jesus I have begotten you through the gospel."*[267]

Many Christians are unwilling to submit to a pastor or elder as a spiritual father who can train them in Christ-likeness. Men often prefer relationships in which they are equal partners or peers, like accountability groups. They can deal with this arrangement because they can take the

---

[264] Romans 1:21 KJV.
[265] Matthew 5:14-16 NKJV.
[266] John 6:63-64 NLT.
[267] 1 Corinthians 4:14-16, KJV.

advice or leave it, but the moment a spiritual leader tries to give them strong direction, they are out of there.

Treat your spiritual father with respect

I often challenge Christians with this question: Do you make your pastor want to quit the ministry? Many pastors' hearts are broken when they have a burden to raise up spiritual sons but they have to spend their time with people who disrespect them and stay stuck on stupid. They are shepherds of dumb sheep.

> *"But if you will not hear it,*
> *My soul will weep in secret for your pride;*
> *My eyes will weep bitterly*
> *And run down with tears,*
> *Because the LORD'S flock*
> *has been taken captive."* [268]

Some people treat pastors the way the Israelites treated Moses. They ask, "Who made you a prince and a judge over us?"[269] However, you need to remember that God's blessing on your ministry outreach will come through respect toward those in authority over you.

Sacrifice to make time for secret prayer with the Father

Revival will come when men sacrifice the time to allow God's Word to penetrate the deepest parts of their lives, discerning the thoughts and intents of the heart (Hebrews 4:12-13).

It is the role of the Holy Spirit to convict you of sin (John 16:8). Even if you are not aware of any specific sin in your life, you need to find a secret place where you can pray alone. Ask God to show you any areas of your life where you are not surrendered and you need to be changed.

Secret prayer is a sacrifice. We would rather do a lot of other things than simple prayer alone with God. It takes focus to stop everything that you normally do and go apart to pray. Jesus did it regularly, even if the only time He could find away from the crowds was in the middle of the night. No man of God ever changed his world without secret prayer.

---

[268] Jeremiah 13:17 NKJV.
[269] Exodus 2:14 NKJV.

What is prayer? It is listening to God. If the only voice you hear in prayer is your voice, you are not praying.

Have faith that you will find souls to father if you go there

Remember that when the Bible says in Hebrews 11 that faith is the substance of things hoped for and the evidence of things not seen it is not just talking about faith and commitment in a vacuum. Faith is real when it rests on the foundation of Who God is by His very nature, and also on what He wants to accomplish. When the things that you are hoping for are grounded in God, you can have hope that they will come to pass. Because God has a heart for the souls of Black Americans, these men will learn how to become fathers again. This vision will come to pass.

If you are in agreement with me that Black men can be rescued and become men of God, here are some ways that you can act on that faith.

ACTING ON YOUR FAITH FOR SOULS

1. Pray for a harvest of inner-city souls—young men needing God.

2. Talk to your pastors and elders about what you are seeing.

3. Go to the streets to find the young men.

4. Speak destiny into the young men's lives.

5. Disciple new converts as a father.

6. Put them to work as ministers.

---

1. Pray for a harvest of inner city souls—young men needing God.

Jesus said, *"The harvest truly is great, but the laborers are few: pray ye therefore the Lord of the harvest, that he would send forth laborers into his harvest."* [270] You might wonder why I focus so much on the men. I believe that they are the key to lasting change. The women will change when the men change and stop chasing after them sexually like dogs.

---

[270] Luke 10:2 KJV.

When the men grow up in God and become husbands and fathers with wisdom and maturity, Black America will change.

2. Talk to your pastors and elders about what you are seeing.

It will be important for you to be under the authority of a local church. Ask your leaders if they are seeing this with you and if they think you should start with some simple street ministry. Find out who would like to accompany you or lead you. As you continue, consult with your leadership on how the church could become more involved.

3. Go to the streets to find the young men.

As you read about in Chapter 4, "Street Revs," if you go to the streets of the inner city, you will find young men who will listen to you. Pray with them to come into the kingdom of God.

Jesus told this story about what a king told his messengers:

> "'The wedding feast is ready, and the guests I invited aren't worthy of the honor. Now go out to the street corners and invite everyone you see.' So the servants brought in everyone they could find, good and bad alike, and the banquet hall was filled with guests. "[271]

4. Speak destiny into the young men's lives.

Regardless of what you see the young men doing on the outside, keep your faith alive. Continue to tell them about Jesus and the good news of the Gospel. Pray for them and keep praying. Tell them that they have value and God has a hope and a future for them.

> "'For I know the plans I have for you,' says the LORD. 'They are plans for good and not for disaster, to give you a future and a hope. In those days when you pray, I will listen. If you look for me in earnest, you will find me when you seek me. I will be found by you,' says the LORD.'"[272]

---

[271] Matthew 22:8-10 NLT.
[272] Jeremiah 29:11-14 NLT.

5. Disciple new converts as a father.

Take them to your church and other churches where they can find spiritual fathers. Play some ball together. Set up neighborhood drop-ins and Bible studies. Have informal rap sessions when you talk about godly principles for living, listen to their hurts and struggles, and give them the peace of God through fatherly wisdom and prayer.

6. Put them to work as ministers.

Once they are converted and discipled, teach them the Bible and encourage them to surrender their lives to God so that He can use them to reach others. When they are stabilized, send them out as missionaries to the streets, the nation, and the world.

Crossing Racial Lines to Be Someone's Father

Are you willing to take responsibility for some area of your city before the Lord? Could the Lord steward a city through your dedication? Two thousand years after the resurrection Blacks are still struggling to find their purpose. They forget that one of the reasons that Jesus came was to make every place on earth like heaven. We have all of the evidence that an entire people group among the poor in our cities right next door is locked in the jaws of the oppressor, and we still wonder if there is anything that we need to do for God!

VISION FOR BLACK
AMERICA:

*THEY WILL FATHER
THE POOR AND THE
OPPRESSED.*

*"I was a father to the poor
and made sure that even
strangers received a fair
trial. I broke the jaws of
godless oppressors and
made them release their
victims."*

Job 29:15-17 NLT

Blessing someone of another race before their change

If you are White, have you ever blessed a Black man? If you are Black, have you blessed someone White, or do you still hold unforgiveness against the people of that race? Most races talk about the negatives they see in other races. Whites ask, "Why are Blacks so divided? Why don't they get along? Why do they have babies out of wedlock?" You haven't blessed them yet. Israel was doing a lot of things wrong but the Lord still blessed them as a people. He didn't bless them *after* their change. He blessed them *so that they could change.*

As a natural father, if you wait to bless your children until after they do something right, they may feel that you are putting pressure on them for the next good deed rather than seeing them unconditionally.

VISION FOR BLACK AMERICA:

THEY WILL RECEIVE GOD'S BLESSINGS THROUGH OTHERS.

"How we praise God, the Father of our Lord Jesus Christ, who has blessed us with every spiritual blessing in the heavenly realms because we belong to Christ."

Ephesians 1:3 NLT

When you love them, you bless your children *first* and then look at their performance later. God called Israel a holy people, a royal priesthood, a peculiar people.[273] That is not where they were already, in the natural. He didn't give them names according to what they were. He called them according to where He ordained them to be.

One day we will stand before the Lord waiting to hear His words, "Well done, thou good and faithful servant." Everything we can do now to please God will be worth it then.

Seeing people with eyes of revelation

You have to see people with the eyes of revelation. That is what God was telling Abram when He said, *"All that your eyes can see, I have given you."*[274] Abraham didn't just look at what he could see geographically. He saw generationally, all the way up to our time. The Bible says that he saw our day. God made him the father of faith. According to what Abraham could see, he is still producing the seed of faith in our generation. He saw that far into the future.

If you let God open your eyes and give you vision beyond your culture, you can reach any culture.

---

[273] See 1 Peter 2:9.
[274] See Genesis 13:15.

Crunch-Time Champions

In the closing weeks of World War II, the 332nd Fighter Group of the United States Air Force faced down the best aircraft that the German Luftwaffe had to offer. On one bold 1,600 mile mission, they successfully escorted U.S. Air Force bombers into the airspace right over the capital of Berlin. They shot down three of the new German jets and did not lose a single U. S. bomber on that mission.

Every one of the pilots in this courageous escort unit was Black. They were known as the "Tuskegee Airmen," mentioned earlier, because they had been trained at Tuskegee Institute in Alabama. The school was chosen in 1940 for an experiment in training Black pilots because of its excellent educational program in aeronautics and its first-class airfield. The men who eventually distinguished themselves in combat in World War II, winning hundreds of medals and citations for bravery, had to overcome incredible trials and faced ongoing racism, but they never lost their commitment to pursue their goal.

When I look at the men of Black America, I see past the darkness of the present into a bright future and light ahead. I see men from the inner city throwing off their sin clothes and putting on robes of righteousness. I see the inner cities becoming a destination place because of the glory of God shining from the inside out in the men of God there. Every family has a father and every child is growing up with the safety and the standards that a father imparts.

PRAYER

My Father, let the transforming power of your Holy Spirit and the privilege of being a father come upon the men of Black America in a mighty way. Let them see the world as an opportunity for them to be developed, launched, and reaching out to those who need them. Give them the gift of your grace. Help them to be an example to one another of love, faith unfeigned, courage, long-suffering, and steadfastness. Help them to take some steps forward today. In Jesus' name. Amen.

CHAPTER 7

PLANNED PARENTHOOD
VS. BLACK AMERICA

"I am the LORD your God,
who rescued you from slavery." [275]

In 1912, James Weldon Johnson, author of *Lift Every Voice and Sing*, wrote *The Autobiography of an Ex-Colored Man*. Although fictional, it is a poignant first-person account of the kind of decisions Black people once made as they tried to survive in society, long after they had legally been declared free. The main character in the book was able to leave behind his true racial identity temporarily because of the lightness of his skin. He "passed" for White. Unrecognized by a vicious lynching crowd, this man witnessed one of the great atrocities of 20th-century racism—a Black man lynched alive in the fire. Johnson wrote:

"There he stood, a man only in form and stature, every sign of degeneracy stamped upon his countenance. His eyes were dull and vacant, indicating not a single ray of thought.

"Evidently the realization of his fearful fate had robbed him of whatever reasoning power he had ever possessed. He was too stunned and stupefied even to tremble. Fuel was brought from everywhere, oil, the torch; the flames crouched for an instant as though to gather strength, then leaped up as high as their victim's head.

"He squirmed, he writhed, strained at his chains, then gave out cries and groans that I shall always hear. The cries and groans were choked off by the fire and smoke; but his eyes, bulging from their sockets, rolled from side to side, appealing in vain for help. Some of the crowd yelled and cheered, others seemed appalled at what they had done, and there were those who turned away sickened at the sight."[276]

---

[275] Exodus 20:2 NLT.
[276] James Weldon Johnson, *The Autobiography of an Ex-Colored Man.* Online at http://www.gutenberg.org/etext/11012. Johnson was the Black author who wrote "Lift

After a major effort by the National Association for the Advancement of Colored People (NAACP), these lynchings finally ended, but today laws are on the books making it legal to kill Blacks once again.

The most effective method of killing Black Americans is abortion.

Lynching, once allowed, has now been stopped. Abortion, once illegal, is now allowed. Lynching of Blacks was done in public, often followed by bizarre rejoicing. Abortions of Black babies, once done in private, are now celebrated as a woman's right. Thanks primarily to Planned Parenthood, millions of Black women can rejoice in the right to kill.

The 20th century may be remembered for the return of Black enfranchisement and other civil rights, but it will also be remembered as the century when it was no longer necessary to mobilize mobs with knives, firebrands, and lynching ropes to kill Blacks. Those weapons were no longer needed. The dark vision of eugenicists was complete.

DID YOU KNOW? Black American Holocaust

Blacks died in Africa and Middle Passage slave trade: approx. 3 million[277]

Killed by lynching in 86 years: 3,446 documented cases of Blacks[278]

Black babies killed by abortion since 1973: more than 17.5 million[279]

Black women are about 13% of the female population of the United States[280] but have 36.7% of the abortions.[281]

Every Voice and Sing," known as the "Black National Anthem." (See also Chapter 1.) He was also an educator, lawyer, U.S. consul, and NAACP official.

[277] Database of Transatlantic Slave Trade online at http://www.slavevoyages.org/ estimates at least 1,464,200 deaths at sea.

[278] Tuskegee Institute, "Lynchings: By Year and Race." Online at http://law2.umkc.edu/faculty/projects/ftrials/shipp/lynchingyear.html. Accessed Oct. 2016

[279] This is a minimum estimate based on 50 million abortions through 2008 with 35% done by Blacks. Online at http://www.cdc.gov/reproductivehealth/data_stats/abortion.htm.

[280] U.S. Department of Health and Human Services, Health Resources and Services Administration, Maternal and Child Health Bureau. Women's Health USA 2012. Online at http://mchb.hrsa.gov/whusa12/search/search.html?zoom_query=women%27s+health+usa.

[281] All statistics are for "non-Hispanic" Black and White women. Source: CDC, "Abortion Surveillance — United States, 2012, Surveillance Summaries, November 27, 2015. Online at http://www.cdc.gov/mmwr/preview/mmwrhtml/ss6410a1.htm?s_cid=ss6410a1_e. Accessed October 2016.

Blacks don't understand that they have bought into the genocidal strategy of Planned Parenthood to decrease the population of the Black race.

Planned Parenthood for "those who should never have been born"

A century ago the founder of Planned Parenthood, Margaret Sanger, wrote *The Pivot of Civilization* to promote birth control to enhance a woman's sex life.

However, Sanger was also a eugenicist. She promoted birth control as a solution to reduce the birth rate of lower classes and diminish the population of "unfit"[282] people whom she considered a drain on the resources of society. Proponents of eugenics believe that some races of people (which includes themselves) are superior to lower races of people (whom they call dysgenics).

Margaret Sanger was a proud promoter of eugenics through her prolific writings. She was a promoter of genocide through birth control and sterilization for "dysgenics" such as the "feeble-minded" and those with "transmissible disease."[283]

Populating the world with "their kind"—Margaret Sanger

> *"Eugenists emphasize . . . the sterilization of the unfit to prevent their **populating the world with their kind** and they may, perhaps, agree with us that contraception is a necessary measure among the masses of the workers, where wages do not keep pace with the growth of the family and its necessities in the way of food, clothing, housing, medical attention, education and the like.*

Margaret Sanger, "Birth Control and Racial Betterment"[284]

---

[281] Ibid.

[282] Margaret Sanger, *The Pivot of Civilization*. Online at http://www.gutenberg.org/files/1689/1689-h/1689-h.htm. Accessed October 2016.

[283] Margaret Sanger, "My Way to Peace," Jan. 17, 1932, Online at https://www.nyu.edu/projects/sanger/webedition/app/documents/show.php?sangerDoc=129 037.xml. Accessed October 2016.

[284] Margaret Sanger, "Birth Control and Racial Betterment," *Birth Control Review* (February 1919). Online at https://lifedynamics.com/app/uploads/2015/09/1919-02-February.pdf. Accessed October 2016.

"Those who should never have been born"—Margaret Sanger

*"Those least fit to carry on the race are increasing most rapidly. People who cannot support their own offspring are encouraged by Church and State to produce large families. Many of the children thus begotten are diseased or feeble-minded; many become criminals. The burden of supporting these unwanted types has to be bourne by the healthy elements of the nation. Funds that should be used to raise the standard of our civilization are diverted to the maintenance of **those who should never have been born.**"[285]*

Margaret Sanger, Founder of Planned Parenthood
"Principles and Aims of the American Birth Control League"

DID YOU KNOW? Black Babies Who Were Never Born (Aborted)[286]

30 percent of Black pregnancies end in death of the baby by abortion.

Black unborn babies are killed by abortion at 3.5 times the number of White babies killed by abortion.[287]

Abortion ratio. 435 Black babies are killed in the womb for every 1,000 babies who survive. The ratio for White babies is 127 per 1,000.

Black women have the highest abortion rate of all races, three times Whites

Abortion rate. Black women have 27.8 abortions per 1,000 women aged 15 to 44 years old. The rate for White women is 7.7 abortions.

". . . the abortion rate for black women has been approximately three times as high as that for white women . . . since 1991 (the first year for which rates by race were published)."[288]

---

[285] Ibid.
[286] All statistics are for "non-Hispanic" Black and White women. Source: CDC, "Abortion Surveillance — United States, 2012, Surveillance Summaries, November 27, 2015 (the most recent data available at the time of this printing). Online at http://www.cdc.gov/mmwr/preview/mmwrhtml/ss6410a1.htm?s_cid=ss6410a1_e. Accessed October 2016.
[287] Ibid.
[288] Lilo T. Strauss, MA, Sonya B. Gamble, MS, Wilda Y. Parker, Douglas A. Cook, MBIS, Suzanne B. Zane, DVM, Saeed Hamdan, MD, PhD, "Abortion Surveillance 2004." Online at http://www.cdc.gov/mmwr/preview/mmwrhtml/ss5609a1.htm?s_cid=ss5609a1_e. Accessed October 2016.

Genocide Became Self-Genocide in the Black Community

Eugenics favors the practice of genocide as defined by the United Nations. In 1951, the United Nations approved the "Convention on the Prevention and Punishment of the Crime of Genocide" that was developed in 1948 after the Jewish Holocaust.

The international crime of genocide described below applies not only to what the Nazis did to the Jews but also to what Whites did to Blacks for centuries in the United States. Eugenics actively carried out against those who demean others as below them is genocide. This crime is one of many tragedies that Black Americans and Jews share in common.

DID YOU KNOW? United Nations Definition of Crime of Genocide

Office of the United Nations High Commissioner for Human Rights

Convention on the Prevention and Punishment of the Crime of Genocide

Approved and proposed for signature and ratification or accession by General Assembly resolution 260 A (III) of 9 December 1948, *entry into force* 12 January 1951, in accordance with article XIII . . .

Article 3

The following acts shall be punishable:

(a) Genocide;

(b) Conspiracy to commit genocide;

(c) Direct and public incitement to commit genocide;

(d) Attempt to commit genocide;

(e) Complicity in genocide.

Article 4. Persons committing genocide or any of the other acts enumerated in

Article III shall be punished, whether they are constitutionally responsible rulers, public officials or private individuals. [289]

---

[289] Online at United Nations website: http://www.ohchr.org/EN/ProfessionalInterest/Pages/CrimeOfGenocide.aspx. Accessed October 2016.

Why Planned Parenthood provides reproductive services for Blacks

Margaret Sanger did not hide her clear purpose for promoting birth control for the poor. It was based on her conviction—common to many people of her day and still true today—that there is something wrong with Black Americans. How many people today believe these things about Blacks?

- They are a drain on society.
- They use up resources.
- Too many are criminals.
- They have too many children.
- They can't be educated.
- They have uncontrolled sex lives.

And on and on. Planned Parenthood is solving the "Negro problem," as it was called, every day by restraining the Black population.

> *Jesus said, "The thief does not come except to steal, and to kill, and to destroy. I have come that they may have life, and that they may have it more abundantly. I am the good shepherd. The good shepherd gives His life for the sheep."*

Black women after slavery loved the chance for "choice"

Margaret Sanger couched her eugenic crusade to reduce the population of Blacks and others in persuasive feminine logic, saying she only wished to relieve poor women of the burden of excessive childbearing, Black women whose grandparents had been slaves welcomed what she said. They had the mentality "Nobody is going to control me."

Sanger's strategy against minorities was so subtle that except in pro-life circles it has not been widely discussed. Feminists and even researchers who should know better routinely deny that she was a eugenicist or claim it was a temporary phase in spite of her decades of prolific writings on the subject of eugenics.

Sanger's plan has been so successful that Blacks are practicing self-genocide of their race through abortion while thinking they are simply exercising their right to plan the size of their families. They have swallowed the lie that women are so oppressed by men that they must seize control of their own bodies, practicing birth control and abortion to maintain their independence. Black women like Faye Wattleton have even taken leadership positions in Planned Parenthood, devaluing their race and perpetuating its destruction.

What began as birth control has become the holocaust of abortion. What began as genocide has become self-genocide. Through the liberalization of abortion laws in *Roe v. Wade,* Black women were released to kill *their own race* through abortion. Sterilization promoted by Sanger and practiced by many states is no longer necessary. Conceiving a child after sex is no longer a problem because society has lost its moral scruples about killing unborn children.

Still strategically located near Black communities

Life Dynamics confirmed that Planned Parenthood strategically locates a number of its centers near Black communities and Historically Black Colleges and Universities. It is no coincidence that Black women have more than three times the abortions of White women. Once they bought into it, Planned Parenthood made it convenient.

Abortion (feticide) and the Black community's spirit of death

The promotion of abortion creates a spirit of death in the Black community because it is a practice of self-genocidal murder. One of the examples of Black achievers in Chapter 1 is Rebecca Cole, the second black female graduate of a medical school. She crusaded to prevent feticide (the killing a fetus, or unborn child) and infanticide. If she were alive today, what would she think of the masses of women of her race who now legally commit feticide daily? Would she see a connection between feticide and the high rate of infant mortality in the Black community (death of a child before the first birthday)?

Other practices of self-genocide include the high rate of homicide in the Black community, deadly diseases like HIV/AIDS transmitted by immoral sex with other Blacks, fatherless families because men have no vision for their race or their children.

Genocide today applies to what Blacks are doing to other Blacks— *Black self-genocide.* If the United Nations has established a penalty for the crime of genocide, what will be the penalty of God?

Favored Races, Eugenics, and Black Genocide

The American government has been trying to deal by law with racism for many years now. More civil-rights laws are on the books than ever before, yet almost everyone acknowledges that deeply entrenched racial problems still exist. The problem is in the way people think. There is still a perceived privilege that comes with being White in America, but it is not a biblical right or privilege. The Bible says that we are all equal, because God "hath made of one blood all nations of men."[290]

"He himself gives life and breath to everything, and he satisfies every need there is. From one man he created all the nations throughout the whole earth." [291]

Black Americans were degraded as slaves and racism is still an unresolved national sin of America that must be dealt with to heal our land.

DID YOU KNOW? Legal Degradation of American Slaves

"Socially dead person" banned from decision making and social activities[292]

A piece of property[293] who could be pursued across state lines after an escape[294]

No right to self-defense against a White person, including beatings and rape

Few, if any, rights; no legal protection; unable to testify in a court of law

Sold into slavery; sold from owner to owner; no ancestral records

No right to income from his labor; perpetual servitude

No ability to make contracts, including marriage; no legal spouse or children

---

[290] Acts 17:26.
[291] Acts 17:25-26 NLT.
[292] Encyclopaedia Britannica's Guide to Black History. Online at http://kids.britannica.com/blackhistory/article-9109538. Accessed October 2016.
[293] Slaves legally affirmed as property by U.S. Supreme Court *Dred Scott vs. John F. A. Sandford* (1857). Online at http://www.ourdocuments.gov/print_friendly.php?page=transcript&doc=29&title=Transcript+of+Dred+Scott+v.+Sanford+percent281857percent29.
[294] Fugitive slave provisions were included in the U.S. Constitution and later laws and rulings.

Darwinian evolution and "favored races" vs. "the unfit"

To understand twentieth-century American thinking about racial superiority, it is important to look not only at the institution of slavery (in a truthful way)—as practiced historically for centuries by the Africans, Arabs, Portuguese, Dutch, English, and then the Americans—but also at a highly touted, hotly defended theory that has contributed significantly to the persistence of racism even in the Church. It's Charles Darwin's theory of evolution.

VISION FOR BLACK AMERICA

THEY WILL REJECT THE THEORIES OF EVOLUTION AND FAVORED RACES.

Charles Darwin subtitled his book on evolution *The Preservation of the Favored Races in the Struggle for Life.*

The Bible says, *God shows no favoritism" (NLT).* "God is no respecter of persons" (KJV).

Acts 10:34

Black genocide and the creation/evolution debate

Before you dismiss this thought of the failure of evolution as absurdly out of date, let me tell you why we must stop avoiding this subject, risk the ridicule of scientists and intellectuals, and return the debate over evolution to the public forum where we can destroy the impact of the evolutionary myth on the minds of Christians.

> *In 1859, a short time before the slaves were emancipated, Charles Darwin [1809-1882] published his book* On the Origin of Species. *It's not widely known, but the book had an ominous subtitle:* The Preservation of the Favored Races in the Struggle for Life.

In his book, Darwin wrote that animal life is composed of two groups, *the fit and the unfit.* Throughout the ages, as these two groups reproduced, he said, they were forced to compete with one another, because space and resources on earth were insufficient to support all human beings who would be born. Darwin wrote that "all groups cannot thus go on increasing in size, for the world would not hold them." [295]

---

[295]Charles Darwin, *On the Origin of the Species by Means of Natural Selection, or the Preservation of Favored Races in the Struggle for Life.* Online at http://literature.org/authors/darwin-charles/index.html. Accessed October 2016.

"Dominant groups beat the less dominant" and Creation is untrue

Here is an excerpt from Darwin's book *On the Origin of the Species* in more detail, with his conclusion that his theory is true and therefore the Bible's story of God's creation cannot possibly be true:

> *"Dominant species belonging to the larger groups tend to give birth to new and dominant forms; so that each large group tends to become still larger, and at the same time more divergent in character. But as all groups cannot thus succeed in increasing in size, for the world would not hold them, the more dominant groups beat the less dominant. . . . **This grand fact of the grouping of all organic beings seems to me utterly inexplicable on the theory of creation.**"* [296]

Darwin based his theory of evolution on several faulty presuppositions that he used as a basis for his thinking. The oldest of his false beliefs originated in the Garden of Eden. It was the lie whispered by Satan that God could not provide for all man's needs. God had not given humans enough resources to sustain life.[297] They would have to take matters into their own hands.

Darwinian evolution and favored races creates a mindset for superiority and inequality of people as well as animals. Darwin's theory of evolution was the stimulus for an aggressive movement of social Darwinism, racial superiority that continues to influence a departure from the Bible's message of the intrinsic worth of every human being according to creative order.

Descent of Man by Charles Darwin specifically addresses man's evolution from primitive stages to his current civilized state. Darwin observed savages in his travels and considered them evidence of his theories that humans are descended from lower forms of animals as well as lower forms of human beings. He also discounted God and said belief in God was not a natural instinct but was actually something that man learned.

> *"The belief in God has often been advanced as not only the greatest but the most complete of all the distinctions between man and the lower animals. It is however impossible, as we have seen, to maintain that this belief is innate or instinctive in man. . . .*

---

[296] Ibid.
[297] See Genesis 3:1-5.

"The idea of a universal and beneficent Creator does not seem to arise in the mind of man, until he has been elevated by long-continued culture."

Charles Darwin, *Descent of Man*

Herbert Spencer read Darwin's *On the Origin of Species* and coined the phrase "survival of the fittest" for human evolution through interaction and competition. He saw it as a progressive process where the weak are dominated and the strong survive.

Thomas Malthus and the myth of scarce resources

Sixty-one years before Darwin's book was released, Thomas Malthus had developed a theory of lack that laid some of the groundwork for the theory of evolution.

In the book by Malthus *An Essay on the Principle of Population (1798),* the author said that people were involved in a struggle for existence because the population was increasing faster than the supply of food. Soon there would not be enough resources to support the population. He said that although the populations on earth increased geometrically (2, 4, 8, 16, etc.), their food increased only arithmetically (1, 2, 3, 4). Eventually, he said, there would be too many eating the resources and not enough food to feed them all. As a result, man would be forced to take on self-centered survival tactics.

Neo-Malthusians say that man's highest goal is an improved standard of living, and this requires decreasing the competition for the earth's scarce resources by limiting the number of births.

Anthropology and Africans displayed in human zoos

In the 19th and 20th century, much of the science of anthropology was built on racist concepts that African people were at a lower level of development in the evolutionary scale than White Europeans. Blacks were considered closer to the apes and monkeys than the Whites. Africans were even displayed in world fairs and zoos as public spectacles, complete with scenery that was supposedly typical of their native environments. Circus owners like P.T. Barnum found that they could draw greater crowds to see these people than the animal exhibits. Anthropologists could perform their tests in these environments without traveling to foreign locations.

These tests included measuring head sizes and drawing conclusions (later disproved) that Blacks had smaller brains than Whites.

Eugenics—well-born and nobler humans of the favored race

In 1883, Francis Galton, a cousin of Charles Darwin, built on the theories of Darwin and their common grandfather, Erasmus Darwin, who pioneered evolutionary theory. Galton also borrowed from Malthus and others to create the pseudo-science of eugenics, which comes from the Greek word for "well-born" or "noble in heredity."

Eugenicists assume there is a noble race and an ignoble race. Eugenicists accept a basic inequality in the worth of human life.

Who determines the value of a person, God or man?

The tragedy of Black genocide and Black self-genocide must be addressed in terms of who determines the worth of a person—God or man.

From God's point of view, every human being has worth.

From the point of view of evolution and the fields of science built on that faulty platform, everyone is in a struggle for survival. Only the strong survive, and sometimes they have to help the strong defeat the weak.

Make sure the lowly don't reproduce—negative eugenics

When the dominant group in America decides that Blacks are a disfavored race competing for scarce money and resources, Whites think they are justified in taking Blacks out. Since there are too many Blacks, they can be killed, jailed, sterilized, placed on birth control pills, and given free abortions—whatever it takes to reduce their population.

Freely available birth control and abortion for Black Americans are types of negative eugenics. They reduce the population of Blacks by millions. If Blacks reproduced according to God's plan and not man's eugenics, they would not remain such a small minority while healthy Hispanic families passed them by. Blacks, too, would have people power.

Make way for the nobler race

In the quote below from an article on "Hereditary Character and Talent," Galton says those who are feeble must give way to the noble, people like himself.

"The feeble nations of the world are necessarily giving way before the nobler varieties of mankind."[298]

Encourage birth rate of the best—"positive eugenics"

The best people on earth—those who are noble—should increase their birth rate, Galton said. This is called positive eugenics.

More of the fit, less of the unfit. In America, positive eugenics has been applied to the White race, especially to intellectuals and those who are successful and have more money. Eugenicists encourage them to have more children while discouraging Blacks and others without money or influence to become less reproductive.

Understanding Eugenics by Studying Hitler's Hatred of Jews

Margaret Sanger strategically placed her first birth control clinic in the Brownsville section of Brooklyn where the population at that time was predominantly Jewish. In Germany, the Jews were for the most part upstanding citizens, but Hitler wanted them killed, so they were killed. Six million Jews were terrorized, abused, and killed on the basis of eugenics.

Once you cross the line and set yourself up as God, saying that some people are more valuable than others, no one is safe from destruction.

In the 1930s and 1940s, Hitler used eugenics to justify his slaughter of Jews. In America, eugenics began decades earlier. The Germans actually credited Americans with helping them develop their theories of eugenics[299] that eventually resulted in the Jewish Holocaust.

---

[298] Francis Galton, "Hereditary Character and Talent," Part I (*Macmillan's Magazine*, vol. 12, 1865, pp. 157-166). Online at http://galton.org/essays/1860-1869/galton-1865-macmillan-hereditary-talent.html.
[299] See *The Nazi Connection—Eugenics, American Racism, and German National Socialism* by Stefan Kuhl (New York: Oxford University Press, 1994).

Eugenics theory began before the Holocaust, then went into hiding

Eugenics as a "science" eventually went into hiding after World War II when the truth emerged about the eugenic Holocaust in Nazi Germany, but eugenic thinking became institutionalized in the way Americans think about race.

Economics became the measure of human worth. In many ways, the lie that a person's worth can be determined in economic terms drives civilization. Parents decide to limit childbearing or abort a child based on their financial condition. Millionaires use their foundations to target the world's poor for population control, based on economics.

Is Jesus thinking what you are thinking? Or is He thinking that the inner cities are a harvest field waiting for the Lord's laborers to wake up?

Long before Hitler discovered eugenics, American eugenics gained momentum from Margaret Sanger. She was an unlikely crusader for the day—this fiery, red-headed woman.

Like all true eugenicists, Sanger set herself up as an expert in assisting the process of human evolution. Since she believed that weaker races—people like poverty-stricken Black residents of the inner-city—are wasting resources and are doomed to extinction, she determined to help them along. One of her most innocent-sounding strategies was to help frazzled, poverty-stricken women to have fewer babies through birth control and abortion. Behind the scenes, however, she rejoiced at her success in discouraging reproduction among the less favored races.

Force society to stop helping the poor—"stupid, cruel sentimentalism"

Sanger wrote openly that charity and ministry to the poor were "stupid, cruel sentimentalism" because those people were a burden on society. Instead of portraying children of the poor as children of God, sons and daughters being born into human families with a mother and father, she used the terminology usually reserved for animals but applied them to people, degrading phrases such as "chance and chaotic breeding."

". . . the most urgent problem to-day is how to limit and discourage the over-fertility of the mentally and physically defective. Possibly drastic and Spartan methods may be forced upon American society if it continues complacently **to encourage the chance and chaotic breeding that has resulted from our stupid, cruel sentimentalism."** [300]

Margaret Sanger, *Pivot of Civilization*

Almost single-handedly, Sanger initiated a program that would eventually reduce the potential population of an entire people group—the disfavored race of Black Americans—by millions. According to abortion statistics alone, millions of Black children never arrived, and never grew up to take their place on God's earth.

Genocide by abortion is much more popular among Black women than it is among White women. *Black women have bought the devil's lie.*

Births of unfit—"greatest present menace to civilization"—Sanger

For years, until the experience with Hitler gave eugenics a bad name and she had to keep her philosophies secret, Sanger's publications were filled with her commitment to eugenics. In her book *Pivot of Civilization,* she spoke of "the lack of balance between the birth rate of the 'unfit' and the 'fit,'

VISION FOR BLACK AMERICA:

THEY WILL STOP THE ELIMINATION OF THEIR RACE.

Margaret Sanger wrote of "the lack of balance between the birth rate of the 'unfit' and the 'fit,' admittedly the greatest present menace to civilization." [301]

The Bible says, "But if you favor some people over others, you are committing a sin." —James 2:9 NLT

admittedly the greatest present menace to civilization." [302]

She said it was urgent to decrease the number of children born to *"inferior classes, . . . the feeble-minded, the mentally defective, the poverty-stricken."* [303]

---

[300] Margaret Sanger, *Pivot of Civilization*. Online at ftp://uiarchive.cso.uiuc.edu/pub/etext/gutenberg/etext99/pvcvl10.txt.
[301] Ibid.
[302] Ibid.
[303] Ibid.

W. E. B. DuBois helps deal with "ignorant Negroes"

Sanger developed a great deal of notoriety from news stories about her disobedience to laws against birth control, and she used her books and publications as powerful weapons to win people to her cause of eugenics.

In 1932, *The Birth Control Review,* a magazine that she had founded but had since left to her successors to edit, devoted an entire issue to the "Negro problem." Even well-known Black leaders like W. E. B. DuBois, a charter member of the NAACP, wrote articles to exhort Blacks to reduce their population.

DuBois compared people to vegetables and accepted unequal value of people as fact. He wrote:

> *"On the other hand, the mass of ignorant Negroes still breed carelessly and disastrously, so that the increase among Negroes, even more than the increase among whites, is from that part of the population least intelligent and fit, and least able to rear their children properly. . . .*

> *"Moreover, they are quite led away by the fallacy of numbers. They want the Black race to survive. They are cheered by a census return of increasing numbers and a high rate of increase. They must learn that **among human races and groups, as among vegetables, quality and not mere quantity really counts.**"*

> W.E.B. DuBois, "Black Folk and Birth Control"
> *Birth Control Review*, June 1932[304]

Other prominent pastors and doctors added their voices to the message. How many knew they were participating in Black self-genocide?

Population research tainted by eugenics

Guttmacher Institute and Eugenics. Sanger founded a research arm that became the Guttmacher Institute, named after Alan Guttmacher. He was a president of Planned Parenthood and a former vice-president of the American Eugenics Society. Eugenics, Planned Parenthood, and

---

[304] *Birth Control Review* issues and many other pro-life resources are available online from Life Dynamics at https://lifedynamics.com/library/. The URL for the June 1932 issue of *Birth Control Review* where this article by DuBois appeared is https://lifedynamics.com/app/uploads/2015/09/1932-06-June.pdf.

Guttmacher Institute research are intertwined and based on the eugenics lie that some people can decide that other people are unfit and determine how to reduce the number of unfit people on earth.

Why People Believe Big Lies

Generations of Black women have been told that Planned Parenthood is their friend instead of an agent of Black genocide. They are told that they should not have to deal with the pain, expense, and frustration of having a baby, except on their own terms. They are encouraged to kill an unseen child in the womb—who already has a beating heart—for the sake of themselves or the children they already have.

Lie: There is a positive benefit to murder of the innocent. Prosperity requires spreading your money among fewer children.

Truth: All life is sacred, and when a baby is conceived in the womb this is a divine trust from God. Prosperity means you have *many* children, and not only those who belong to the "favored races."

The LORD will grant you abundant prosperity--in the fruit of your womb, the young of your livestock and the crops of your ground--in the land He swore to your ancestors to give you.[305]

Blacks are victims of a classic propaganda technique—the big lie

Some lies are so big that people suspend disbelief. They can't believe anyone would tell such a whopper, so they swallow the lie—hook, line, sinker, fisherman, fishing boots, and fishing pole.

---

[305] Deuteronomy 28:11 NIV.

Lie: Sanger said birth control was only about women's rights to have fewer babies—or none. Barren sex is best—free from submission to men and devoid of children.

Truth: Sanger wanted Black women and other poor women of lower races to have fewer babies because she was a eugenicist who believed in fit and unfit races, and Blacks were not members of her favored race. She used lies about women's choice and sexual pleasure to persuade descendants of slaves to practice self-genocide.

Buying into the lie. Black women fight to have abortions and to keep them easily accessible. All the time, they are dooming themselves and their generation to the wrath of God and the decline of their race at the rate of millions of people. They are denying their God-given instincts to love their husbands and nurture their children.

Eugenics covered up by the big lie

Sanger wrote prolifically and spoke with great clarity about her passion for decreasing the birth rate of people she considered unfit because they were poor, involved in crime, or apparently incapable of being educated. She blatantly exposed her motives to the world, in print, apparently assuming that the victims of her diabolical plan would be too ignorant or unexposed to ever read her writings.

Through birth control and abortion, Planned Parenthood, the organization she founded, continues to devalue unborn Black babies as non-persons, just as the U.S. Constitution and the Confederate Constitution described slaves.

Slavery has been referred to as the "peculiar institution." Planned Parenthood is a peculiar name for an organization that prevents millions of people from becoming parents through Black self-genocide.

Don't you see it, Black America?

Somebody planned that you would not have a race.

Do the research!

Jewish Eugenics by Hitler Covered by His Big Lies

Adolph Hitler, Germany's leader who started World War II, was a master of using lies as propaganda to accomplish his purposes, but initially he claimed that his enemies, the Jews, were the liars.

In Hitler's book *Mein Kampf* (usually translated "My Struggle"), he said that the Aryans were the Master Race and the Jews were the unfit race who must be dominated in the struggle of life.

Hitler claimed that Jews were dangerous liars. However, in describing their supposed characteristic of lying he was actually describing himself. His propaganda chief, Joseph Goebbels, had no scruples about truth and few restrictions from Hitler on what he could publish as long as it dominated the minds of the German people.

The purpose of Hitler's propaganda was achieving the power necessary to push through his goals. It did not have to be true. It only had to be persuasive.

Hitler explained about big lies and then used them

There are lies, and then there are big lies. Hitler wrote this in *Mein Kampf* about why people believe big lies:

> "*. . . in the big lie there is always a certain force of credibility; because the broad masses of a nation are always more easily corrupted in the deeper strata of their emotional nature than consciously or voluntarily; and thus in the primitive simplicity of their minds they more readily fall victims to the big lie than the small lie, since they themselves often tell small lies in little matters but would be ashamed to resort to large-scale falsehoods. It would never come into their heads to fabricate colossal untruths, and they would not believe that others could have the impudence to distort the truth so infamously. Even though the facts which prove this to be so may be brought clearly to their minds, they will still doubt and waver and will continue to think that there may be some other explanation. For the grossly impudent lie always leaves traces behind it, even after it has been nailed down, a fact which is known to all expert liars in this world and to all who conspire together in the art of lying.*

These people know only too well
how to use falsehood for the basest purposes. *"*[306]

Facts are irrelevant when big lies are believed

Again, excerpting a portion from the quote above, Hitler said that facts will not change the mind of someone who believes a big lie.

> *"Even though the facts which prove this to be so may be*
> *brought clearly to their minds, they will still doubt and*
> *waver and will continue to*
> *think that there may be some other explanation."*[307]

When Black Americans hear the truth that there is a diabolical plan of eugenics targeting them for extinction, they are usually so sold out to the lie that they dispute plain facts. They can even read Margaret Sanger's own words and still insist that she didn't really mean what it seems. Black women think she was for them when she was actually against them, and she said so plainly.

Lie: Satan told the woman in the Garden that she would not die if she disobeyed God. She would become like God.

> *"'You won't die!' the serpent hissed. 'God knows that your*
> *eyes will be opened when you eat it. You will become just*
> *like God, knowing everything, both good and evil.'"*[308]

Truth: Satan is the father of lies, as Jesus said.[309] Everyone who opposes the direct commandments of God will die.

---

[306] Adolph Hitler, *Mein Kampf,* Chapter X, "Why The Second Reich Collapsed." Published in two volumes in 1925 and 1926 by Franz Eher Nachfolger. Online at http://gutenberg.net.au/ebooks02/0200601.txt.
[307] Ibid.
[308] Genesis 3:4-5 NLT.
[309] See John 8:44.

God Judges Sin—If You Die in Sin You Have No Redress

Sometimes God's judgment for sin brings sudden death, as in the case of Ananias and Sapphira[310] in the New Testament or Achan's sin[311] in the Old Testament.

At other times His judgment is delayed, but it always comes. Why risk His wrath by defying His standards?

"I call heaven and earth to record this day against you, that I have set before you life and death, blessing and cursing: therefore choose life, that both thou and thy seed may live."[312]

"And if it seem evil unto you to serve the LORD, choose you this day whom ye will serve; whether the gods which your fathers served that were on the other side of the flood, or the gods of the Amorites, in whose land ye dwell: but as for me and my house, we will serve the LORD.[313]

No excuse for buying into the lie. The German people claimed ignorance in spite of irrefutable evidence that Hitler was attempting to exterminate the Jews. They heard his racist rhetoric. They saw the businesses of their Jewish neighbors being destroyed and even threw the rocks themselves on *Kristallnacht*. They knew that Jews disappeared in the night. Hitler's propaganda machine spit out such big lies that they couldn't seem to connect the dots.

The Planned Parenthood propaganda machine is so effective that the federal government and major foundations spend hundreds of millions of dollars to kill children of all races, and especially Blacks. About 43 percent of Planned Parenthood's annual income, $553.7 million, came from government grants and reimbursements.[314] Millions of dollars of your tax money are being used for Black genocide.

---

[310] See Acts 5.
[311] See Joshua 7.
[312] Deuteronomy 30:19 KJV.
[313] Joshua 24:15 KJV.
[314] "Summary of Financial Activities" (Planned Parenthood Federation of America, Inc., *Annual Report 2015-2016*), p. 16. Online at their website: https://issuu.com/actionfund/docs/2014-2015_annual_report_final_20mb/1

Six million Jews died in the tragedy of the German Holocaust. Seventeen million Blacks have died from abortion alone since 1973. Planned Parenthood has far surpassed *"Der Führer"* in its pursuit of a master race.

Reproduction v. Depopulation

When the population of a nation or a people group is in a state of "depopulation," it is below the level where it can reproduce itself. It will eventually die out. Some nations of the world are on the brink of a depopulation crisis, such as Russia, France, and the Nordic countries. The rate of childbirth is below the level of deaths. They are not replacing themselves. Black Americans could have produced so many more great men and women of God, statesmen, inventors, and literary geniuses.

Time to act now—the land is desolate and houses lack a man

The Lord says that we will know that the times are urgent when "the cities are laid waste and without inhabitant, the houses are without a man, the land is utterly desolate."[315] That describes the fatherless, spiritually destitute wasteland of America's inner cities today.

> *"And He said, 'Go, and tell this people: "Keep on hearing, but do not understand; keep on seeing, but do not perceive. Make the heart of this people dull, and their ears heavy, and shut their eyes; lest they see with their eyes, and hear with their ears, and understand with their heart, and return and be healed."' Then I said, 'Lord, how long?' And He answered: 'Until the cities are laid waste and without inhabitant, the houses are without a man, the land is utterly desolate.'"[316]*

Blood on the hands of Christians

What should Christians do? We should warn the perpetrators of Black genocide—both the mothers and their mentors—that judgment awaits if they do not turn to God and repent.

---

[315] Isaiah 6:11 NKJV.
[316] Isaiah 6:9-11 NKJV.

*"So you, son of man: I have made you a watchman for the
house of Israel; therefore you shall hear a word from My
mouth and warn them for Me. When I say to the wicked, 'O
wicked man, you shall surely die!' and you do not speak to
warn the wicked from his way, that wicked man shall die in
his iniquity; but his blood I will require at your hand.
Nevertheless if you warn the wicked to turn from his way,
and he does not turn from his way, he shall die in his
iniquity; but you have delivered your soul."*[317]

The Church must again provide alternatives for women such as homes for those who are poor and pregnant out of wedlock and adoption agencies encouraging couples to adopt a Black baby. Before a child is conceived, the Church can teach the virtue of chastity and the importance of marrying and raising a family together. That is our challenge and responsibility to this generation.

God Favors the Weak, Not the Strong

Evolution. In the evolutionist mentality, because Blacks are a disfavored race, they are locked into failure. The most that can be hoped for is that a few can be trained for some useful purpose, but what about the masses? Forget it. They have no purpose so their deaths are welcomed. They have been caught up in this wave of false teaching, but they need to create a new wave based on the teachings of God.

Creation. The Bible teaches the value of all human life. Every person can have the favor of God. He or she starts out with equal worth because they are created by God, in His image and likeness. [318]

Salvation. Jesus died for the sins of the whole world—not just the dominant race. He gave every individual the power to become like God. Jesus especially reached out to the lowly and said that the meek will inherit the earth.[319] Any person can become great through Christ.

*"But as many as received him, to them gave he
power to become the sons of God,
even to them that believe on his name."*[320]

---

[317] Ezekiel 33:7-9 NKJV.
[318] See Genesis 1:26 KJV.
[319] See Matthew 5:5 KJV.
[320] John 1:12 KJV.

Favoring the weak and despised. Paul said "the foolishness of God is wiser than men" and God favors the "base things of the world," not the strong. He chooses those who are "despised," not the "mighty."[321]

> *"God chose things despised by the world, things counted*
> *as nothing at all, and used them to bring to nothing what*
> *the world considers important, so that no one can ever*
> *boast in the presence of God."[322]*

Seed of God inside. Our value is not determined by brute survival but by the seed of God inside of us.

PRAYER

My Father, help us to prepare in our spirits and our minds for divine commitment and a step of faith that will end Black self-genocide in our lifetime. May people seek Your face as never before. Let the fire of God fall. Help them to walk according to the standard of Your Word. Give them a sense of divine destiny—that You have chosen them and have a purpose for their lives.

What you're going to do next is beyond measure. I come against every work of darkness; I speak healing to every wounded spirit. Devil, loose them and let them go. I forbid you to touch them any longer.

Thank You, Father. It's done. In Jesus' name I pray. Amen.

Cry out to God for Black America,
Please don't die!

---

[321] Excerpts from 1 Corinthians 1 KJV.
[322] 1 Corinthians1:28-29 NLT.

APPENDIX

APPENDIX CONTENTS

Scripture References Included in the Book

Sources in Each Chapter from Footnotes

Index

Vision for Black America Series from the Book

Author's Bio

SCRIPTURE REFERENCES

1 Corinthians 1:18-20 NLT

1 Corinthians 1:20-21 NLT

1 Corinthians 1:26-29 KJV

1 Corinthians 14:39-40 NLT

1 Corinthians 15:46 KJV

1 Corinthians 4:14-16, KJV

1 Corinthians 4:9 NLT

1 Corinthians1:28-29 NLT

1 Corinthians 14:1-2 NLT

1 John 1:7 NKJV

1 John 5:14

1 Peter 2:10 NLT

1 Peter 2:9

1 Samuel 17:24, 26 NLT

1 Thessalonians 1:7-8 NLT

1 Thessalonians 5:12-13 NLT

2 Chronicles 7:14 NLT

2 Corinthians 5:9-19

2 Timothy 2:1-2 KJV

2 Timothy 4:2 NLT

Acts 5:20-30 NLT

Acts 10:34 NLT

Acts 14:23 KJV

Acts 17:25-27 NLT

Acts 2:1 NKJV

Acts 26:19 NKJV

Acts 5

Acts 6:4 NLT

Acts 26:17-18 NLT

Colossians 2:15 NKJV

Colossians 3:1-3 NLT

Daniel 12:3 NLT

Deuteronomy 5:16 NLT

Deuteronomy 8:18 NLT

Deuteronomy 28:9-11

Deuteronomy 30:19 KJV

Ecclesiastes 3:1, 11 KJV

Ecclesiastes 4:1 KJV

Ephesians 1:3 NLT

Ephesians 3:20 NLT

Ephesians 3:21 KJV

Ephesians 4

Ephesians 4:11-16 NLT

Ephesians 5:25 KJV

Ephesians 6: 1-3 NLT

Ephesians 6: 11-12 NLT

Exodus 2:14 NKJV

Exodus 8:22 NLT

Exodus 20:2 NLT

Exodus 20:12

Ezekiel 16:43-45 NLT

Ezekiel 33:7-9 NKJV

Ezekiel 37:3-10 NLT

Galatians 2:19-20 NLT

Galatians 4:19-20 KJV

Genesis 1:26 KJV

Genesis 3:1-5

Genesis 3:4-5 NLT	John 1:1-12
Genesis 4:10	John 13:14-15 KJV
Genesis 13:15	John 14:16-17 KJV
Genesis 22:17-18 NKJV	John 17:21 NLT
Habakkuk 2:1 NKJV	John 3:3
Hebrews 5:14 KJV	John 3:16 KJV
Hebrews 11:1 KJV	John 5:5-9 NLT
Hebrews 11:35-40 NLT	John 6:63-64 NLT
Hebrews 12: 1	John 8:34
Hebrews 2:9 KJV	John 8:44
Hebrews 7:24-26 NLT	John 15:16 NKJV
Hebrews 11:1 NLT	Joshua 7
Isaiah 6:9-11 NKJV	Joshua 24:15 KJV
Isaiah 40:3 and	Jude 22-23 KJV
Isaiah 53:3	Leviticus 19:2-3
Isaiah 40:12	Luke 1:13-17 NLT
Isaiah 53:11 KJV	Luke 1:37
Isaiah 58:12 NKJV	Luke 4:8
Isaiah 61:3	Luke 4:18-19 NKJV
Isaiah 62:11 NLT	Luke 6:38 KJV
Isaiah 66:7-9 NLT	Luke 10:2-3 NLT
Isaiah 66:8, 14 NLT	Luke 13:26-28 NKJV
James 2:5	Luke 14:21-23 NLT
James 2:9 NLT	Luke 15:11-27 NLT
James 5:20 NKJV	Luke 17:4 NLT
Jeremiah 13:17 NKJV	Luke 18:1
Jeremiah 29:11-14 NLT	Malachi 4:5-6
Job 29:15-17 NLT	Mark 10:8 NLT
Job 38:4-11 NLT	Mark 10:27 NLT

Mark 16:15-18 NLT

Matthew 3:3

Matthew 11:4-5 NLT

Matthew 16:18-19 KJV

Matthew 17:21 KJV

Matthew 18:19-20 NLT

Matthew 19:28 NLT

Matthew 22:8-10 NLT

Matthew 25:10-13 NLT

Matthew 28:18-20 NLT

Matthew 5:5 KJV

Matthew 5:10-16

Matthew 5:42 NLT

Matthew 6:13 KJV

Matthew 9:10-13 NLT

Matthew 9:35-38 NLT

Matthew 15:4 NKJV

Matthew 23:31, 36 NLT

Nehemiah 1:8-9 NLT

Nehemiah 9:27 NLT

Numbers 11:12 KJV

Numbers 11:26-30 NLT

Numbers 11:29 NLT

Numbers 27:18-21 NLT

Proverbs 8:1-6 NLT

Proverbs 29:18

Proverbs 30:11-14 NKJV

Psalm 24:1-2 NLT

Psalm 34:17 NLT

Psalm 50:5 KJV

Psalm 60:1-4 NLT

Psalm 73:16-19 NLT

Psalm 85:3 KJV

Psalm 85:6-7 NLT

Psalm 123:1-2 NLT

Psalm 127:4-5 NLT

Psalm 133:1 NKJV

Proverbs 22:7 KJV

Proverbs 29:18 KJV

Revelation 3:8-9 NLT

Revelation 3:19-21 KJV

Romans 1:21 KJV

Romans 2:11

Romans 3:23

Romans 6:6-11 NLT

Romans 8: 18-28

Romans 8:29-37

Titus 3:5-6 KJV

Zechariah 3:2 NLT

Zephaniah 3:18 KJV

Zephaniah 3:19 NKJV

SOURCES IN EACH CHAPTER FROM FOOTNOTES

INTRODUCTION

Library of Congress exhibit on the 50th anniversary of *Brown v. Board of Education*. Online at http://www.loc.gov/exhibits/brown/brown-brown.html.

Brown V. Board of Education, 347 U.S. 483 (1954). 347 U.S. 483. Online http://caselaw.lp.findlaw.com/scripts/getcase.pl?court=US&vol=347&invol=483#f10.

Kiri Davis, "A Girl Like Me." Online at https://www.youtube.com/watch?v=z0BxFRu_SOw.

CHAPTER 1

John Winthrop, "A Modell of Christian Charity" (1630). Hanover Historical Texts Project. Corrected to match modern usage. Original online at http://history.hanover.edu/texts/winthmod.html.

Declaration of Independence. The full text is online at http://www.archives.gov/exhibits/charters/declaration_transcript.html.

"Teaching with Documents: The Fight for Equal Rights: Black Soldiers in the Civil War." Online at https://www.archives.gov/education/lessons/blacks-civil-war/.

J. David Hacker, "Disunion. Miscounting the Dead." New York Times, September 20, 2011. Online at http://opinionator.blogs.nytimes.com/2011/09/20/recounting-the-dead/#more-105317. Accessed October 2016. This source also includes a bibliography.

The Civil War death statistics estimated a century ago were too low because of many difficult conditions in those days for recording facts. The Confederacy was in disarray. There were no systematic ways to count the dead or even bury them all. Many died after the war was over from wounds suffered and disease.

The Confederate Constitution is available online at the University of Georgia http://www.libs.uga.edu/hargrett/selections/confed/const.html.

Jefferson Davis, President of the Confederate States of America, "General Orders, No. 111" (Richmond, Virginia, December 24, 1862). Source: The Freedmen and Southern Society Project. Online at http://www.history.umd.edu/Freedmen/pow.htm.

"Emancipation Proclamation." National Archives. Online at http://www.ourdocuments.gov/doc.php?doc=34.

The text of Patrick Henry's speech is online at https://www.history.org/almanack/life/politics/giveme.cfm.

The full text of our national anthem is at the Smithsonian, online at http://amhistory.si.edu/starspangledbanner/the-lyrics.aspx.

National Association for the Advancement of Colored People.

James Weldon Johnson, "Lift Every Voice and Sing." Online at http://www.pbs.org/black-culture/explore/black-authors-spoken-word-poetry/lift-every-voice-and-sing/.

William H. Carney's personal account is available on the website of the elementary school in New Bedford, Massachusetts, that is named after him. Online at http://www.newbedford.k12.ma.us/elementary/whc.htm.

Jane Waters, "William H. Carney." New Bedford Black Heritage Trail. Online at
http://nbhistoricalsociety.org/Important-Figures/sergeant-william-h-carney/. Accessed September 2016.

Thomas Sowell, *Ethnic America: A History* (New York, Basic Books, 1981), p. 186-190.

All quotations from the United States Constitution online at
http://www.ourdocuments.gov/doc.php?flash=true&doc=9&page=transcript. Accessed October 2016.

Dred Scott vs. John F. A. Sandford (1857). Online at
http://www.ourdocuments.gov/print_friendly.php?page=transcript&doc=29&title=Transcript+of+Dred
+Scott+v.+Sanford+percent281857percent29.

"Madame C. J. Walker." Online at http://www.biography.com/people/madam-cj-walker-
9522174#success-and-philanthropy.

"The Black Population:2010. 2010 Census Briefs." Online at
https://www.census.gov/prod/cen2010/briefs/c2010br-06.pdf.

CHAPTER 2

Allison Pohle, "Massachusetts is the 8th most popular destination for college students." Online at
http://www.boston.com/news/education/2015/09/01/massachusetts-is-the-8th-most-popular-destination-
for-college-students.

Phillis Wheatley, *Memoir and Poems of Phillis Wheatley, a Native African and a Slave. Dedicated to
the Friends of the Africans* (Boston: Geo. W. Light, 1834). Online at
http://www.vcu.edu/engweb/webtexts/Wheatley/brought.html.

William W. Layton, "The Spring of 1863—A Call to Arms" (The Smithsonian Associates Civil War
E-Mail Newsletter, Volume 2, Number 3). Online at
http://civilwarstudies.org/articles/Vol_2/layton.htm.

Carter Woodson, *The Mind of the Negro* (Washington, D.C., 1926), 544. Quoted in History Matters,
the U.S. History Course on the Web. Online at http://historymatters.gmu.edu/d/6215/.

Clara Merritt DeBoer, "Blacks and the American Missionary Association" Online at
http://www.ucc.org/about-us_hidden-histories_blacks-and-the-american.

MDAH "Sovereignty Commission Online: Agency History." Online at
http://www.mdah.ms.gov/arrec/digital_archives/sovcom/scagencycasehistory.php. Home page
http://www.mdah.ms.gov/arrec/digital_archives/sovcom/.

General Laws of the State of Mississippi, 1956, Chapter 365, 520-524.
http://www.mdah.ms.gov/arrec/digital_archives/sovcom/notes.php.

Reconstruction was the period of time after the North won the Civil War and the U. S. Congress
mandated and enforced conditions of liberty for the freed slaves in the South.

Douglas O. Linder, "Bending Toward Justice: John Doar and the Mississippi Burning Trial." This is
an excellent resource for understanding the struggle. Online at
http://law2.umkc.edu/faculty/projects/ftrials/doaressay.html. Accessed September 2016.

Matt Schudel, "John M. Doar, top federal prosecutor during civil rights era, dies at 92." Washington
Post, November 11, 2014. Online at https://www.washingtonpost.com/national/john-m-doar-top-
federal-prosecutor-during-civil-rights-era-dies-at-92/2014/11/11/31399db0-69c5-11e4-a31c-
77759fc1eacc_story.html.

John F. Kennedy, "Civil Rights Address" delivered 11 June 1963. Online at American Rhetoric http://www.americanrhetoric.com/speeches/jfkcivilrights.htm.

Douglas O. Linder, "Bending Toward Justice: John Doar and the Mississippi Burning Trial." Originally published in Mississippi Law Journal (Volume 72, No. 2, Winter 2002). Online at http://www.law.umkc.edu/faculty/projects/ftrials/trialheroes/doaressay.html.

Lewis Tappan, *The Life of Arthur Tappan*, pp. 230-231. Hurd and Houghton, 1870. Available online from Google books.

"Statement of the reasons which have induced the Students of Lane Seminary, to dissolve their connection with the Institution. Cincinnati: 1834." The Liberator, vol. 5, no. 2, Jan. 10, 1835, pp. [5]-6. Online at http://oberlin.edu/external/EOG/LaneDebates/RebelsDefence.htm .

CHAPTER 3

Charles H. Spurgeon, "Open-Air Preaching: A Sketch of Its History and Remarks Thereon." Online at http://www.biblebelievers.com/StreetPreaching2.html.

J. Edwin Orr, *The Light of the Nations* (Grand Rapids, MI: Eerdmans, 1963).

Thomas Lewis Johnson, *Twenty Eight Years a Slave*, pp. 14-16. Online at https://archive.org/details/twentyeightyears00johnrich.

Katharine Lee Bates, "America the Beautiful." Online at Library of Congress site http://lcweb2.loc.gov/diglib/ihas/loc.natlib.ihas.100010520/lyrics.html.

Maggie Gallagher, "Fatherless Boys Grow Up Into Dangerous Men" (Wall Street Journal, December 1, 1998). Report of a study by the University of California's Cynthia Harper and Princeton's Sara McLanahan. Referenced online at http://www.fathermag.com/news/2770-WSJ81201.shtml.

CHAPTER 4

Francis Asbury, "Letter to James Quinn" (a Methodist preacher for nearly 50 years). Wesley Center for Applied Theology. Online at http://wesley.nnu.edu/holiness_tradition/asbury_journal/vol_II/ch13.htm.

Ezra Squier Tipple, *Francis Asbury: The Prophet of the Long Road* (New York, Cincinnati: The Methodist Book Concern, 1916). Public domain. Available online at www.Archive.org.

Source of statistics—Asbury University website, www.asbury.edu.

CHAPTER 5

Winston Churchill, "Withhold No Sacrifice." Chateau Laurier, Ottawa, 9 November 1954. Online at http://www.winstonchurchill.org/resources/quotations/499-famous-quotations-and-stories.

109th CONGRESS, 1st Session, S. RES. 39, "Apologizing to the victims of lynching and the descendants of those victims for the failure of the Senate to enact anti-lynching legislation." Online at http://thomas.loc.gov/bss/109search.html. Enter search using text from above title.

U.S. Bureau of the Census, "Living Arrangements of Black Children Under 18 Years Old" (1960-2005). Online at http://www.census.gov/population/socdemo/hh-fam/ch3.pdf.

Patrick F. Fagan and Christina Hadford, "The Fifth Annual Index of Family Belonging and Rejection. Family Research Council Marriage and Religion Research Institute, February 12, 2015. Online at http://downloads.frc.org/EF/EF15B28.pdf.

Gaines, W. J. (Wesley John) (1840-1912), *The Negro and the White Man* (Philadelphia: AME Publishing House, 1897), pp. 143-144. Electronic Edition online at http://docsouth.unc.edu/church/gaines/gaines.html. Gaines was a Bishop in the African Methodist Episcopal Church and a co-founder of Morris Brown College in Atlanta. He also served as vice president of Payne Theological Seminary.

Allen Parker, *Recollections of Slavery Times* (Worcester, Mass.: Chas. W. Burbank & Co., 1895), Chapter 7. Online at http://docsouth.unc.edu/neh/parker/menu.html.

"Like Something the Lord Made." Longform Reprints. Originally published in the Washingtonian. Online at http://reprints.longform.org/something-the-lord-made-mccabe.

Harriet Beecher Stowe, *The Key to Uncle Tom's Cabin* (Boston: Jewett, 1854), p. 41. Online at http://jefferson.village.virginia.edu/utc/uncletom/key/kyhp.html.

Josiah Henson (1789-1883), *The Life of Josiah Henson*, Formerly a Slave Now an Inhabitant of Canada, as Narrated by Himself:. Online at https://archive.org/details/lifeofjosiahhens00hens.

Dennis Adams and Grace Morris, "Robert Smalls—War Hero and Legislator (1839-1915)" (Beaufort, SC, County Library). Online at http://www.bcgov.net/bftlib/smalls.htm.

William J., Simmons, *Men of Mark: Eminent, Progressive and Rising* (Cleveland, OH: Geo. M. Rewell & Co., 1887). Online: http://docsouth.unc.edu/neh/simmons/simmons.html.

Robin Mazyck and Charlene Israel, "An Unlikely Hero." CBN News, April 21, 2007. Online at http://www.cbn.com/CBNnews/138685.aspx.

Benjamin Brawley, *A Social History of the American Negro*. Online at http://www.gutenberg.org/files/12101/12101-h/12101-h/12101-h.htm.

Thomas Wentworth Higginson, "Negro Spirituals" (Atlantic Monthly, June 1867). Online at http://xroads.virginia.edu/~HYPER/TWH/Higg.html.

Julia Ward Howe, "Battle Hymn of the Republic." "The hymn appeared in the Atlantic Monthly in 1862. It was sung at the funerals of British statesman Winston Churchill, American senator Robert Kennedy, and American presidents Ronald Reagan and Richard Nixon." History and words to the song online at http://www.cyberhymnal.org/htm/b/h/bhymnotr.htm.

Nat Turner, *Confessions of Nat Turner* (1831). Full text online at http://etext.virginia.edu/toc/modeng/public/TurConf.html.

John Brown, "John Brown's Last Speech, November 2, 1859." Online at http://www.iath.virginia.edu/seminar/unit4/brown3.html.

Wellington Boone, *Breaking Through* (Nashville, TN: Broadman and Holman, 1996), p. 206.

"Racial Reconciliation," PCA 30th General Assembly, 2002, 30-53, III, Items 14 - 16, pp. 262 - 270. Online at http://www.pcahistory.org/pca/race.html.

"Mathematician and Astronomer Benjamin Banneker Was Born November 9, 1731." America's Story. Library of Congress. Online at http://www.americaslibrary.gov/cgi-bin/page.cgi/jb/colonial/banneker_2.

"Copy of a Letter from Benjamin Banneker, &c. Maryland, Baltimore County, August 19, 1791." Online at http://etext.virginia.edu/readex/24073.html.

Thomas Sowell, "Random Thoughts" (Townhall.com, Thursday, June 24, 2004). Online at http://www.townhall.com/columnists/ThomasSowell/2004/06/24/random_thoughts.

E.R. Carter, *The black side: a partial history of the business, religious and educational side of the Negro in Atlanta, Ga.* Online at http://fax.libs.uga.edu/E185x93xG4xC323/#/ .

Booker T. Washington, *Up from Slavery.* Chapter VII, "Early Days at Tuskegee." E-text online at http://xroads.virginia.edu/~HYPER/WASHINGTON/ch07.html.

Booker T. Washington Papers, University of Illinois. Online at http://www.historycooperative.org/btw/Vol.6/html/370.html.

Fisk Jubilee Singers history online at http://www.fiskjubileesingers.org/our_history.html.

"Quotes from Dr. Carver." George Washington Carver National Monument. Online at http://www.nps.gov/archive/gwca/expanded/quotes.htm.

William J. Federer, George Washington Carver: His Life & Faith in His Own Words (St. Louis: Amerisearch, 2003), p. 54.

The Narrative of Bethany Veney, A Slave Woman. Worcester, MA, 1889. Press of Geo. H. Ellis, 141 Franklin Street, Boston. Online at http://docsouth.unc.edu/fpn/veney/veney.html.

CHAPTER 6

U.S. Census Bureau, C3. Living Arrangements of Children Under 18 Years1 and Marital Status of Parents, by Age, Sex, Race, and Hispanic Origin2 and Selected Characteristics of the Child for All Children: 2015. Online at http://www.census.gov/hhes/families/data/cps2015C.html.

Cynthia C. Harper and Sara S. McLanahan. "Father Absence and Youth Incarceration." Annual Meeting of the American Sociological Association (San Francisco). 1998. Referenced online at http://www.smartmarriages.com/factsheet.html.

Larry L. Bumpass and James A. Sweet. 1995. "Cohabitation, Marriage and Union Stability: Preliminary Findings from NSFH2." NSFH Working Paper No. 65. Center for Demography and Ecology: University of Wisconsin-Madison. Referenced online at http://www.smartmarriages.com/factsheet.html.

Eileen Patten and Jens Manuel Krogstad, "Black child poverty rate holds steady, even as other groups see declines." Pew Research Center (July 14, 2015). Online at http://www.pewresearch.org/fact-tank/2015/07/14/black-child-poverty-rate-holds-steady-even-as-other-groups-see-declines/.

Jo Blanden, "'Bucking the trend:' What enables those who are disadvantaged in childhood to succeed later in life?" Working Paper No 31 Corporate Document Services. London: Department for Work and Pensions. Online at http://dera.ioe.ac.uk/7729/1/WP31.pdf. Accessed October 2016.

Margaret Sanger, *The Pivot of Civilization.* Entire book available online at http://www.gutenberg.org/files/1689/1689-h/1689-h.htm#2HCH0004.

U.S. Supreme Court, *Roe V. Wade,* 410 U.S. 113 (1973), 410 U.S. 113, *Roe Et Al. V. Wade, District Attorney Of Dallas County,* Appeal From The United States District Court For The Northern District Of Texas. No. 70-18. Argued December 13, 1971. Reargued October 11, 1972. Decided January 22, 1973. Online at http://caselaw.lp.findlaw.com/scripts/getcase.pl?court=US&vol=410&invol=113.

"Response," in *Percy Lavon Julian, A Tribute* (Jacksonville, Illinois: MacMurray College, 1972), pp. 24-25. Quoted in Percy Lavon Julian. National Academy of Science Biographical Memoirs. Online at http://www.nap.edu/html/biomems/pjulian.html#REF1.

"Tips for Parents." U.S. Department of Health and Human Services. Online at http://www.hhs.gov/ash/oah/adolescent-health-topics/reproductive-health/teen-pregnancy/tips-for-parents.html.

Bill Albert, "Who Most Influences Teens' Decisions about Sex? Parents: New Survey Findings Released" (October 4, 2016). The National Campaign to Prevent Teen and Unplanned Pregnancy. Online at https://thenationalcampaign.org/blog/who-most-influences-teens%E2%80%99-decisions-about-sex-parents-new-survey-findings-released.

Rob Schwarzwalder and Natasha Tax, "Daddy's Girl: How Fatherlessness Impacts Early Sexual Activity, Teen Pregnancy, and Sexual Abuse." Family Research Council. Online at http://downloads.frc.org/EF/EF15L32.pdf.

"New Study Finds Abstinence Pays Off in the Long Run." Article online at http://www.lifesite.net/ldn/2005/may/05050607.html. Study by Focus on the Family Medical Issues Analyst Reginald Finger, M.D., M.P.H.; Tonya Thelen, B.S.; John T. Vessey, Ph.D.; Joanna K. Mohn, M.D.; and Joshua R. Mann, M.D., M.P.H. Full study at Adolescent and Family Health website at http://www.afhjournal.org/toc.asp?issue=0304.

CHAPTER 7

James Weldon Johnson, *The Autobiography of an Ex-Colored Man.* Online at http://www.gutenberg.org/etext/11012. Johnson was the Black author who wrote "Lift Every Voice and Sing," known as the "Black National Anthem." (See also Chapter 1.) He was also an educator, lawyer, U.S. consul, and NAACP official.

Based on several recent estimates. Database of Transatlantic Slave Trade online at http://www.slavevoyages.org/ estimates at least 1,464,200 deaths at sea. (Database sponsors include Emory, Harvard, National Endowment for Humanities, and others.)

Tuskegee Institute, "Lynchings: By Year and Race." Online at http://law2.umkc.edu/faculty/projects/ftrials/shipp/lynchingyear.html.

This is a minimum estimate based on 50 million abortions through 2008 with 35% done by Blacks. CDC notes there is "no national requirement for data submission or reporting." Online at http://www.cdc.gov/reproductivehealth/data_stats/abortion.htm.

U.S. Department of Health and Human Services, Health Resources and Services Administration, Maternal and Child Health Bureau. Women's Health USA 2012. Rockville, Maryland: U.S. Department of Health and Human Services, 2013. Online at http://mchb.hrsa.gov/whusa12/search/search.html?zoom_query=women%27s+health+usa.

All statistics are for "non-Hispanic" Black and White women. Source: CDC, "Abortion Surveillance — United States, 2012, Surveillance Summaries, November 27, 2015 (the most recent data available at the time of this printing). Online at http://www.cdc.gov/mmwr/preview/mmwrhtml/ss6410a1.htm?s_cid=ss6410a1_e. Accessed October 2016.

Margaret Sanger, *The Pivot of Civilization.* Online at http://www.gutenberg.org/files/1689/1689-h/1689-h.htm.

Margaret Sanger, "Birth Control and Racial Betterment," *Birth Control Review* (February 1919). Online at https://lifedynamics.com/app/uploads/2015/09/1919-02-February.pdf.

All statistics are for "non-Hispanic" Black and White women. Source: CDC, "Abortion Surveillance — United States, 2012, Surveillance Summaries, November 27, 2015 (the most recent data available at the time of this printing). Online at http://www.cdc.gov/mmwr/preview/mmwrhtml/ss6410a1.htm?s_cid=ss6410a1_e.

Lilo T. Strauss, MA, Sonya B. Gamble, MS, Wilda Y. Parker, Douglas A. Cook, MBIS, Suzanne B. Zane, DVM, Saeed Hamdan, MD, PhD, "Abortion Surveillance 2004." Online at http://www.cdc.gov/mmwr/preview/mmwrhtml/ss5609a1.htm?s_cid=ss5609a1_e. Accessed October 2016.

Online at United Nations website: http://www.unhchr.ch/html/menu3/b/p_genoci.htm.

Encyclopaedia Britannica's Guide to Black History. Online at http://kids.britannica.com/blackhistory/article-9109538. Accessed October 2016.

Slaves legally affirmed as property by U.S. Supreme Court *Dred Scott vs. John F. A. Sandford* (1857). Online at http://www.ourdocuments.gov/print_friendly.php?page=transcript&doc=29&title=Transcript+of+Dred +Scott+v.+Sanford+percent281857percent29.

Charles Darwin, *On the Origin of the Species by Means of Natural Selection, or the Preservation of Favored Races in the Struggle for Life.* Online at http://www.literature.org/Works/Charles-Darwin/index.html.

Francis Galton, "Hereditary Character and Talent," Part I (*Macmillan's Magazine*, vol. 12, 1865, pp. 157-166). Online at http://galton.org/essays/1860-1869/galton-1865-macmillan-hereditary-talent.html.

See *The Nazi Connection—Eugenics, American Racism, and German National Socialism* by Stefan Kuhl (New York: Oxford University Press, 1994).

Birth Control Review issues and many other pro-life resources are available online from Life Dynamics at https://lifedynamics.com/library/. The URL for the June 1932 issue of *Birth Control Review* where this article by DuBois appeared is https://lifedynamics.com/app/uploads/2015/09/1932-06-June.pdf.

Adolph Hitler, *Mein Kampf,* Chapter X, "Why The Second Reich Collapsed." Published in two volumes in 1925 and 1926 by Franz Eher Nachfolger. Online at http://gutenberg.net.au/ebooks02/0200601.txt.

"Summary of Financial Activities" (Planned Parenthood Federation of America, Inc., Annual Report 2015-2016), p. 16. Online at their website: https://issuu.com/actionfund/docs/2014-2015_annual_report_final_20mb/1.

INDEX

VISION FOR BLACK AMERICA

The logo of Wellington Boone Ministries that appears with the "Vision for Black America" series throughout *Black Self-Genocide* (see also list below) shows Jesus washing His disciples' feet. *(See John 13.)* Christian humility is a key to revival and restoration in resolving America's racial crisis.

Prayer Affirmations to Declare on Behalf of Black America

Page 2. All Americans will finally see how previous racism against Blacks has caused cultural self-hatred. ". . . to separate them from others of similar age and qualifications solely because of their race generates a feeling of inferiority as to their status in the community that may affect their hearts and minds in a way unlikely ever to be undone." (*Brown v. Board of Education*).

Page 54. Black Americans will inspire a new wave of students to work with them for lasting change. John 15:16 NKJV.

Page 65. Black Americans will see killers convicted and pray for their salvation before it is too late. Psalm 73:16-19 NLT.

Page 69. Black Americans will become benefactors like Arthur and Lewis Tappan to finance next movement of college students. Luke 6:38 KJV.

Page 83. Black Americans will receive the comfort of the Holy Spirit's truth. John 14:16-17 KJV.

Page 84. Black Americans will experience God's mighty power and receive hope. Ephesians 3:20 NLT.

Page 85. Black Americans will know that God hears and answers prayer. Psalm 34:17 NLT.

Page 92. Christ will live in them. Galatians 2:19-20. NLT.

Page 96. Black Americans will see the Church unite across all the dividing lines. 1 Corinthians 14:1-2 NLT.

Page 144. Black Americans will overcome the past to champion human rights at home and abroad.

Page 145. Black Americans will not be afraid to obey God publicly. Acts 5:29-30 NLT.

Page 146. Black Americans will raise up Davids willing to fight the pagans who defy God. 1 Samuel 17:24, 26 NLT.

Page 150. Black Americans will no longer be poor and ruled by the rich and lenders. Proverbs 22:7 KJV.

Page 152. People who help them will discern what Black Americans need and provide help as to mature men of God. Hebrews 5:14 KJV.

Page 154. Black Americans will turn from Satan and take God's light to the darkness. Acts 26:17-18 NLT.

Page 155. Black Americans will go and make disciples of nations instead of always staying where they are. Matthew 28:19 -20 NLT.

Page 159. Black Americans will press through the pain to develop Christ-like people. Galatians 4:19-20 NLT.

Page 161. Black Americans will fast as a sacrifice for others' release. Psalm 50:5 KJV.

Page 166. Black Americans will stay strong in their ability to forgive. Luke 17:4 NLT.

Page 167. They will stay right with God and up to date on their repentance. Luke 13:26-28 NKJV.

Page 178. They will be an example of the respect due to a man of God. 1 Thessalonians 5:12-13 NLT.

Page 179. They will be leaders in a new movement for Christians to respect the Church. Matthew 16:18-19 KJV.

Page 191. They will have faith for their future families. Hebrews 11:1 NLT.

Page 197. They will love their children. Psalm 127:4-5 NLT.

Page 198. All the nations of the world will be blessed because they obeyed God. Genesis 22:17-18 NKJV.

Page 200. They will remember that babies in the womb have fathers. Luke 1:13-14 NLT.

Page 205. They will honor fathers once again. Deuteronomy 5:16 NKJV.

Page 206. They will get new vision and no longer perish. Proverbs 29:18 KJV.

Page 207. They will end the curse that came with dishonoring fathers. Matthew 15:4 NKJV.

Page 211. They will accept rebuke and be encouraged. 2 Timothy 4:2 NLT.

Page 212. They will become spiritual fathers teaching others. 2 Timothy 2:1-2 KJV.

Page 222. They will father the poor and the oppressed. Job 29:15-17 NLT.

Page 223. They will receive God's blessings through others. Ephesians 1:3 NLT.

Page 233. They will reject the theories of evolution and favored races. Charles Darwin subtitled his book on evolution *Preservation of the Favored Races in the Struggle for Life*. However, the Bible says, "God shows no favoritism." Acts 10:34 NLT. "God is no respecter of persons" (KJV).

Page 239. They will stop the elimination of their race. Margaret Sanger wrote of "the lack of balance between the birth rate of the 'unfit' and the 'fit,' admittedly the greatest present menace to civilization." The Bible says, "But if you favor some people over others, you are committing a sin." (James 2:9 NLT).

AUTHOR'S BIO

BISHOP WELLINGTON BOONE

Bishop Wellington Boone is a widely respected Christian leader with an unwavering commitment to Jesus Christ, his family, unity in the church, and his country, the United States. He stands on the truth of biblical principles. For the past three decades he has been a sought-after international speaker on racial reconciliation. For more than 40 years he has inspired and trained Christian men and women to become leaders with Christ-like character, faithfulness in marriage, and a zeal to transform society.

Researcher George Barna named Bishop Wellington Boone one of the 17 most influential Black Americans of the 20th Century because of his leadership in racial reconciliation and his resource books, including *Breaking Through,* published by the Southern Baptists to emphasize their repentance after 150 years of racism. The debut of his Black American Christian Embassy (BACE) and his book *Black Self-Genocide* will have a global impact in the 21st century.

Bishop Boone is the founder and chief prelate of the Fellowship of International Churches, a cross-cultural, global network of bishops, pastors, and Bible-based churches and Bible schools.

He established Goshen Learning Centers for children in South Africa led by his daughter, Nicole Boone. Beginning in the 1980s, New Generation Campus Ministries and Global Outreach recruited and trained multiracial college leaders.

Bishop Boone is known as a man of integrity and is a respected consultant to mega church boards and international ministries. He is a former board member of the leading Christian rating organization, Evangelical Council for Financial Accountability (ECFA), and the former chairman of the board of March for Jesus in the United States, which mobilized millions of people to take a bold public stand for Jesus Christ in major cities.

The Wellington Boone Collection—four decades of archives from his published and unpublished books, articles, manuscripts, recordings, research, and other materials demonstrating the impact of Bishop Boone on this generation—is included in the Special Collections of the Regent University Library in Virginia Beach, Virginia.

More than a million men have heard Bishop Wellington Boone preach in stadium events for Promise Keepers and many other Christian organizations as he has taught them biblical principles of Christ-likeness for a successful life.

He is a national and international speaker for groups as diverse as the African Anglican Church, Billy Graham Evangelistic Association, CRU (Campus Crusade for Christ), CBN, TBN, Daystar, Family Research Council, Focus on the Family, Liberty University, MorningStar Ministries, NRB (National Religious Broadcasters), Regent University (where he served many years on the Board of Trustees), Salvation Army, World Changers (Creflo Dollar).

His books for men, like *Your Wife Is Not Your Momma,* and for women, like *Women Are Kingmakers* (which became the international Kingmakers women's movement) are recommended reading by national leaders of marriage ministries. Other acclaimed books include *Dare to Hope, Holy Ghost Is My Friend, Low Road to New Heights, Your Journey with God* (a personal accountability journal for serious Christians), and *A Man's Journey with God*, a vital resource for Bishop Boone's ManHunt men's discipleship movement.

Bishop Boone has been married to his high school sweetheart, Katheryn, for 43 years. In March 2015, after more than 40 years of developing leaders in the churches that he has founded, he commissioned Bishop Garland Hunt to replace him as senior pastor of The Father's House in Norcross, Georgia, to become a full-time Biblical Strength Coach.

He now travels internationally, training pastors and leaders in the church, university, and business communities how to grow closer to God through private consecration, how to recruit and develop leaders, and how to have an impact on the culture without compromising on the Word.

 The logo of Wellington Boone Ministries that appears with the "Vision for Black America" series throughout *Black Self-Genocide* shows Jesus washing His disciples' feet. *(See John 13.)* Christian humility is a key to revival and restoration in resolving America's racial crisis

Wellington Boone Ministries
5875 Peachtree Industrial Blvd Ste 300
Norcross, GA 30092
http://WellingtonBoone.com

APPENDIX

CPSIA information can be obtained
at www.ICGtesting.com
Printed in the USA
LVOW13s2313060717
540524LV00008B/155/P